Jumping the Line

Also by William Herrick

The Itinerant (1967)

Strayhorn, a Corrupt Among Mortals (1968)

¡Hermanos! (1969)

The Last to Die (1971)

Golcz (1976)

Shadows and Wolves (1980)

Love and Terror (1981)

Kill Memory (1983)

That's Life (1985)

Bradovich (1990)

Publication of this book has been assisted by a
grant from the Program for Cultural Cooperation
between Spain's Ministry of Education and Culture
and United States' Universities

Jumping the Line

The
Adventures
and
Misadventures
of an
American
Radical

William Herrick

With an
introduction by
Paul Berman

**The University
of Wisconsin Press**

Wisconsin Studies in American Autobiography

William L. Andrews
General Editor

A list of titles in the series will be found on pages 281–83.

The University of Wisconsin Press
2537 Daniels Street
Madison, Wisconsin 53718

3 Henrietta Street
London WC2E 8LU, England

5 4 3 2 1

Printed in the United States of America
Permission has been granted by Second Chance Press to quote
from *¡Hermanos!*

The author and publisher are grateful to Sylvia P. Marro, widow of
Joe Gordon, for permission to publish the letter on pages 230–32.

Library of Congress Cataloging-in-Publication Data
Herrick, William, 1915–
    Jumping the line: the adventures and misadventures of an American rad-
ical / William Herrick; with an introduction by Paul Berman.
        308 pp.   cm.—(Wisconsin studies in American autobiography)
        ISBN 0-299-15790-3 (cloth: alk. paper)
        1. Herrick, William, 1915–   —Biography. 2. Novelists,
    American—20th century—Biography. 3. Radicalism—United States—
    History—20th century. 4. Radicals—United States—Biography.
    5. Radicalism in literature. I. Title. II. Series.
    PS3558.E75Z47   1998
813′.54—dc21
    [B]   97-34639

To Jeannette
Nicholas and Lea

They want to get
out of themselves
and escape from
the man. That is
madness: instead
of changing into
angels, they
change into
beasts, instead of
raising themselves,
they lower them-
selves.

—Michel de Montaigne

Jumping the line: hobo slang for hopping a freight, hitting the road, copping a beat, skedaddling.

Author's Note

Conversations that lack quotation marks embody the gist and thrust of what was said as best I remember.

I have already thanked many people for their help, but there are some, no offense meant, who are more equal than others:

Nathan Shlechter, a moral man.

Sol Levitas because he published *The New Leader* and made his pages available to Boris Nicolaevsky and David Dallin, who, decades before the Soviet archives were opened, told us with great insight and astounding accuracy what was going on in that poor land.

Theodore Draper and Harvey Klehr for their objective and superb histories of, and writings on, American Communism.

Burnett Bolloten and Stanley Payne for their respective histories, *The Spanish Revolution*, fully researched and brilliantly interpreted.

Verle B. Johnston for his *Legions of Babel*, and Cecil Eby for his *Between the Bullet and the Lie*, histories of the American volunteers in the International Brigades. The Comintern archives now prove their accuracy.

Victor Alba and Stephen Schwartz for their history of the POUM, *Spanish Marxism versus Soviet Communism*, a solid work that brings the POUM to life.

Victor Serge for *The Case of Comrade Tulayev* and Gustav Regler for *The Owl of Minerva*, the first a novel, the second a memoir, both of them moving and memorable.

And, of course, George Orwell.

William Herrick: an Introduction

Paul Berman

William Herrick is our American Orwell. Like Orwell, he went to Spain during the Civil War of the 1930s to fight against the Fascists. Like Orwell, he was shot at the front and was lucky to survive. Like Orwell, he saw horrifying goings-on behind the lines in Spain—saw the Communist forces, who claimed to be the champions of democracy, try to impose a dictatorship of their own, Soviet-style, on the Spanish people. The biggest of the anti-Fascist organizations in Spain was a trade union federation led by anarcho-syndicalists. Orwell saw the Communists gun the anarcho-syndicalists down. Herrick saw something similar. Orwell saw foreign supporters of Spanish Communism come to Spain and embroider the sheerest lies about the Communists and the war. Herrick saw that, too.

Orwell was supremely dedicated to the cause of freedom and social justice, and he went home to England no less dedicated than before. But his ideas about freedom and justice grew more precise as a result of his Spanish experience. He realized that Communism was as much a danger as Fascism; that people could be manipulated by systematic falsehoods and propaganda machines; that truth was no less important than freedom and justice. He also discovered that in Britain and not just in Spain the authoritarian wing of the left—the Communists and some of their supporters among the intellectuals—were determined to keep any criticisms of their activities from being known. Herrick went home to New York, came to the same appreciation of truth, and discovered that in New York, too, the authoritarian left wanted to shut him up. Over the next several years Orwell found himself facing some difficult decisions in his fight against the authoritarians of the left: whether to cooperate with a British government that, in earlier times, he might have regarded as less than legitimate. Orwell came to realize that black-and-white moral choices are not always at hand. Herrick faced the same difficult choices regarding the American government, and during the McCarthy era he found himself in the same gray zone, not always to his own satisfaction.

Naturally the parallels between Herrick and Orwell go only so far. Orwell received the education of a certain kind of privileged Englishman, and by the time he went to Spain he was already a mature, independent thinker, and a great writer. Herrick, when he went to Spain, was a young man from the Jewish working class in New York. He was a trade union organizer, a sometime communard on an anarchist farm, and, most of all, a militant of the Communist Party USA (and when he fought in Spain, it was in a unit that was organized and led by the Communist Party). It took Herrick many years to work his way into circumstances where he, too, could devote his energies to writing. His first book, *The Itinerant,* came out only in 1967, and his best-known work, *¡Hermanos!,* in 1969, when he was well into middle age—and those were novels, not memoirs. He did not feel the impulse to speak in his own name about his personal experiences, the way that Orwell did in *Homage to Catalonia.* I suppose that Herrick has never been as political as Orwell, except now and then, when the mood strikes. Orwell took a serious interest in political theory (*Nineteen Eighty-Four* was nothing if not political theory, rendered into a fable). That was never Herrick's inspiration.

Still, Herrick's books, a number of them, touched on political themes. He wrote about a super-politicized Jewish working class in America during the 1920s and '30s, about the young Communists and anarchists from that background, about the American volunteers who fought in Spain—wrote about those topics with a wonderful rough-and-ready vividness that always seemed drawn from life, exactly as if he were telling us historical truths, and not just inventing stories. But was that the case? There was no way to be sure. For it is only now, more than sixty years after he went to fight in Spain, that Herrick, too, has finally produced a memoir, his *Jumping the Line*, about the whole of his life, not just about the Spanish Civil War—and only now can we see, in the pages of his book, a number of the sharply etched scenes from the novels re-compose themselves, as it were, into the real-life shapes that had been their origin.

Naturally the reader will want to know how reliable is Herrick's memoir—will want to know this as a matter of course, but also for a second reason that attaches to any memoir dealing with Communism from a critical perspective. The Communist movement has been with us since the days of Lenin, and during the whole of that period, whenever someone has stood up to offer a damning eyewitness account of Communist principles or actions, a chorus of voices has responded with accusations about mendacity, conspiracy, immorality, swinishness, greed, pay-offs, and every possible purple insult intended to make the hostile eyewitness appear to be a miserable fraud. Orwell met exactly that response. The most horrible things were said about him—still are, from time to time. In Herrick's case, he has been offering harsh judgments about Communism ever since a moment in 1939, well described in his memoir, when, infuriated by Stalin's fateful pact with Hitler, the young veteran of the war in Spain went parading up and down the garment district of Manhattan (where the Communist Party was strong in several of the trade unions) denouncing Communism in the iciest terms. From that moment until today, a chorus of voices, consisting mainly of his own former comrades from the Spanish Civil War, has vilified him in every possible way. And so, the reader, in opening the pages of Herrick's memoir, can hardly avoid wondering if the dreadful accusations that are routinely thrown at the author have some basis.

I can answer that question by telling a little story about my own experience with Herrick and with his accusers. In 1986, on the occasion of the fiftieth anniversary of the outbreak of the Spanish Civil War, I was a columnist at the *Village Voice,* and I decided to look up Herrick and write about him. I had read *¡Hermanos!* and a couple of other books, plus a few reviews that he had contributed to *The New Leader,* and I had found him to be an interesting and sympathetic personality with a gravelly exuberant prose style and an air of having seen everything, and I wanted to know more. I reached him on the phone. We began to talk. And—I don't know why—on an impulse he decided to tell me things that he had never told anyone, not even his wife, about his time in Spain.

What he told me ought not to have surprised anyone who had read *¡Hermanos!* or some of the other novels and could remember Herrick's descriptions of the Soviet secret police, the GPU (the ancestor of the KGB), in Spain. Those descriptions, he told me over the phone, were based on personal experience. His unit in Spain was the Abraham Lincoln battalion, which answered to the Communist chain of command, which included the GPU. One day he himself was put under a GPU command. He was ordered to accompany a GPU execution squad and to stand among them, unarmed, as the squad coolly put to death three Spanish leftists. That was a terrible revelation for Herrick to make—in a sense, more terrible than anything that Orwell had revealed, given that Orwell had merely witnessed the Communists in action, and had never stood among them. Herrick and I held a second conversation, which I taped, and in the July 22, 1986, issue of the *Village Voice,* I published excerpts of our discussion in the pristine form of a Q & A. And the response to that piece was amazing.

Ever since the war, Herrick's former comrades from the Lincoln battalion have kept up an energetic little organization with the slightly inaccurate title Veterans of the Abraham Lincoln Brigade (inaccurate because the battalion was inflated for reasons of sonority into a brigade), whose business is to burnish the memory of the volunteer fighters, except for the several volunteers who, like Herrick, went on in later life to oppose Communism. The VALB, it must be said, has performed this task brilliantly. The organization has generated a vast stream of books, articles, public testimonials, salutes from politicians, pamphlets, newsletters, film homages, and testimonial dinners, all rehearsing the single message that, during the Spanish Civil War, the Lincoln soldiers and the Communist forces in general were fighters for freedom and democracy, not for Communism.

The publicity campaign has been enormously successful, too, with the effect that, in the minds of many people who would never think of themselves as sympathetic to Communism, the Lincolns have come to embody the cause of simple idealism, pure and democratic and courageous. As late as 1996 the *New York Times* managed to run a front-page story describing the VALB in the most admiring terms—quite as if there were never any dark controversies surrounding the Lincolns' Communist provenance and the connections to the GPU and the battalion's role in advancing Stalin's foreign policy. The VALB has always been feisty, too. Anyone who, like me, participated in the giant antiwar demonstrations of the Vietnam era or in the demonstrations against the Reagan foreign policy of the 1980s will remember the VALB at those marches, smartly dressed and displaying its banners with a dapper military pride. And that same feistiness went into action when the *Voice* published my Q & A with Herrick.

The exact focus of the VALB's indignation surprised me. Herrick, in his interview, had not only confessed to accompanying the GPU executioners but had proposed some pretty severe criticisms of the Communist role in general. He knew very well that the Lincoln battalion fought for Communism and for Stalin in Spain—not for democracy—and he felt no compunction at saying what he knew. Looking back on his own experiences in the Spanish war, Herrick had come to admire the anarcho-syndicalists and an independent, non-Stalinist Marxist party called (in its Spanish acronym) the POUM, in whose military ranks Orwell had fought. Those were the genuine anti-Fascists and champions of the Spanish people, in Herrick's estimation. That was his main point. In passing, though, he discussed a scene from ¡Hermanos!, where some American volunteers frag (kill, that is) their own officer at the Spanish front. That scene, he told me in the interview, was likewise based on real life—not on what he had witnessed with his own eyes but on what had been told to him by his closest friends in the battalion. There was an officer in the battalion named Oliver Law, and Herrick's friends and several other men had felt that Law was hopelessly stupid and incompetent and was sending them to their deaths, and they had killed him in a mad fury during the Brunete Campaign.

Was there anything implausible about this story? It is worth observing that the execution of soldiers was a notable trait of the Lincoln battalion, which stood closer in that respect to the traditions of the Soviet military than to those of the American military. The story about Oliver Law, in any case, was not especially new. A history of the Lincolns by Cecil Eby, *Between the Bullet and the Lie,* published in 1969, had reported two different versions of Law's death, with no way to choose between them: a version that conformed to what Herrick had told me in the interview, and an "official" version, according to which Law had died a heroic death attacking the Fascists. In preparing my interview with Herrick, I spoke to a number of Lincoln veterans, including an important figure, John Gates—a commissar during his time in Spain, with a link to military intelligence, later on a top figure in the Communist Party USA until he quit—who told me that, although he remained skeptical, he had heard the rumor about Law's death, and, for that matter, had heard rumors about men from the battalion killing other officers, too. So the story was old news.

This single aspect of Herrick's interview with me, the passing mention of Law getting killed by his own men, nonetheless became the focus of a VALB campaign against the *Village Voice.* The organization wrote and telephoned the editors to demand a retraction of my column or, short of that, the publication of an article by the VALB. The editors offered, in response, a place on the letters page, which the VALB was not at first eager to accept. One of the leaders of the VALB, Steve Nelson—another major figure in the Communist Party USA during the Stalin era—went out for coffee with me and pleaded with me to back off what I had published about Oliver Law. Nelson reminded me that Law was black, and he made the case that black people in America have very few heroes and that I was besmirching the name of one of them—even if, as Nelson said, "maybe Law wasn't a genius" (which I thought was an odd point to volunteer). Next the VALB organized a picket line at the *Voice*. It was the strangest picket I have ever seen. A group of ten or fifteen elderly white-haired men, some of them decidedly short, plus a white-haired woman, walked in a circle in front of the *Voice* office and shouted slogans, one of which rhymed my name with "vermin." The picketers hurled insults at Herrick and denounced the interview as racist and called for me to be fired, and when they figured out that I was among the people observing their demonstration, they thrust their faces upward into mine and shouted and shook their fists.

The atmosphere was weirdly violent, as if at any moment the picketers were going to burst into the *Voice* city room with bare knuckles and start overturning furniture. Yet these people were going on seventy-five or eighty years old, and the violent air exuded a pathos of extreme fragility. The picketers came back for a second day of protests, and the astonished *Voice* staffers wandered down to the sidewalk to see what the uproar was about, and the fear was great that on the street in front of our newspaper an entire squadron of elderly mythic veterans of the Spanish Civil War was going to drop dead of heart attacks, caused by the vehemence of their rage and their slogans. And as the picketing went on, the VALB campaign against the Herrick interview advanced in other ways—in a New York black newspaper, on a radio talk show, and, most of all, through letters to the *Voice*.

The first of those letters came from someone named Harry Fisher. I must say, when I first read Fisher's letter, the hair stood up on my journalist's head. I had considered that I was justified in publishing the interview with Herrick because of his literary achievements, because of the confluence of his view of the Spanish war with that of various historians, and because I had spoken to a number of other veterans, at least three of whom had expressed admiration for him, in degrees that varied from forthright to begrudging. Still, I had no way to judge for myself how accurate was Herrick's recall of particular details from the 1930s. The letter from Harry Fisher began, "I was shocked, appalled, and outraged by the Herrick interview," and went on to say this: "I was in Spain for nineteen months, sixteen of them at the front with the Battalion. I fought under Commander Law and was an eyewitness to his death." Fisher in his letter said that he had watched Law stand up in the middle of battle and shout to the Lincolns, "Let's chase them off that hill! Let's go!"—and then Fisher watched as Law was shot. I will admit that, after reading this letter, I began to worry about that one brief section of the Herrick interview.

Then I learned a couple of curious facts—about the picket line and about Harry Fisher's letter—from one of the other Lincoln veterans. This other veteran, who wished to keep his name out of print, told me that some of the old men in the VALB were not happy about having to spend two days picketing the *Village Voice*. But these men were pensioners of businesses—a travel agency, a publishing house—that were associated with the Communist Party USA, and they had been ordered to go out and picket, and they had no choice in the matter. As for Harry Fisher and his letter, was I aware that Fisher had spent his life working for the New York office of Tass, the Soviet news agency?

That struck me as a relevant bit of information, given Tass's reputation for dishonesty. In my reply to Fisher on the *Voice* letters page, I mentioned the Tass affiliation. But I did think it was my obligation to push Herrick to provide a few details to show why he believed that Fisher's version was untrue. Herrick explained that the heroic story of Law's death was a myth invented by the Communist Party for political purposes, in order to cultivate an image as the champion of racial integration, and that his own version of the death came from his two best friends in Spain, Doug Roach (who was black) and Joe Gordon. Roach and Gordon had been part of the group that killed Law. Both men were dead, however, which meant there was no way to confirm Herrick's recollection of what they had told him. I included those additional details in my reply to Fisher on the *Voice* letters page. Then another letter arrived at the *Voice*.

It began, "I am the sister of Joe Gordon, who was maligned by William Herrick and Paul Berman as one of those who murdered Captain Oliver Law." The letter said, "My brother lost an eye at Jarama and was sent home before the start of the Brunete offensive. He could not have witnessed or participated in the events described, since he was not even in Spain at the time." The sister demanded an apology. This letter, too, was a little unnerving. If Gordon's sister was right and Joe Gordon was not in Spain, then Herrick would appear to be unreliable. I pressed Herrick on this question, which irritated him no end. He testily assured me that he knew exactly when his dear friend Joe Gordon had left Spain. The two men, Herrick and Gordon, had taken the same train to France. Still, I wanted further reassurance, and I glanced at one of the histories of the Lincolns, Arthur H. Landis's *The Abraham Lincoln Brigade,* published in 1967. And in that book, by remarkable chance, I came across a mention of Gordon and the dates of his time in Spain. The dates were consistent with Herrick's version, not the sister's. Herrick's memory was not faulty at all—so far as I could see. This information, too, I published in the *Voice,* in a reply to Gordon's sister.

Now came the most remarkable letter yet. It was on VALB stationery and was signed with twenty-three names—actually, twenty-four, since Harry Fisher's name appeared twice. The letter read in full: "I am a Veteran of the Abraham Lincoln Brigade. I knew both Oliver Law and Joe Gordon, and I took part in the Brunete offensive in July 1937 in Spain.

"Joe Gordon received a serious eye wound at Jarama in February 1937. He was not present *at any time* during the Brunete Campaign. He did not take part in that campaign in any manner, shape or form.

Therefore it was impossible for him to have participated in the alleged murder of Captain Oliver Law as charged by the self-confessed informer William Herrick.

"Oliver Law was the first Black American to command a *completely integrated* American military fighting unit. He died honorably leading an attack on a strongly fortified fascist position on July 9, 1937.

"The *Village Voice* should publicly apologize for the scurrilous article written by Paul Berman."

I was definitely worried about that particular letter. Gordon might well have been in Spain at the right moment (as I had discovered), but if twenty-three people signed a statement saying with absolute conviction that Gordon was not exactly where Herrick had said he was, at the Brunete Campaign, then surely Herrick's recollection was wrong, and I had done a bad thing in publishing his particular remark about Law. That seemed all but certain. Still, I poked around in the library a little more, just to see what could be learned. I looked up the old journal of the volunteers in Spain, *The Volunteer for Liberty,* glanced through a few issues, and stumbled on a pertinent article called "Joe Gordon: Jarama Volunteer Returns," in the issue of July 1, 1938. The article explained that Gordon had been in the hospital for many months because of a wound. But he had returned to the Lincoln battalion just in time to participate in the Brunete Campaign. The men were ordered up a hill in order to beat off a Fascist attack. The article explained, "As is already well known, the job was done with full success. But Joe Gordon's group was the first to reach the ridge, and Joe himself was the first American to open fire. For that reason, when all was quiet later, the Spanish brigade commander came over and thanked Joe for the service rendered by the battalion."

So Gordon was not just in Spain. He was exactly where Herrick had said he was. Not just that: Joe Gordon was *famous* for having been there. The Spanish commander had thanked him. The *Volunteer for Liberty* had reported on his deeds. Everyone who was paying attention to these things must have known about Joe Gordon at the Brunete Campaign.

22

He was the man of the hour. The American fighters at Brunete must have known all about it. Yet in reply to my interview with Herrick, twenty-three of those doughty individuals, the militants of the VALB, had signed a letter to the *Voice* saying that Gordon had not been there "in any manner, shape, or form."

There had been a lot of letters-to-the-editor by then—not just from Herrick's detractors but one from a fellow Lincoln veteran who saluted Herrick for telling the truth and another, equally positive, from an American volunteer who had gone to Spain to work with the anarcho-syndicalists. The editors were getting a little tired of the Spanish Civil War, and they decided to call a cease-fire—which meant not publishing the letter from the twenty-three members of the VALB. I could understand the decision, but I regretted it. There was something instructive in the whole elaborate campaign against the Herrick interview and especially in that single letter with the massed signatures. Why, after all, had twenty-three war veterans endorsed such a document? It was easy to work out the rationale. Herrick had spent a lifetime telling truths about the Communists in Spain, and now he was doing it in a newspaper of the left, and the VALB wanted to stop him. The VALB people did not try to argue against his larger contentions. They did not have the nerve to go against his most shocking revelation, which recounted his personal experience. They decided instead to focus their attack on the single point in Herrick's interview that, in their estimation, could be shouted down: his account of Law's death, which, by his own frank acknowledgment, was drawn merely from a conversation with friends who had subsequently died.

The VALB must have figured that, if they could assemble enough people to make Herrick look like a liar (and a racist) on this single point, a shadow would fall across every aspect of his recollections and judgments, and their own vehemence and the mythic prestige of the VALB would overwhelm everything else that Herrick had said. So the VALB fired away on the single story about Oliver Law. The people who marched on the picket line and signed those letters never asked themselves if they were right. They had made a political decision, and in the bright light of their decision, questions of truth or falsehood faded into nonexistence. That was why twenty-three loyal veterans signed the letter. They did it for the cause (except, of course, for any veterans who may have signed because they were forced to do so by the higher-ups who controlled their pensions). Some of those elderly signatories had broken with the Communist Party long before, and others of them were still associated with it (according to everything I had heard). But all of them retained the old spirit of ferocity, group-think, discipline, and disdain for truth. The spirit of Stalinism, in a word. They were disciplined liars. They could swear to a falsehood in a thunderous massed chorus, fists in the air. Orwell would have recognized those elderly militants at a glance. He wrote about them in *Animal Farm*.

I never worried that the VALB would get me fired. The VALB was definitely prestigious in 1986, especially at a leftwing paper like the *Voice*, yet it was an organization of very old people whose prime had been long ago. The curses and demands of those ancient militants had all the windy force of their physicality in picketing. But their campaign did offer, in a safely miniature version, a lesson in what life had been like back in the 1930s and '40s, when the Lincoln veterans were young and muscular and the Communist Party and its network of organizations had a lot of power in certain Manhattan streets and a few other places. The campaign showed me what Herrick has been up against ever since the Spanish Civil War—the fierceness of his opponents, their organizational sophistication, their determination, their scary unscrupulousness. And the experience filled me with admiration for him—the unstoppable truth-teller, just as brave in his older years as when he enlisted for the war against Franco, unwilling to shut up no matter what.

Herrick's memoirs express a bitter rage against the Communist movement. I am told that some people think his anger excessive. I think it is appropriate. To have given an articulate expression to his natural and authentic emotional response to the Communists he has known is, I think, Herrick's finest literary achievement. Yet what I have come to admire most in Herrick is how he has borne up under these circumstances, not just during his little escapade with me but throughout the decades. Someone else might have fled from the doctrinaire world of the authoritarian left into the welcoming arms of the doctrinaire right. Herrick was never tempted to do anything of the sort.

His particular fate has been to find himself in the middle of each of the great battles of the twentieth century. The battle for workers' rights: he worked for the trade unions, even organized and led a union of his own. The battle against racism: he went down South during the early 1930s and organized people to oppose Jim Crow, when it was not so easy to do anything of the sort. The battle against Fascism: he fought as a soldier. A Fascist machine gun bullet from Spain, unextractable by surgery, remains in Herrick's neck even now. (He feels it when it rains.) The battle against Communism: he fought, pen in hand, as tenaciously as anyone you can mention, without reaping huge rewards for it, either. Herrick's memoir of these many painful struggles must be the most thoroughly twentieth-century book ever written. Yet his battles never shriveled him into a mere fighter, as sometimes happens to people. Herrick fought his battles because that was his destiny, but he was always bigger and livelier than politics and wars, was always more of a lover than a fighter. Gusto for life is written across his face. You'll see it for yourself in his memoirs.

Jumping the Line

1

I was born too late to be a Wobbly, one of the I Won't Work guys, the Industrial Workers of the World. Too bad. Over my crib hung a piece of tin embossed with the stern physiognomies of Vladimir Ilich Lenin and Leon Trotsky. It hung on one wall or another until I was in my teens. Finally, it was replaced by another piece of tin, this one stamped with the benign image of Joseph Stalin.

In Willa Cather's *Death Comes for the Archbishop,* Father Latour asks his Indian guide, Jacinto, why the Ácomas would live on the high rock, and Jacinto answers, "A man can do whole lot when they hunt him day and night like an animal. Navajos on the north, Apaches on the south; the Ácoma run up a rock to be safe."

Cather goes on to say, "And the Hebrews of the Old Testament, always being carried captive into foreign lands—their rock was an idea of God, the only thing their conquerors could not take from them."

What is my rock? What notched stones do I climb for sanctuary?

A man stands among piles of wallpaper rolls as the sun slants in through a wide-open store door. He opens a slender tin and withdraws a small brown cigarette, tamps it on the lid and puts it in his mouth, strikes a match and lights it. He sees me climbing up and down one of the wallpaper piles and smiles. He is my father. I climb down and run to him and hug his leg. It is night. I am sitting in a highchair as my older brother and parents sit at the table under a glaring light. My parents are quarreling, shouting at each other. I begin to cry. They stop and look my way. They smile, kiss each other, then kiss me, first one, then the other. My brother Harry has never stopped spooning his soup. I remember running wildly across the back yard and starting up the outdoor stairs and losing it and feeling so ashamed. As she wiped me clean, my mother sang a Russian song. She sang a lot, sometimes old Russian songs, sometimes others from the Yiddish theaters in New York. She was an energetic woman, always singing, dancing, a coquette. Her flirtatiousness infuriated my father. Then he was dying; I remember that, too. It was 1919. I was four. He lay in the bed in their room off the kitchen. Doctors came and went. There were whispers. My mother began to cry frequently. Then one night she screamed. It was like the keening of a hound in pain. The entire neighborhood heard her. The white light in the kitchen was blinding. Neighbors came, relatives. People brought their own chairs. It was like an arena; in the center, death in an open coffin, people seated in circles around it. My father had died. My brother Harry, nine years old, cuddled me in his arms. My mother wouldn't stop screaming. She was thirty years old. Tante Golda, my father's sister, hovered over her. At the cemetery, while I watched a farm boy throw stones at a tree, wanting to join him, my mother tried to jump into the grave. She was restrained by Golda's husband, Uncle Dave, and his brother Charlie.

My father, Nathan Horvitz, was thirty-six when he died. All I know about him is that in 1909 he left Byelorussia, now Belarus, and came to Trenton, New Jersey, leaving behind my pregnant mother, who came a year later. He also left his mother and several sisters behind, exactly how many I don't know. After World War II my mother told me they and their families had been murdered by Hitler. As a young man, my father drank a concoction to weaken his heart in order to escape conscription into the tsar's army. That was probably what killed him at his early age. In Trenton he owned a wallpaper store and was himself a wallpaper

My father

hanger. We lived over the store. His only kin I ever knew was his sister, Tante Golda, who had come to America several years before him.

In Europe his name was Gurevich—Gu-RE-vich. The immigration officer at Castle Garden transliterated it into Horvitz, and Horvitz became Herrick when my brother Harry worked in the main office of the Metropolitan Life Insurance Company at Madison Avenue and 23rd Street. Every year Harry took competitive examinations given by the Met and came out first or second but they never gave him a titled job, though they did give him a raise. Then in 1939 he decided to translate his Jewish name into Anglo-Saxon, and sure enough when he came out first at the next competitive examination he got a title. It wasn't that they were anti-semitic, they just didn't like Jews. When Harry changed the family name, he included me in the application. My sister Natalie refused and remained Horvitz until she married. In later years, I regretted the change, but at the time I had already used different names as a Communist, so it didn't seem to matter. What's in a name?

Cry today, smile tomorrow, my mother always said. Still, it took her several years to stop crying. She's buried in an Arbeiter Ring cemetery in New Jersey, on the other side of the George Washington Bridge.

Since her burial, I have never visited her grave. Mourn a stone, a yard of earth? She herself said that to me. Austere rules to live by. She loved often and rarely wisely. From the age of thirty-four to the time she died at eighty she suffered four cancers: sarcoma, uterine, breast, and lungs, and it was only the last which finally put her in her grave. Periodically over forty years she traveled to Montefiori hospital in the Bronx for radium treatments. She cried, she danced, she loved. When you give yourself, she said, hold nothing back. Give it all you've got. Enjoy every moment of it, store up the happiness, you will need it for the bad times.

It scared me. Why didn't she settle down with one man, live a normal life like everyone else? She was never at rest, never at peace. It infuriated me. Once when I was about eleven, a man with glossy black hair

My older brother with me

and greedy eyes sat on her bed to watch her comb her hair. I didn't like him much. I ran to the kitchen, picked up a long knife and came at him with it. Fortunately he was quick. My mother kicked him out of the room, sat me on her lap, and sang a Russian song to me. It was a love song, of course, she rarely sang anything else. In later years, I would run away, never even leaving her a note or writing to her while I was on the bum. When I became an adult I questioned her about it. She had an excuse. She loved Nathan so much she could never find another. It was, she said, like Anna and Vronsky. I laughed at her.

Finally, when I was about fifty, I arrived at a place of rest with her. It was too late. She had become paranoid, senile, crazy, the doctor said. She accused me of stealing money from her. When she became ill, I literally had to fight her off, carry her down four flights of stairs from her apartment, throw her—yes, throw her—into the back of my car, lock the doors, and drive her to the hospital. She didn't stop cursing me all the way and threatened to jump out the window if I didn't take her home. When I visited her she screamed so hysterically I had to stop coming. She was quiet during my wife Jeannette's visits, however, asking about the children and even about me. Three weeks later she died. The doctor said the lung cancer had spread to her brain. I buried her, we were

My mother at work

at peace. It was 1968. Though she was an unbeliever, a rabbi said the prayer for the dead.

She was born Mary Saperstein, the youngest of eighteen children, many of whom died in early childhood, some of whom lived to old age, and not a few of whom perished at the hands of Hitler, including my grandmother. At ninety-five she was bayonetted to death by a Nazi soldier infuriated by her stubborn refusal to board a cattle car.

My mother went to work as a seamstress when she was ten, and stopped at the age of sixty-nine. In between she lived a life of great gayety and also of great bitterness, filled with tragedy—the death of her husband, my father; her son, my brother Harry, in the prime of his life; Paul, my sister Natalie's son; and Seth, my son, in early childhood. That she herself managed to live her full life after her many illnesses was a tribute not only to medical science but to her personal will and courage.

She was one of the finest dressmakers in New York, a woman whose talented hands made dresses and gowns for the wealthy and the aristocrats of our world, yet she was the best dressed of them all. During her good years she was considered the gayest, among the most beautiful and vivacious women of the Yiddish art world. She was sought after by the leading Yiddish poets and actors of the time to read their poems, to sing their songs.

For me to think of her alive is to see her at the sewing machine, the silks and the satins and the brocades and the spools of thread of many colors and the needles and the pins and the shears. It would be easy to say that she was a silk thread herself, and that the thread had run out and all that remains is the wooden spool.

But that wouldn't be true at all. The thread of her life goes on in her children and their children, her kin for whom she sang her songs and for whom she labored a lifetime.

She was a vain woman, a sharp-tongued woman, a woman of gaiety and wit, a very generous woman. She suffered all the faults of being human, and enjoyed all the virtues.

My mother as a young woman

Mother as Pocahontas

2

I wish I could write a book like Fred Exley's *A Fan's Notes*.

Scoop out my guts, scream at the fucking world out of a drunken frenzy, half crazy. I can never get drunk enough for the simple reason that I do not like hard liquor and never drink beer other than to quench my thirst on an extremely hot day, and no matter how hard I try to go crazy, it never works. I can get very angry, mad, but usually live to regret it. I am one of those people who can't forget every bit of evil they've committed in moments of white hot anger or sheer stupidity.

In a fury because of a surge recently of African-American anti-semitism, I wrote a friend a splenetic letter using the word "nigger"—and worse— several times, and now can't allow myself to forget the loosing of that shit from my bowels. I could have my friend tear up the letter or return it to me so I could flush it down the toilet, but how do I flush it out of myself? It is there, an unflushable stink along with other unflushable stinks, to remind me that I am not crazy, just a sane, stupid son-of-a-bitch.

Forgive me, I plead on bended knee with downcast eyes, but, please, don't call me a dirty Jew, you idiotic bastard.

Once, a long time ago, I did get drunk. It was in late 1934, when I'd come off the road and through a friend got a job as a busboy in the Roumanian Paradise. Paradise was Stanton and Rivington in lower Manhattan. The boss was a marvelous man who enjoyed watching me eat and ordered the chef to feed me all I wanted. One night I was bussing a banquet and emptying into my mouth every bottle of Sweet Tokay as I removed it from the long festive table. The more bottles I emptied the better it felt, and by the end of the night I was happier than I'd ever been. And happier still when I received a twenty-dollar tip from the banquet-giver, a sweet wine barrel of a man. I kissed him on both cheeks to his belly-rolling laughter, then headed home. Halfway up Second Avenue to where we lived on East 22nd Street, I finally lay down in the gutter for a short nap. A cab driver found me, wakened me, loaded me into his cab, and, digging out my address from my semi-delirious murmurs, drove me home. Still drunk, still grateful, I dug out the twenty and gave it to the cabbie, but he handed it back. You're drunk, kiddo, he said, the ride's on me. An honest man who probably had to drive his cab two weeks to earn twenty bucks.

It seems to me during the Great Depression people were more honest than they are in today's affluent times, or am I just dreaming?

I dream a lot, half awake, staring into space, wishing I could drink myself into a stupor or go round the bend. In his craziest moments Fred Ex knew he was nuts, so would you say he was really nuts, or was he faking it so he could have a good excuse for concealing himself in a nuthouse? All of his escapes were useless, at most momentary, so his pain, his Doppelgänger, never stopped confronting him.

And who is my Doppelgänger? A self-righteous Eagle Scout. Honesty is the best policy. Love your country. Respect your mother and father. Cleanliness is Godliness. If you screw a whore, give her an extra buck to assuage your conscience. If you cheat on your wife, tell her. Is there a more antiseptic way to kill her? Or her, you?

As I say, I relive every lie, relive every hurt given or received. Let us not forget the received.

It took me forty years to forgive my father for dying when I was four. The bastard. Left me without a male role model. Poor me. Poor Pop.

It took me almost as long to forgive my mother her amorous perambulations during her long widowhood. I am a free woman, a widow, I have a right, she said to me when she thought I could understand. Whenever I would have a childish fit of jealousy, she would sit me on her lap, hold my head to her billowing breasts, and sing songs to me. I never loved a woman who couldn't sing and who didn't have a sweet alto voice. Is there a better way to tame the wild beast?

Miss Veronica was my third-grade teacher. Time has made her darkly beautiful with very red lips and a slender desirable body. I was obsessively in love with her. Every morning I couldn't wait to leave Rosie, my sister's and my guardian, and go to school. Miss Veronica knew I was an orphan who only saw his mother once a month. Rosie gave all her love to Natalie, my little sister; me she fed and kept clean. Love is what I wanted. Miss Veronica knew. Every day, after the rest of the class was dismissed, she would sit me on her lap, place my needful hand on her breast, and rock me back and forth. When she dismissed me, my little cock was as stiff as a steel rod. Today, against my protestations, Miss Veronica would be hauled in for child molesting.

Six months after my father died, my mother gave birth to my sister, a plump redhead named Natalie after my father, Nathan. Everyone oohed and aahed. I did not realize I was jealous of her and guilty for my father's death until I was in my thirties and suffered an emotional crisis. At my therapist's I had a hallucination and saw my father staring at me with bloodshot eyes. Weeping bitter tears—are tears other than bitter?—I told him it wasn't my fault that he died, I had had nothing to do with it. He smiled kindly and forgave me. It took me ten years, though, to appreciate it.

Shortly after my mother gave birth to my sister, she became ill with her first cancer, the sarcoma. She was admitted to Mt. Sinai hospital, in

New York. My Tante Golda, who had six children of her own, turned Natalie and me over to the guardianship of Rosie and Jake Ross, an orthodox Jewish couple in Trenton, New Jersey. Jake made a comfortable living peddling fruit and vegetables off a horsedrawn wagon, and Rosie did as well, cooking for bar mitzvahs and weddings. His son from a previous marriage was a prizefighter for a time, Kid Ross, who married a shiksa, and Jake and Rosie wore ashes on their heads, as for the dead, until the marriage broke up. We were supposed to live with them for only several months, but it turned out to be five years. Rosie and Jake fell madly in love with my baby sister, and tolerated me only as part of a tie-in sale. I understood I was merely tolerated and resented it deeply; so deeply that I didn't realize it until, again, I was in my late thirties. That was when I began a long process of growing up. Now that I am past eighty, I dream of Miss Veronica, her warm lap and plump breast. I am back to the beginning. The circle is closing. However, the rod is lacking in steel, only the arteries are hard.

3

Tante Golda's lap was particularly pleasing. She would kiss my head, my ears, my neck, giggling all the time, embarrassed at her overflowing love.

She was as round as she was tall, not quite five feet. She had red hair and a sweet smile and always gave me candy and pennies. She said I looked like poor Nathan. My sister Natalie grew up to be Golda's spitting image; pretty, with flaming red hair. Very smart. Her greatest ambition was to become a modern dancer, like Martha Graham or Anna Sokolow. Her dance teachers tried to dissuade her because, they said, she was "too short." She should not have listened.

Golda was my father's sister, his only relative ever to leave Minsk. Those of our kin who remained perished at the hands of Adolph Hitler—may he burn in hell, as Mama always said. It is possible some might have died at the murderous hands of the wisest man who ever lived, Joseph Stalin, since several were known to have been members of the Jewish Socialist Bund. We all know now that Stalin hated none more than Socialists, since they were able to read him best of all. Why do we detest most those who read us best?

Tante Golda was my lifeline. My mother was ill and trying to eke out a living in New York, and Rosie's love for my sister left little for me. She deserved all the love she got. On Saturdays, after shul and lunch, I would leave Jake and Rosie's house on Fair Street, which paralleled the Delaware River near the bridge with its sign, "TRENTON MAKES AND THE WORLD TAKES," turn left and walk to Fall Street, again turn left, pass the narrow side streets where most of Trenton's Negroes lived, arrive at the corner having passed several small Jewish stores, and upon reaching the corner at Union Street, nod respectfully to our shul across the street, turn left yet again onto Union, skip past the Bailiss fish store, hoping to chance upon the three little Bailiss daughters with whom I played every chance I got (one brother, incidentally, had killed the other accidentally with their father's gun), then pass Klempner's Hotel, nod to Paul Klempner, who was to become a great basketball star at Penn, then slip hurriedly by the building which housed our old wallpaper store and apartment, afraid to see my father's ghost, and then make a right turn onto Market Street, up a hill on the left side of which was the Caplin tailor shop, disappointed if I did not see Pearl Caplin, one of the girls I was in love with, and on the right side of which was the Siegel delicatessen where Alex Siegel lived upstairs, and who was to become a famous actor/director on Broadway and in Hollywood, and right after the Siegels came the Grads, whose father, an insurance agent, died young leaving his children orphans, one of whom was my peer, also named William, then up the hill to Broad Street, and left turn to Loft's Candy Store, where if I had a penny or two I would stop to buy a chocolate finger, and where upstairs lived my sort-of relatives, Charlie and Minnie Cohen and their son Danny, my age, and his older sister Ida, with whom I was also madly in love, and as I walked up Broad Street and its many shops I would pass the Josephson shoe store, one son, Barney, grew up to own Cafe Society Uptown and Downtown, and another son, Leon, was to become a Soviet spy, and when I reached State Street I would turn right and go to the State Theater and beg pennies until I had ten for the top gallery and go up to see William S. Hart or Tom Mix or Hoot Gibson in a cowboy movie, after which I would leave the movie house and turn left and go way up State Street and—now I am lost, but up there somewhere I would make a right turn and find my way to Oak Lane, to Uncle Dave's and Tante Golda's new house, and as soon as I entered she would sit me on her ample lap and lavish me with kisses and sweets.

Before Golda's family bought the new house on Oak Lane in north Trenton they lived in south Trenton, where Golda ran a grocery store. The neighborhood was mostly Polish. One Saturday afternoon when I arrived after my long walk from Rosie's I saw a gang of kids chasing another kid and yelling after him, "Kill the Jew, kill the Jew!" I was stunned to see Arnold, Golda's youngest child, among this gang of little bullies. The boy they were chasing got away, and I don't think he even was Jewish. When Arnold returned to the house I told him he was Jewish, didn't he know that? It hadn't occurred to him. I don't believe his family ever lived in a Jewish neighborhood. Arnold never quite knew who he was. An intelligent man, an excellent student, he became a psychiatrist. In his early forties, he was found dead in his bed.

Golda had six children, two of whom had already left home: Emil, born Isadore, who was to become a doctor, and Clara, a school teacher. Arnold was my age. He would cry when I sat on his mother's lap a bit too long. Golda, however, had enough love for everyone. Arnold and I got along fine unless I lost my temper, which was fast and loose as well as envious and nasty.

I remember sitting on Tante Golda's lap at a meeting. There was a lot of yelling. Uncle Dave, Golda's husband, was standing on a platform with his brother Morris. They were having an argument. Years later, Uncle Dave told me about it. He was speaking on behalf of the Socialist Party, and Morris on behalf of those who wished to split off and become the Workers (Communist) Party. Dave stuck with the Socialists, and Golda became a fellow traveler of the Communists. On one or another holiday, when Dave's many siblings and their families gathered at his new house on Oak Lane—Dave was one of the Metropolitan's top insurance agents in Trenton—it would become a raucous mishmash of Socialists, Communists, and Anarchists. The blood pressure would ascend with the decibels. Dave's brother J. J., Joe to his familiars, was the leader of the Yiddish Anarchists. Morris led the Communists of Trenton, and later, Philadelphia. Dave, who became a Social Democrat when the Socialists split yet again, was responsible for the erection of Trenton's Labor Temple. My mother was a charter member of the Communist Party. She always said if my father had lived, he, too, would have been a Communist. Uncle Dave said that was not so, he would have been a Social Democrat. Tante Golda, wanting to please everyone, said, Who knows?

More than forty years later, at Dave's funeral in Trenton—Tante Golda had died, to my profound sorrow, a few years before—his brother Morris showed up at the cemetery, climbed one of those short ladders commonly used for street corner meetings, and harangued the mourners, trying to convince us that in his heart Dave had been a Communist. We all showed our backs to him.

My first act as a revolutionary occurred when I was seven or eight years old. On November 7, the anniversary of the Bolshevik Revolution, I was directed by Hymie Cohen, the eleven-year-old son of Morris (they were renting the second floor of Jake and Rosie's house) to hand out leaflets at the gates of Roebling Cable Company, Trenton's largest factory. It was during lunch hour, when most of the workers sat in the factory yard with their lunch pails. We ran among them handing out the leaflets and yelling, Long live the revolution! Mostly the men laughed and threw their sandwich wrappings at us. Long live sandwiches!

My wife Jeannette's revolutionary career began at age ten, when her brother would get her up early in the morning to help him hand out leaflets in front of the U.S. Steel plant in Worcester, Massachusetts. Our families took politics very seriously. We both grew up spending endless hours at meetings, and it didn't take too long before what we detested most was going to one.

When I was about nine, I became an organizer. I attribute it not so much to the urging of my relatives as to the strength I gathered sitting on Miss Veronica's warm lap.

To get to our public school in Trenton, most of us had to pass under a railroad bridge. The Polish toughs in the neighborhood would gather underneath it and bully the black and Jewish kids as we tried to pass through. Usually it was verbal abuse—niggers, kikes, and the like. Some of the meaner bullies would trip us up, push us around. A tall, thin, black boy in the fifth grade named Miles and I met one afternoon to scheme our revenge. He lived off Fall Street not too far from us, and he used to come early on Saturday mornings to light the huge cook stove for Rosie, who was orthodox and refused to let me do it. Miles and I discussed our common problem. We agreed to get our cronies, Negro and Jew, to hoard stones near the bridge and prepare for battle. On D Day, we got to our cache of stones just after the school bell rang. We ambushed the bullies, threw fusillade after fusillade at them, and then as they panicked we attacked with broomsticks. Dirty cocksucking fucking bastards! We routed them, chased after them for blocks. They never bothered us again. I gloat even now, more than seventy years later.

Miles and I became friends. He would visit me at Jake and Rosie's house on Fair Street near the river, and I would visit him at his poor ramshackle dwelling in the shadow of Trent House, a grand colonial mansion, pristine white and colonnaded, taken care of by a poor white family whose sons would not join Miles and me in a game of one o' cat because we were a nigger and a hebe. To this day I can remember Miles, that long drink of water with his long, serious face. I also remember what I have always thought of since as the odor of poverty, the overwhelming stink of bacon fat or lard. Twelve years later when I helped a Party organizer work with black sharecroppers in southern Georgia, I encountered the same smell. I remembered Miles then and wished he were with me, because our Trenton campaign was more successful.

When my mother became ill after my father died, my brother Harry, who had a brooding face under his heavy black hair and was five years my senior, was sent to live at Tante Golda's. After a couple of years there, he went to live in Englewood, New Jersey, with Golda's eldest daughter Clara, a school teacher, and her family. At Clara's he became a live-in baby sitter for her two sons. As my mother recovered from her sarcoma operation and settled down in the Bronx, working as a draper for a Fifth Avenue dress shop, he moved back to live with her, going to high school and working after school. Then the happiest day of my life thus far arrived. My mother came to Trenton and gathered my sister and me up in her arms, and took us to her apartment on Dawson Street in the Bronx. At last, after five long years, an eternity, we were together as a family.

Before I left Trenton I said goodbye to Miles. We never saw each other again, even though I returned to Trenton many times, hitching from New York to visit Tante Golda and her family.

Rosie and Jake were traumatized by the loss of Natalie. After all, they had raised her from infancy. So badly were they hurt that they forgot their decency, came to New York, and offered to buy Natalie from my mother. To this day I can remember Rosie, tears streaming down her plump dark cheeks, pleading, begging my mother to relieve her pain. Of course, my mother, standing tall, all five feet of her, her eyes stern, refused Rosie's dreadful offer. I must say I was of two minds about it.

4

My mother's mother arrived from Europe. She was seventy-five years old.

Why she came to live with us, I don't know. She had two other daughters living in America, one in Cleveland and the other in Brooklyn, both orthodox who kept kosher homes, as my mother, who was an atheist, did not. Perhaps it was because my mother was her youngest. I don't remember her name, and now there is no one I can ask.

She was a tall, forbidding woman who wore a wig over her shaven head as required by her religion. As we stood before her she examined us with sharp, unsmiling eyes. I was immediately afraid of her, though my sister managed to evoke a smile from her firm lips. In Minsk she and my grandfather Daniel, already long dead, had owned a jewelry store. Daniel had been a yeshiva *bocher,* studying Judaic law and lore most of the time, and tending the store when my grandmother went out on the road to sell jewelry. She would return when her time came to give birth to another child. A child brought into the world, impregnated again, she would pick up her jewelry cases, say goodbye to her children and husband, and again trudge forth on the dusty roads of White Russia, leaving her family in the hands of older daughters and maids. Grandpa did little but study. We are, of course, people of the book and the word.

My mother instructed us that as long as her mother resided with us we were to observe the kosher rules. Natalie and I already knew those

My maternal grandfather

rules since Rosie had kept a kosher home, but Harry did not. A few days after she arrived, as I was walking home from school, P.S. 52 on Kelly Street, I saw my grandmother on her knees in an empty lot near our house. She was *shirering,* polishing, our pots with earth and stone to cleanse them of *traifness,* making them kosher. I was ashamed in front of the other kids and pretended not to see her. Two days later, either out of meanness or because he simply forgot, Harry took the butter dish

My maternal grandmother

out of the icebox and placed it on the table as we were eating a meat meal. As my grandmother stared impassively at him, he buttered his bread and bit into it. She said not a word. The following day her daughter Becky came from Brooklyn and left with her. I saw her again a few times before she decided that even Becky's home wasn't kosher enough and she returned to Minsk.

That was in 1927. Some sixteen or seventeen years later, when she was in her nineties, she and the rest of our family there were taken by the Nazis. My mother told me the story of how she refused to enter a cattle car headed for one of the hellholes in Poland, or perhaps the Ukraine, and had been bayonetted to death. I do not know how true the story is, but I insist on believing it. She was a tough old lady, and I am proud to be her grandson.

5

Dawson was a wide street. It was our playground.

Kids of every age populated the street; Jews, Italians, Irish. There was an older and tougher Irish kid who kept bullying me and the other Jewish kids until an even bigger and tougher Italian kid beat him up. Dawson Street was a League of Nations.

In season we played touch football, what we called throwing association, punchball, stickball, one, two, three and over, buck, buck, how many horns are up. I was skinny and the kids kept telling me I was stronger than I looked. I hated punchball because I could never get the hang of punching the ball with my fist. I would slap at it, which was an automatic out. Good field, no hit. I was good at the other games, so I loved them. Why not? I would be difficult with my friends until they gave in and played the game I wanted to play.

I played hard, always keeping an eye on my kid sister while she hopscotched on the sidewalk with her friends until my mother and brother returned from work. I loved her, I hated her. Even at Rosie's I'd been her protector, her big brother, her father, for God's sake. Now, again. Once, playing throwing association, I caught a pass and ran hard into one of the big guys we were playing with, a football guard at Morris High, and was knocked cold. When I woke up in the corner drug store, Where's my sister, where's my sister? She, oblivious to what went on right before her in the street, was still playing hopscotch.

It would already be dark when my brother called us in for supper, and even then I'd have to tear myself away from whatever game we were playing. I loved it, loved the excitement of the game itself, of the competition. I hated losing and would try to find an excuse to fight, throw my fists. My mother would make food which was easy and quick to prepare. Chops, meatballs, chicken soup from the chicken she'd boiled the night before, bananas or berries in season with sour cream, fresh Jewish rye or rolls. I relished the heel of the rye and of the rolls it was the crescents I preferred. Jell-O. Lemon Jell-O, orange Jell-O, grape Jell-O. Jell-O.

Harry worked after school in a large stationery store, Goldsmith's, on Nassau Street in Manhattan. He worked five afternoons a week and all day on Saturday. Still he came home with all A's. Natalie was already in school and also bringing home all A's. I was a lousy student, glad to get B's. I had a good excuse, I couldn't understand my teachers. Where I said law, bird, New Jersey, they said lawr, boid, New Joisey. On a spelling test, how would you write lawr, boid? A talented dressmaker, my mother worked in one or another Fifth Avenue shop. This was in the twenties, so she worked steady. Right after school Natalie and I had to go to the Sholem Aleichem Yiddish Shule on Bathgate Avenue, the Orchard Street of the Bronx, with pushcarts and open stands and always crowded with sellers and buyers. In shule we learned to read and write Yiddish. I played Judas Maccabeus in a Hanukkah play and halfway through forgot my lines and had to be prompted. Five years later, on the bum, I'd fight a man for calling me a dirty kike, and when back in New York City would proclaim proudly that I wasn't a Jew, I was a bolshevik. What really was I?

On Saturday nights my mother would have parties with many friends, mostly Party comrades, Yiddish poets, writers. Natalie and I would dance among the grown-ups. Mama was the life of the party. She would sing songs from Yiddish musicals and do the Charleston and the Black Bottom. We were very proud of her. And there were men, of course. One, then another.

Finally there was just one, and I loved him. Lyovka. Leo. A love of a man. Soft-spoken, attentive to me, asked me questions and then listened patiently to my answers. Natalie loved him too, and my mother was the happiest I'd ever seen her. We rejoiced. Marry him, Mama, please. Lyovka would come to the house, we would get dressed up in our best and go to a restaurant, or a soda parlor, or the Bronx Zoo. Then there was a crisis. Always there were crises. From the beginning of Day One. The apple. Cain and Abel. The Flood. The Philistines. World War I. Coxie's Army. Papa dying. President Wilson having a stroke, and dying, too. He looked like Papa, and for a while I would confuse them. Mama sick. Now another crisis. Lyovka wanted to marry Mama and take the whole family to live in the Soviet Union, the land of the proletarian revolution. Mama, let's go. I'll drive a tractor, become a leader in the Party. Mama hedged. Give me time, she said. Harry didn't want to go, he had a girlfriend. I would have gone to hell just so long as Mama married Lyovka. I wanted a papa, I wanted Mama to have a husband. All night long from behind our closed bedroom door Natalie and I could hear them arguing, talking, discussing, kissing.

We went to Trenton so that Mama could discuss it with Tante Golda, with Uncle Dave, with Charlie and Minnie Cohen, with Morris and Tillie Cohen. Uncle Dave said, Don't be a fool, Merril, things are terrible there. People are starving, dying by the thousands. Morris, Charlie, Minnie, good Communists, said, Go, go, Merril, it will soon be a paradise there, and Lyovka is a nice man, will be a good father to your children. Five years later, Charlie and Minnie's daughter fell in love with a Russian engineer visiting New York on a mission, and returned with him to the Soviet Union. He died of cholera during the war, as did her two children, and she ended up the wife of the KGB agent who ran Estonia—or was it Lithuania? It was said in the family that when her brother Danny came to visit her after the war she refused to kiss him at the airport because it was forbidden to kiss Americans.

Mama did not marry Lyovka and go off with him to the workers' paradise. He went alone. I was furious with her. I loved Lyovka, he was a love of a man.

He wrote Mama long letters. One day a picture postcard arrived. It showed Lyovka leading a May Day parade, red flags flying, pennants and banners, too. It was the last Mama was to hear from him. She waited and waited, rejecting all other men, and then learned—how I never discovered—that Lyovka, who'd been an admirer of Trotsky, had been eaten for breakfast early one morning by the man with the insatiable appetite, Comrade Stalin, the Father of All Peoples.

My mother went on to a Mr. Brown. I disliked Mr. Brown, as did Natalie. He was loud. He was crude. Always trying to kiss Mama, hug her, in front of us. She got rid of him.

Mama never mentioned Lyovka again. She became deaf when purges were mentioned. She was a denier. The world is full of deniers. Uncomfortable truths make them uncomfortable. Poor, sensitive souls. I hid Lyovka deep in my heart. He had been a sweet, kind man. I had seen it in his face, in the way he carried his slender body, in his smile. You know, damn it, you know. I, too, denied, forgot him until he emerged from deep in my heart for a swift short moment one bitter dawn in the city of Murcia, Spain, as I stood before a Party security chief, his lethal black gun staring me straight in the face.

6

1929. October. The crash.

Who cared? Who had stocks? Only the rich, and to hell with them! What was important was that the Yanks did not win the pennant again, and the Babe did not break his own home-run record that year. A few years later, in 1932, I was standing outside the pool parlor on Brighton Beach Avenue in Brooklyn with a hundred other people, watching the large diagram of a ballfield on the window being manipulated by Louie the Goniff to simulate what was going on in Chicago, when the loudspeaker yelled that the Babe was pointing to right center, and next, BANG! he hit one over the fence, just where he had pointed. Good old Babe. There was a man who never let you down. God, I loved the Babe, and lived and died with the Yankees.

So unlike the Party and its leaders. Every year another split. My mother and her friends were always at each other's throats, screaming at each other, and splitting, too. When Charles Ruthenberg died, we mourned him. Then we raised our fists to our beloved leader Weisbord.

The next year on May Day, in our bleached white shirts and red kerchiefs, Union Square mobbed, the Cossacks on horses pushing us
around, we raised high our fists to the Soviet Union and Ben Gitlow.
Sure enough, he too, like Weisbord, betrayed the working class, and we
huzzahed for Jay Lovestone, our new beloved leader. And just as soon
as we hailed him, down he went and up went our fists to BrowderFoster.
First Weisbord refused to follow the line laid down by Russia, then
Gitlow, then Lovestone. Russia. Russia. Russia. Didn't Stalin know best?
Didn't the Russians? Hadn't they made a revolution? Trotsky had betrayed the revolution, and now these guys.

Three years running, Natalie and I went to a Young Pioneer camp in
Lumberville, New Jersey, on the Delaware River, not too far from Philly.
I won all the races on field day. I became official campfire tender.
Natalie learned all the Joe Hill songs. I loved sneaking into the girls'
tents at night to scare them. Peeked through a knothole in the outhouse when one of them went in to pee. Made cigarettes out of corn silk
and smoked and jerked off simultaneously.

The first summer we were there, in 1928, I was thirteen, star athlete,
a tough kid. Malya, one of our counselers, had to go to Philadelphia for
a night; she was hitching, would I accompany her? Sure, I was proud to
be her protector on the road. She was a tiny woman, just barely taller
than I was that year. Malya spoke with an accent, had come from Russia
as a child, was now about nineteen. We left after lunch, made good time,
and arrived at her house about four o'clock.

Her husband, Bill Lawrence, was already there. He was a nice looking fellow with a kind face. We had a quiet supper, then I was sent up to
bed. No sooner was I undressed than they began to argue. I never really
got any sleep. They argued all night. I heard every word they said—they
spoke loud and clear. Bill's life was in crisis. His whole life was at stake:
he was going to quit the Party, he was a follower of Jay Lovestone, each
country's Party had a right to interpret Marx and Lenin according to its
own history and traditions, something about Nicolai Bukharin's theory
of exceptionalism. Malya said it didn't matter, you can't leave the Party,

the Party is the vanguard of the proletariat, Stalin knows best, you are politically immature, Lovestone is an opportunist—"politically immature" and "opportunist," words of obloquy, I already knew, were enough to send one to hell. Back and forth they went all night. I would fall asleep, awake to shouting, to weeping, Malya's, Bill's, life or death, everything we believed or did not believe was life or death. In the morning, as the sun rose—of course—Bill acceded. He would stick with the Party, right or wrong, the Party. The Party. It was to be his life until he died. Malya's life, my mother's life, the life of most of her friends; only Uncle Dave stood adamantly against it.

Me? The Party may have been my church, but I would rather play ball. I hated meetings, yet every Saturday morning I sat with other Young Pioneers and listened to how John D. Rockefeller robbed and stole, how the first J. P. Morgan made a fortune selling defective rifles to the Union army, and how the steel bosses used thugs to kill striking workers and how William Z. Foster, our beloved leader, stood up to them.

How do kids do it? I went to school, did my homework, cleaned our apartment, shopped from a list my mother left, played ball, went to Young Pioneer meetings, bummed around with my friends on the street corner, went to the library to pick up an armful of books—large tomes, Feuchtwanger, Romain Rolland Andersen-Nexo's *Pelle the Conqueror*, *Anna Karenina*, Nick Carter, Frank and Dick Merriwell, Jack Reed's *Ten Days That Shook the World*—and had enough time left over to daydream about girls and their breasts and that exciting secret between their legs. And still get in eight hours' sleep.

In 1929, when Natalie and I were at camp again in Lumberville, my mother arrived to stay at the adjoining adult Camp Hulyit, which I now interpret as Camp Have a Ball. She came with a man she told us she was going to live with. She loved him. She had met him that summer, and we had never seen him before. We were also moving from Dawson Street to the Communist Co-ops on Bronx Park East, where she had bought a four-room apartment. She also had to sell her little dress store on Prospect Avenue because she employed one woman, and the Co-operative would not sell an apartment to anyone who exploited labor. She would, she said, find employment with one of the Fifth Avenue shops. Okay, Mom, that's nice but I got to go, got a ball game to play. I didn't care anymore. She could do as she goddamned pleased. Who was this fat guy? Natalie stayed to eat with them in Camp Hulyit. I ran away as fast as I could to our camp next door. I was Red Grange, stiff-arming onrushing tacklers, swivel-hipped, as fast as greased lightning, until I got to my game. Then, with my new glove bought with Raleigh cigarette coupons stolen from the coat pockets of our boarder on Dawson Street, I played second base, Tony Lazzeri, Poosh-em Up Tony, my mother and her new free love lover shunted aside. I hit a double which I ran into a triple, and then stole home. Who cared what she did? Who cared?

Rieback was the man's name. Fat-faced. Red-faced. Never saw the prick before, now he was going to live with my mother, move in with us. I called him Rieback because that is what my mother called him. It is not my intention to denigrate free love marriages. Nearly all the couples in our milieu, whether Communist, Socialist, or Anarchist, lived in free love marriages. They were no less enduring, stable, and responsible than state-certified marriages, and their children grew up to become Nobel laureates, win Pulitzer prizes, and to shoot Brinks armored car guards.

My mother sold her tiny store on Prospect Avenue. We moved to a brand-new four-room apartment in the Coops, as we called it, and Rieback settled in with my mother in the bedroom next to Natalie's and mine. Harry slept in the living room, on a couch that, when covered with a beautifully fitted velvet cover made by my mother, served as a sofa during the day.

Across the park were the co-ops erected by the Amalgamated Clothing Workers Union, and on our side, not too far from us, were the National Co-ops owned by the Labor Zionists. The Bolshevik Revolution profoundly affected even those radicals who had no love for bolshevism as "played out on the stage of history" by LeninTrotskyStalin. Revolutions, collectives, cooperatives were in the air. Brotherhood. The Universal City of Man. Didn't everyone believe in revolution? I wondered.

I guess not. Not far away, between the National and the Communist Co-ops, sprawled a large Italian district. Before we moved there, a gang of young Italians armed with stones and clubs had come to raid the vanguard of the revolution, you goddamned dirty red bastards, but were repelled with stones and baseball bats. They got the living shit beat out of them, lumpen proletarians that they were, and they never returned. The Aces, our teen-age social and athletic club, played baseball with them and we could never beat them.

We wore red jerseys with Aces in white scrawled across our chests, and we had our own clubroom where we taught each other how to do a fast Lindy Hop and where, in the darkness on old sofas scrounged and bought from secondhand furniture stores, we necked with girls from the Coops or the neighborhood, and we played football in Bronx Park and baseball in French Charlies Oval, and went to Young Pioneer meetings, then YCL meetings (when we remembered), and marched on May Day, running back each time after reaching Union Square to march with the painters, the dressmakers, the tailors, the teachers, so that the *Daily Worker* could say 100,000 marched when it was only 25,000, and because we forgot more frequently to attend meetings were called in by a functionary named Wilson or Fox and scolded, simultaneously being told we were "overexposed politically" and "politically immature" and should be paying more attention to the Party, the Cause, the Movement, the Good Fight, the Soviet Union. There was also school, listening to ball games, turning on Rudy Vallee, then Bing Crosby and Kate Smith, and reading, and reading, and reading. Meanwhile my mother and Rieback were not getting along. Once I saw him with another woman walking in Bronx Park, but of course I didn't tell my mother. I didn't care for the man; he was a cold fish, and after two years or so he moved out and my mother was single again.

The Party began simultaneously to split unions and form the Trade Union Unity League. That's called the unity of opposites in the dialectic. Magic. More and more Party leaders began to call for revolution. I was at a buddy's house once when Israel Amter, our Abe Lincolnesque leader, said in his quiet voice that perhaps we ought to capture City Hall and take command of the Brooklyn Bridge. I was all for it. Even kids knew things were bad and getting badder and soon would be baddest of all. Yes, who gave a damn the market had crashed, or that capitalists were jumping out of windows? Workers did not jump out of windows. I never heard of one jumping out a window because he was broke. He suffered. His family suffered. But my family got lucky. Uncle Dave, because of his high rating as an agent, was able to get Harry—who had just graduated from high school—a job in the Metropolitan Life office on Madison Avenue for twenty-one dollars a week. My mother, who had been making a good living working for Hattie Carnegie full time as a draper, began to have her season shortened. First to forty weeks, then to thirty, then to twenty, and in the mid-thirties to as low as five weeks a year.

Harry's twenty-one dollars a week began to attract every unwed girl in the Bronx, and he was having a ball. He was a great dancer, had many girl friends, was the family's breadwinner, and attempted—after a fashion—to be a father to Natalie and me. We were not to read in bed at night because he had heard it hurt your eyes. And he was strict about it. His slaps came quick and sharp. Then we were to chew our milk, not just swallow it, because he had read you are supposed to eat milk, not drink it. Try it sometime. Then he read that bacon was good for you, and we had to eat bacon several times a week. Though my mother wasn't kosher, she couldn't endure the smell of pork, but Harry had said bacon was good for you, so she bought bacon and covered her nose and mouth with a hand towel when she fried it for us. I loved it. Then Harry said we had to have warm milk with Ovaltine every night before we went to sleep, so we had Ovaltine. Who cared, if only he hadn't slapped so quickly and so sharply. Natalie and I began to fear his every step when he entered the house. For five years after my father's death we had rarely seen him; then, when we at last lived together, he was busy with school and an afternoon job; and now he was bossing us around.

Rieback moved out; a boarder—thin, small, hairy Daniel—moved in. He played the cello. My mother moved into our bedroom to sleep with Natalie. I had my own bed.

It was not healthy. Though my mother was modest and careful, I caught glimpses of her naked breasts, her behind, a few times her pubis. In addition there was Natalie, now eight or nine, and an occasional girl friend of hers who would come to sleep over, three in a bed with my mother, naked little bodies and one thirteen- or fourteen-year-old, girl-crazy boy. In the second bedroom, Daniel played his cello and gave lessons to young women behind the closed door—at times more silence than cello. I was going to Morris High then, to which I commuted by trolley car. Because Morris was overcrowded it had both a morning and an afternoon session. I attended in the afternoon. In the morning, my mother and Harry would go off to work, and Natalie to grade school. I would do my homework, clean up the house—a task I had begun even at Rosie's—take a shower, have my lunch, and leave for school.

One morning, my work done, while I was enjoying the shower and its usual delights, a hairy hand reached in between the shower curtains and gently grasped my penis. Frightened, I punched it away and snarled in my original tongue, Fuck off! Daniel let go and returned to his room. I was scared and felt queasy. Of course I said nothing to my mother and brother, and nothing to him the next time I saw him.

A week or so later, again while I was taking my shower, Daniel entered the bathroom, parted the curtains, and, as I stepped back, paralyzed, he fell to his knees and pleaded with me to let him suck it. Scared, reluctant, mute, I let him draw my body close to him as he took my penis in his mouth and worked at it until I ejaculated.

I was thirteen, fourteen years old. Girls—in the street, on the movie screen, in magazine and newspaper ads—excited me. Once a week or so, Daniel would enter the bathroom, and, not a word said, play my flute. I can't say I didn't enjoy it, but I wasn't satisfied; I felt guilty, dirty. Finally one day I broke our silence and said, No more unless you get me a girl. I want a girl. I was certain he could produce one for me. He promised he would, and I permitted him to proceed, which he did, expertly, as I felt guiltier and dirtier. No girl appeared. I reiterated my demand that he find me one, and he reiterated his promise that he would. So it continued for several months, once a week or so. I began to look more closely at girls, women in the street, my sister, her friends, my female classmates. I fell in love with one and wrote "Libby, my Phantom Sweetheart" on my sneakers. With my eyes I probed their breasts, the bigger the better. In the movies I watched Joan Bennett fall into a pond while wearing a tight white sweater, and when she emerged I saw the tell-tale large brown marks where her nipples were. I dreamt of her, masturbated to her. Girl-crazy my friends called me. Luckily I kept busy doing other things. School, playing football for the afternoon session team, playing ball on Saturdays with the Aces—I caught a pass for a touchdown and forever after was called Dick, for Dick Merriwell, by my chums. And Daniel played my flute, which did not stop me from talking to my street buddies about fags and whores, and making silly remarks to passing young women on the corner, cigarettes drooping from our oh-so sophisticated lips; or from looking obliquely at a woman named Ruby Bates, who lived in the Coops and who was one of the girls the Scottsboro Boys were supposed to have raped. The Party lawyers were coddling her to keep her honest as the judicial proceedings continued. None of us and none of the big guys in the Coops tried anything with her; she was a sad, pasty-faced, slope-shouldered thin girl whom we felt sorry for, but that didn't stop us from wondering was she a whore, and were any of the Party big shots fucking her.

In Worcester, when Jeannette (who was to become my wife) was about eight years old she remembers her family talked, it seemed endlessly, about the Scottsboro Boys, who were in jail for allegedly having raped two white women. The Negro boys were being framed, there was no doubt about that.

One night her father came home from work and told the family that a little girl would be staying overnight. Her name was Lucille Wright, the sister of one of the Scottsboro Boys. Because she was about the same age as Jeannette she would sleep with her, and Jeannette's two sisters, Eva and Dora, with whom Jeannette shared a bed, would sleep elsewhere, on the floor or perhaps at a comrade's house. (She had two more sisters, the oldest and the youngest, Evelyn and Freda, and two brothers, Eddie and Woofie.) In any event, a black, very shy little girl was soon brought by a comrade, had supper, and they went to sleep.

Lucille didn't talk very much to Jeannette, just that she was scared because she had to make a speech the next day at some outdoor meeting, and she snuggled close to Jeannette during the night and held on very tightly.

The following morning one of the Party's leading comrades in Worcester came to the Wellin house and Jeannette was told she must go along to City Hall because Lucille had asked that Jeannette stay with her.

A small crowd gathered around the soap box outside City Hall and Lucille trembled as one speaker after another got up to denounce the capitalist system and the frame-up of the boys.

When Lucille stood on the soap box her voice could barely be heard, she could not remember the speech that had been written for her. All she could say, and she repeated it over and over again, was, "The bosses are no good, . . . the bosses are no good, . . . the bosses are no good. . . ."

Jeannette felt sorry for Lucille, who was taken away by car after the rally, to go to another city, and another rally.

I was saved from further iniquity. Daniel gave my mother notice; he was vacating his room and going to Paris, where, he told me, he could live freely as a homosexual and not be afraid, like me. I told him he was the fairy, not me. I liked girls. He tried one more time before he left, but I refused him because, I told him, I wanted to be pure for Miriam, a girl in my Yiddish shule with whom I'd fallen in love. He begged and grabbed at my penis, and though I had an erection I told him I would kill him if he touched me. I was already taller than he, and twice as muscular. I told him I hated him, and goodbye and good riddance. Miriam had her appendix out and I went every day after school to visit her in the hospital, to the sentimental smiles of her co-patients in the ward. When Miriam returned home, she allowed me small favors; a kiss, a quick feel. But it turned out she loved another kid in our Yiddish class. He did the Kazatsky better than I did during the rehearsals for the Yiddish school concert. Still, when we sang the "Internationale," though she held his hand, she also held mine. Small victories are better than none.

My cousin, Emil Conason—the son of Golda and Dave Cohen—opened his doctor's office on Sherman Avenue, not far from Yankee Stadium. I played hookey often and thus saved the trolley fare to and from high school; I was fourteen, in the ninth grade. After I had enough for the bleachers at the Stadium and knew the Babe was due for a homer, not having hit one for three or four games, I would go. It astonishes me now how many times I guessed right. The Babe was truly very reliable. After the game, I would go to Emil's, where it was always a pleasure to eat, since every meal was a feast. Emil was an ebullient, gregarious man, charismatic, and had many friends who, like me, came to eat at his table. As I recall, we were all a very hungry lot, though Emil ate more than any of us. One of those doctors who never followed his own advice, at that time he was just beginning to become obese. At sixty-five, his obesity killed him. One of his skinny, hungry friends was a tough-speaking guy from Brooklyn, a know-it-all named Henry. He was always broke and nearly every time I was there I'd hear him asking Emil for a tenner. He could be very funny and we would always be laughing when he ate with us.

One time after a ball game—the Yanks lost but I saw the Babe make a fantastic running catch—Henry was there with his wife, with whom I immediately fell in love. I'd have picked her over Joan Bennett any time. They were quarreling when I walked in, quarreled during supper, quarreled after supper; neither Emil nor Celia, Emil's long-suffering wife, could stop them. Henry was very nasty, obscenities flowed from his mouth without interruption. His wife was no slouch herself, and I was titillated by such dirt emanating from those gorgeous lips; I'd never heard a woman curse so fluently.

They were still at it when Emil reminded me it was time to go home, and not to play hookey so much. Ceil and Betty, Emil's sister and my favorite cousin—she never forgot to give me a quarter—kissed me goodnight, and then, to my everlasting joy, so did Henry's wife. A real kiss, too, not one of those tight-lipped buzzes. I could barely keep my hands off her.

Years later, when Henry became Henry Miller to me, Betty told me about his fight with June that night. When June had affairs with other men, Henry, a true anarchist, didn't care too much, since he was always screwing around with other women, but June had fallen in love and was having a red hot affair with a woman. Henry flipped, went totally nuts. Couldn't take the competition, I guess.

When *Tropic of Cancer* appeared, Emil was featured in the novel as Dr. Krankheit, a not very pleasant portrait of the man who had fed and bankrolled Henry when he was down and out. Emil was so infuriated he forgot himself and thought of suing Henry for slander. We all told him to forget it, artists had license, et cetera. Fuck Henry, we said. No, Emil laughed, June fucked him—but good.

I loved *Tropic of Cancer* even though it did vilify my most generous and beloved of cousins. Though Ernest Hemingway influenced the style of an army of writers who came after him, it was Henry who broke all the barriers. There's no one way to write a novel, he seemed to say. And, remember, you little bourgeois swine, conventions are for the dull-witted. I tried to follow his tongue-in-cheek wisdom with *The Itinerant,* my first published though third-written novel, and was terribly disappointed when Henry, after I had air-mailed a copy to Big Sur, sent me a card saying he was sorry he couldn't read it now, his eyes were just about blind. What a soft put-down.

A mystery. Most of my life I believed that, during those early days when I used to visit Emil and Celia, I met there, and sat on the lap of, Emma

Goldman, the Anarchist leader and lover of Alexander Berkman, the would-be assassin of Henry Clay Frick, the steel magnate. Recently I learned that Emma, who resembled somewhat my Tante Golda, resided in Canada from 1919 onward and was not allowed into the United States. Our loss. So when did I sit on her plump lap? Certainly not before the twenties, and not in Canada. Did she used to sneak into the States and spend a night or so at Emil's? It's possible. My cousin Betty, Emil's kid sister who lived with him and Ceil before she married, confirmed it for me. I would have been a pretty big kid to be sitting on Emma's lap, ten, eleven, perhaps. I have always loved sitting on women's laps, since even before Miss Veronica. And Emma was a loving lady. It's possible and I prefer to believe it happened, but I present you with all the possibilities.

7

Politics means power, and what power does, Lord Acton
told us.

As if we didn't know. We do, but refuse to acknowledge it. We are, as I repeat and will repeat again, expert
at denying what may upset us. Is that because we are cowards or because, sentimental me, our lives are difficult
enough, poor us?

The more violent the politics, the more violent the
power when achieved, and so the more violent the rot
when it sets in. Because of the sheer mendacity of those
infected, the only antitoxins are total confession, or total
silence. Though when it is total, can one believe it?

An image—I have no idea whether it is apposite to the
above—comes to mind: the face of a man. It was in the
communal dining hall of Sunrise Farm, the anarchist
commune organized by Uncle Dave's brother, J.J. Cohen,
in the early thirties, some sixty years ago as I write. Mostly
Anarchists, but some Socialists, Communists, Labor
Zionists, Yiddishists lived together in what could be called

an uneasy truce. But not for long. At least when the truce was broken no one was killed, though there were several physical confrontations. Oh, yes, one old Anarchist, shotgun in hand, went in search of a young Anarchist who had betrayed the cause by joining the Communist Party and fleeing to Detroit. Fortunately, he never caught up with the fellow. Old Angelo was still seeking vengeance for the slaughter of the Kronstadt sailors by the Red Army led by Leon Trotsky. We were at lunch when suddenly a small group of commune brothers escorted a slight, very smooth-faced man into the hall and to a table which had been reserved for them. The silence in the large hall was sudden and we were pervaded by a collective awe. I heard someone at the table whisper something about an execution and I was sure what I heard was that the man had been among those who had killed the tsar and his family. Slight as he was, he now assumed the proportions of a giant in my eyes. Christ, the man was a great revolutionary, he had executed the tsar, had made history. My, how I admired his heroism.

But now all these years later another face intrudes—how tricky memory, is it really the same face?—and this face belongs to a man also feted for his bravery. He had, it was said, assassinated the infamous Petlura, the Ukrainian murderer of Jews. He tailed Petlura for two weeks in Paris, then shot him dead. At a dramatic trial, he proclaimed his deed openly, did not plead the Fifth, if such they have in France, and was acquitted to popular acclaim. If ever I knew his name I did not remember it, but recently I learned that the man who killed Petlura was a Russian Jew named Samuel Schwartzbard, a poor watchmaker. Or was it Volodine, a Ukrainian Anarchist, who aided and abetted the assassination?

Is it possible there were two different visitors to Sunrise who had killed for our great cause, or am I mistaking the man who killed Petlura with the man I thought at first he was, the man who among others killed the tsar?

At that time, we were much taken with revolutionary heroes; I hoped to be one myself, or at least I imagined so.

8

I hate politics. It always manages to get in the way of romance.

I was sixteen years old. We were getting ready to flee the Coops. My mother owed five months' maintenance and she would have to lose her investment of sixteen hundred dollars, since a buyer could not be found. I would transfer from Morris High to the brand-new Abraham Lincoln High School on Ocean Parkway, because my mother had found an apartment in Brighton Beach. And I fell in love with Anna Goldstein, who had black hair, large brilliant black eyes, very red lips, and not so great skin. She was very quick-witted, smart, eighteen years old, and a budding actress. She didn't give a shit whether I went to meetings or not.

Anna spoke beautifully, as budding actresses should. Though she had no interest in my politics, she did bother me about the language I spoke. She said it was not necessary for me to say fuck every other word, shit every third word, and cocksucker every fourth. My attempt to sound like a proletarian from the gutter, she said, was false, and falser still for someone who boasted he read the great works of the finest writers who ever lived. I tried, though it was difficult, to avoid fuck, shit, and cocksucker when I was with Anna.

She was the daughter of my mother's new boy friend, the theater critic for the Jewish daily, *Der Tag*. My mother was a little embarrassed about that, since *Der Tag* was, as she said, a bourgeois reactionary rag, always telling lies about the Soviet Union. How come, he once twitted her in my presence, you keep saying what a great country Russia is, and yet you're always asking me for money for the starving peasants there? A denier, like so many of her friends, my mother refused to answer Mr. Goldstein's question. She forgave him, however, because he took her to the openings of all the Jewish plays on Second Avenue and the English-speaking plays on Broadway. Then they would taxi to the Cafe Royale, where my mother would be ogled by all the men and sneered at by all the women. My mother gloried in it. Goldstein was a very handsome man and she was the best-dressed woman in the place. She made her own dresses from patterns copied at Hattie Carnegie's. As for Goldstein, he was possessed of a great mane of white hair and wore black spats. A capacious black cape swirled about his elderly shoulders, and a black pearl-handled cane supported his well-manicured hand. A real Parisian boulevardier. They made a handsome pair.

My mother was a very busy woman. She worked at Hattie Carnegie's when work was to be had, and picketed struck shops on Fifth Avenue which the union was trying to unionize. I still have a clipping from the *Daily News* showing my mother being escorted into a paddy wagon because she and her sister unionists had physically attacked a scab. Bailed out, she came home with a bandage on her leg where she said a cop had beaten her with his club. In addition, she attended Party meetings regularly, did dress and coat alterations at home for friends and their friends and comrades, made sure Natalie and I were fed, clothed, and kept clean, and galavanted with Mr. Goldstein, whose first name I no longer remember. He had a wife with whom he seemed to be on the outs, and he had at least one child, Anna. Anna became friends with my mother, even though she lived with her mother on Ocean Parkway in an apartment house I passed every day as I went to Lincoln High.

At the time I first met and fell for Anna, she was playing with the Davenport theater company in an old clinker called *Bells* at the Cherry Lane theater. Once I got all dolled up in some of my brother's clothes: suit, white shirt, tie, polished shoes, camel-hair overcoat with sporty raglan sleeves, and subwayed down to the Village to see Anna in the play. I just about swooned at the sight of my love onstage, and yet again when I went backstage at play's end to be kissed by her in her make-up, smelling musty and womanish and so, to me at least, terribly sexy. On my way home afterwards I had to admit to myself that Anna was better looking onstage than off. That is part of the magic of the theater, I suppose, and the movies, too. When I worked with Orson Welles in the forties, first as he and Cole Porter put on *Around the World* as a musical on Broadway, and then in Hollywood when he wrote, produced, directed, and starred in *Lady From Shanghai* with Rita Hayworth, I discovered the same truth. Except for Rita. She was just as beautiful on, off, and in between. Incidentally, the same was true for the men as well as for the women. Off, Welles had the physiognomy of a refined pig—a very big pig, of course. The voice, however, was the same on, off, and in between: that of God as recorded by Cecil B. De Mille.

Shortly after my theater date with Anna, we moved to Brighton and I left behind all my Aces buddies and the Young Communist League branch which I had recently joined; left behind football in the park, baseball in French Charlies, and meetings, meetings, meetings.

After we moved to Brighton, twice a week I would stop at Anna's on my way home from school. At first Anna said I was too young—she was no more than two or three years older than my sixteen—for us to be close friends. I was insistent, however, and she relented. She taught me many things. First and foremost was that I must always defer to a woman's wishes. I must always carry a condom; I was strong, so I must always, always be gentle; and, don't you ever forget it, never insist on doing what a girl does not want to do.

For the two years we lived in Brighton—when we owed six months' rent we moved again, this time to Second Avenue between Tenth and Eleventh Streets in Manhattan—Anna instructed me. She was a marvelous teacher. In addition to her, I had only one other close friend, a boy I'd met in the Coops who had also moved, not because of lack of rent money, but because his parents were Lovestoneites and the new Party leadership had made life difficult for them there. His name was Natie Shlechter; we were close friends in the Coops, and we were close friends in Brighton. I will return to Natie, who was to be a very important person in my life.

After we moved to Second Avenue Anna would come to visit us, but now she had a boy friend and he would accompany her. Once he did not come with her, and since no one else was home she again gave me instructions, after which she said I had been an excellent student. I was very proud.

The world, mostly politics, intervened, and we never saw each other again. Well, not for a good twenty years anyway. It was in March 1953, shortly after the demise of one Osip Djugashvili. I hadn't had much time to celebrate because a small union I had helped organize, the Federation of Shorthand Reporters, was on general strike, and I was worried about it. I was thirty-eight then. I ran into a tired, sallow-faced Anna on Park Row, across from City Hall. We stopped in a coffee shop for a cup. I had hardly said a word before Anna told me she had just learned that she had cancer and did not have much longer to live. No wonder she looked so tired, so worn out, wan, drawn. I could find but few words to say to her, I just held her hand. She did not want to talk. I never learned if she was married, had children, what had happened to her father, who the last time I had seen him was on his knees begging my mother to take him back after she had discovered he was seeing another woman. I kissed Anna's pale cheek, then watched her as she slowly crossed the street and entered the subway kiosk in City Hall Park.

If this were a work of fiction, I would try to create a life for Anna based on what I did know about her, but since it is not a work of fiction, I am not permitted to do that. I do not know if she ever became a professional actress, or ever had a husband and children. I don't even know how long she lived after that.

All I do know is that she adored her father, a man who gave her little time, a dandy who always wore spats, a swirling black cape, and a soft black fedora over his wild mane of gray hair. And that she had been exceedingly kind to a young man starved for love, and who loved her as much as any sixteen-year-old could possibly love. Anna.

9

Natie Shlechter was a powerfully built boy, handsome, with the high cheekbones and slit eyes of a Tatar nomad. When we played football, I was the back asked to catch a pass or run the field, but Natie was the one asked to crack the opponents' line for a needed yard or two. Though I frequently failed, he rarely did. He was a bull. He was also intelligent, an A student at Clinton High School and then at City College, quick-witted, and I was jealous of him. He had a father and mother. We were best friends.

Up to the time I met Natie at the Communist Coops, I believed everything I was told by the Party. I didn't really have to be told anything, I inhaled it. If I was bothered by one or another contradiction—how could a man be my great leader last year and a traitor to the cause this?—I attributed it to weakness on my part, I was just sucking up to the bourgeoisie: the simplest yet greatest ploy for self-delusion and denial ever invented by ancient magician or modern agitpropnik.

In a word or two, I was a believer. More, I was a fundamentalist. Which does not mean I was a fundamentalist in Marxist or even Leninist theory, far from it; I merely skimmed the surface, I was never a good student. I was a fundamentalist in my belief that the Soviet Union and the Party were the answer to every single problem faced by the human race. When we made the world revolution, which was inevitable, there would no longer be any car collisions, because people would no longer be nervous, competitive, and in a hurry—because, naturally, it would not be necessary to be nervous, competitive or in a hurry in a socialist society. Voilà!

Greed, envy, brutality, power; all would vanish from the earth. We were, and Stalin meant it, the engineers of the human soul (even though we did not believe in the human soul). I knew adults—workers, college graduates, Ph.D.'s—who believed all this; great poets, world-class novelists, people with genius I.Q.'s. We believed beyond reason, and pretended that what we believed was founded on pure reason. We believed what we believed so profoundly that our beliefs became the very foundation of our existence. Our minds were closed to all else. And if you combine a closed mind with a predilection for action it is not difficult to say with Sergei Nechaev, "Whatever aids the triumph of the revolution is ethical. . . ."

Excuse me. I repeat myself. It is like one of those viruses, a plague, you wipe it out in one place, it appears in another in a different guise. First it is a law of the dialectic, then it is a commandment of God.

When I was a boy two daydreams ran in parallel lines: one to be a great broken-field runner like Little Boy Blue, Albie Booth of Yale; and the other to be chosen by the Party to become a Cheka agent ordered to track down and kill an enemy of the revolution and the Party, which were one and indivisible. There I would stand, steely-eyed, a .45 in my fist, staring down the enemy, and then putting a bullet between his cowardly eyes. The enemy was always cowardly, and we were always brave. It took me quite a while to learn that bravery knows no creed, even fascists could be brave; it is wisdom, not bravery, which is unique, and the greatest virtue.

I never had the talent to run a field like Albie Booth, but I think it's possible, despite a queasy stomach, that I could have realized the second dream, if not for Natie Shlechter. We were best friends. We played ball together, went to the library together, talked books, exchanged books. I rooted for the Yankees, he, ever the iconoclast, for the Detroit Tigers. His parents owned an apartment in the Coops. Like me he had been born into the Communist Party, but his parents had split—or been expelled, more likely. His father, a little pock-faced man who made his living delivering papers door to door, once said to me in his broken English, "A great revolutionary is someone who thinks for himself." He and his wife were Lovestoneites, and thus ostracized by most of our parents, who, though they themselves had been followers of Lovestone when he led the Party, were now Browderites, as ordered by Stalin, leader nonpareil, one of the greatest men who ever lived, a man who never—well, hardly ever—made a mistake.

I am not joking. I knew a dear man, decent, intelligent, a Marxist, by God, who would stare me in the eyes and say that Stalin was probably the greatest man of the twentieth century, a man who never made a mistake, and what he did in Russia was necessary because the Russian people just did not know any better and needed an iron fist to guide them. He also exclaimed, out of the other side of his mouth, that what we needed in America was true democracy, not ruling class democracy. This man was not a fool, nor was he cruel. He himself could never shoot a man in cold blood, but for the cause, he exulted in another man doing it for him. He was a fundamentalist, a true believer, a killer by proxy. I still cringe; so was I, until the gun was pointed at my very own nose.

In the Aces we ignored political differences. We were, as we had been informed by our political leaders, overexposed; what we wanted was to play ball and dance and neck with girls in our dark cave of a clubroom. Natie was a bit slower with girls, I a bit faster—thanks, no doubt, to Miss Veronica, and Daniel, the flute player. (On the bum, where realism ruled, it was called playing the piccolo, a shorter and more slender instrument.)

But Natie and I were best friends. We discussed the books we read, and we had to discuss politics. Whatever contradictions I attempted to conceal, he attempted to expose. It seems to me now, more than sixty years later, that there was one point about which we argued endlessly.

If the workers, referring to the Soviet Union and the Party, don't have a say in decisions governing their lives and livelihood, if there is no free labor market and there are no free trade unions, then it is just plain peonage. Read Marx. He showed me the page in Volume I of *Das Kapital*.

> And my response: That will come later, give it time.
> How much later?
> When the entire world is socialist.
> But up to then I have to accept the life of a peon, right?
> If in the end we'll have socialism.
> Is that a promise?
> Yeah, it's a promise.
> Thanks, I appreciate that.
> Then, both angry, we would force a laugh.

To a fundamentalist, it would be the laugh that would prove us both guilty of betraying the cause. A true believer does not laugh. To be an engineer of the human soul is very serious business.

Even at seventeen, Natie thought of himself as a free thinker, a skeptic. He wanted you to prove every damn thing you said. I hated doubt. I needed to believe completely. Order was what I required, there was enough chaos in my life. I didn't want to talk about—whatever it was.

If we can't talk about it, how can we be friends?

Aw, shit, let's walk to Coney Island and get a Nathan's hot dog.

Together we would manage the five pennies for a hot dog, though most of the time it would be his four against my one. We shared equally, and there was many a time when I could hear him whisper to his mother to ask me to stay for dinner because he knew there was little to eat at my house.

When we moved to Second Avenue in Manhattan during my senior year in high school, I commuted to school in Brighton. I would stop in to see Anna, and, on rarer occasions, Natie. When it comes to friendship, the penis is more equal. When I did see Natie it was as if we'd seen each other the previous day. Who you reading? Sigrid Undset. Knut Hamsun is a hell of a lot better. When the intervals stretched out, we wrote each other long letters. He was kind. Your letters are very good, you ought to think about becoming a writer. I thought he was, as usual, just being nice. He kept insisting he meant it. It made me feel very good, of course, but I put it out of my mind, until about twenty-five years later.

Several times during my commuting days, when I returned to our flat on Second Avenue I would find a woman friend of my mother's, a Comrade Lazarowitz, on our stoop, standing guard. She would tell me I couldn't go up. When I questioned her, she said to just wait, I would find out soon. Sure enough, a half hour or so later, there was Comrade Earl Browder coming out the door, nodding to Comrade Lazarowitz, giving me a cold stare, departing. Still she kept me waiting. Five minutes later, a man I didn't recognize departed, also nodding to Lazarowitz, and yet again she held me back. I was to meet him several years later; he was a Comrade Alpi, Comintern rep to the American Party. In another five minutes, Jack Stachel, another leader—famous or infamous, according to which split you favored—emerged. He nodded to her, and to me, too. He and my mother were friends. He had been to visit. I had no love for him.

I was, of course, very proud that our apartment had been chosen for secret meetings of the Party high muckamucks. Thereafter, and it occurred four or five times, Browder also acknowledged me when he left our house. Though I could now boast to my comrades that I knew Earl Browder, I could not say how I knew him because Lazarowitz had warned me not to mention it.

By the time I was graduated from high school in June 1932, the Great Depression was just about fully depressed. My brother Harry got married, moved out, and had a wife to support; and my mother eked out but a few weeks work at Hattie Carnegie's. Even the rich were hurting badly; they didn't buy new dresses so readily, and brought in their out-of-style gowns for alterations. We moved again. My mother would pay the first month's rent, pay the requested month's security, then not pay for five or six months. It cost, as I remember, about twenty-five dollars to move because by then I was able to help the moving man. The rent was around thirty dollars a month. We had so little food in the icebox that when some of my old friends from the Coops came to visit for a day I could give them very little to eat, and what little I did give them caused my mother to scream at me for a good half hour, since it left us without food the next day.

I finally got a job selling cigarettes and candy at a stand in one of the private beaches near Brighton. It paid two dollars a day. If it rained, I didn't open the stand and thus received nothing. It seems to me it rained a lot that summer. Then I was hired through an employment agency to haul bolsters of silk for a wholesaler in Manhattan, using a hand truck. For this I received a weekly wage of eleven dollars, and for overtime, a corned beef sandwich and a coke. I would come to the job at 8 A.M., and overtime would begin after 6 P.M. I put in a sixty- to seventy-hour week for the eleven dollars and the sandwich. By that time we had moved again, this time to East 15th Street, across the street from Stuyvesant High School and next door to a refuge for delinquent—read pregnant—young girls. I would stare at them from one of our windows, and several repaid my lack of courtesy by revealing their naked breasts to me. In return I would blow them passionate kisses.

Laid off in the spring, I was rehired to sell cigarettes and candy in Oriental Beach for two dollars a day.

Then my cousin Arnold came to visit with an offer I couldn't refuse. Utopia was at hand.

10

Sunrise Cooperative Farm, Saginaw Valley, Michigan.

Utopia.

In a cooperative you own your own land individually, and you make your own profit or loss. Most of the time you work the land yourself. You buy your seed and equipment cooperatively, because it's cheaper when you buy in bulk. You might sell cooperatively in order to protect the price of your produce, gaining or losing according to the market, and in proportion to what you have invested. Cooperatives were and are acceptable in American society. Co-ops allow for individual initiative. Salute the flag.

Sunrise called itself a cooperative farm, though it was in fact a commune, a collective, words that would have disturbed the natives. In a collective, as an individual you own nothing, except perhaps your clothes and toothbrush. It is a kibbutz. You own whatever is to be owned as a group, and everything owned is owned equally. Whatever gain or profit is made is shared equally. Unlike Orwell's *Animal Farm*, no one is more equal, not even the person democratically chosen to superintend the enterprise. I am speaking of a voluntary collective, not the forced variety as in Red Russia or Red China which, as my friend Natie Shlechter would say, resulted in peonage. There are no leaders in a voluntary collective; there are spokesmen, or -women, for different points of view. There are a great many meetings in a collective, and final decisions are made by each and every member casting a vote. No one wields power over anyone else, since power presupposes superiority. Each individual in a collective wields individual power. There is no human organization on earth that respects the rights of an individual more than an anarchist commune.

I do not mention children. They are treated with respect, but even among anarchists children must go where their parents go, do as they are told. Since it is in childhood that the seeds of rebellion are sown (or so we assume, but do we really know?) the harvest will be a new generation of anarchists. A perfect circle. Utopia.

There is a worm in this apple, what some call the human equation. In that equation, as Dostoevsky said, two plus two does not equal four.

Sunrise Farm was a collective enterprise organized by J. J. Cohen—editor of the *Freie Arbiter Shtimme,* the Free Voice of Labor, a Yiddish Anarchist newspaper—and a group of Anarchist friends. In 1932–33, as he traveled about the country to lecture among working class organizations, he inventoried the hardships the Great Depression imposed on the working and unemployed poor. And as FDR, just elected, began his efforts to save American capitalism, Uncle Joe Cohen decided to begin his anarchist experiment in America's heartland, the Middle West.

The Owosso Sugar Company wanted to sell Prairie Farm, ten thousand acres of the finest muck soil in the country, with irrigation canals, a schoolhouse, post office, assembly hall, workers' shacks, barns, silos, several thousand head of sheep, some pigs, teams of Belgian drays, and a 1927 blue Buick coupe on which I was to learn to drive. It was a perfect set-up for an anarchist commune. The price was about $200,000. As J. J. wrote, "The farm is a highly productive one and can easily feed a thousand families. . . . No one will have to work too hard and the community will have an abundance of things that are needed to make life attractive and worthwhile."

The initial proposal was for 150 families of four to pay $500 each. One hundred families subscribed almost immediately. There were some from Chicago and Detroit, but most were Jews from New York's needle trades, and were Anarchists; a few were Communists, like myself. I was to be the fourth member of Tante Golda's family, along with her, Uncle Dave, and Arnold. There were also several Labor Zionist families, some Yiddishists, a few Socialists. J. J. did not want active Communists because, as he said, their main activity "was disrupting labor organizations," with the thought of taking them over. Well, he got me and several others. We never established a branch or cell, so I can say we never conspired to take Sunrise over.

Since 100 families at $500 each equalled only $50,000, I don't know where Uncle Joe obtained the remainder. It was rumored that Beanie Baldwin, an undersecretary of the Department of Agriculture in the New Deal and a friend of Richard Gilbert, Joe's son-in-law and an economist, was able to obtain a grant for Uncle Joe and his comrades. After all, Sunrise was a producer of peppermint, sugar beets, wheat, barley, and sundry vegetables in large quantity. Ten thousand acres is a lot of land. It was a place where no one would ever go hungry. For unemployed dressmakers and tailors, it looked like heaven.

No one, as far as I know, elected J. J. Cohen to be our spokesman, leader, president, chairman. He was just plain Genosse Cohen, but he found the farm, organized its purchase, and planned the recruiting campaign, so he was the man who ran the collective. He hired a man named DeGus, a Belgian who had been the superintendent for Owosso Sugar, to run our farming operations as well.

Opening day was June 26, 1933. I arrived with six other people from New York a week or so later.

The sight of the farm was overwhelming. Everything we could see, from horizon to horizon, belonged to us. Us. Not only would we now never go hungry, but we would live in collective joy as proud, respected individuals. We exulted, and were exalted. Only my entrance into revolutionary Barcelona in early January 1937, in a parade with newly arrived International Brigaders, was to surpass the exultation, and in Barcelona what seemed to be the entire population of one million people turned out to greet us. We were going to create a new world—here, and there.

We knew nothing, here or there. We hired, or our Belgian superintendent did, farmers who had worked on Prairie Farm for years to help us.

Our first collective job was to weed our forty-acre parcels of peppermint. A single acre is about 220 by 200 feet. A forty-acre square, we soon figured out, meant a single row of peppermint would run about 2800 feet, a half mile and counting. Peppermint is so good a crop each leaf is very valuable so it must be weeded by hand, since machines waste your money.

You get down on your knees between two rows and crawl, pulling out weeds on either side of you. You have never done this before. You are a dressmaker, a presser, a failed storekeeper, now you are on your knees under a broiling sun pulling weeds. Every once in a while someone comes along with a water pail and a ladle. A momentary respite. At twelve noon, trucks appear to carry you back to the large assembly hall, which has been transformed into a messhall. The kitchen brigade has prepared borscht, baked bread, cold milk from our own cows, milked by our brothers and sisters just recently taught how to milk cows. Lunch concluded, back to your weeding station. Two rows per person take a whole day. Some of the younger and spryer finish early and move over to the next two rows. It is hard, grueling work.

Still, our adrenalin is flowing, we are amazed at the bounty that awaits us. All this is new, all this property is ours, we love each other, we love our farm, we love our adventure, we are idealists, we are living what we have dreamed all our lives. It is now *tochiss afn tisch:* literally, your ass is on the table; you talked a good fight, now prove it. All our lives we fought for the eight-hour day, now we work ten hours, twelve if rain threatens, and we don't care, we love it. The little kids go to school, taught by a young couple, Esther and Joe Swire, who follow the principles of Ferrer and Dewey, anarchistic, progressive, free; and those my age, proud of their youth and strength, weed faster, and of course that is natural, the older are not expected to do as much. Who notices, who cares? New families keep arriving almost daily. Houses—shacks really, formerly occupied by Owosso Sugar employees, Mexicans and Slavs—are assigned. It seems we are on perpetual holiday. Weeding in the hot sun is like being on vacation. We are getting tan. On Sundays, many of us are trucked to Bay City, the Saginaw River, for a picnic and a swim. Of course weeding is harsh work, but on holiday, who cares? We sing Joe Hill songs, Halleluja, I'm a bum.

We eat a lot of borscht. Pigs are slaughtered, old sheep. Mutton, mutton, borscht, borscht. Who cares? We work hard and we eat what we are given, though the kitchen people are far from professional. Who cares? We work long hours in the sun, we are on holiday, we are camping, we are making do in the Catskills, we are living in rundown houses on Coney Island. This is all ours; we are building a new society, right smack in the middle of capitalist depression America. Men and women are equal, work equally, share equally. (I have no recollection of any women being on the farm board.) Everyone has promised to leave his or her sectarian differences behind. No fanaticism would be tolerated. Open minds are demanded. The kids are being taken care of during the day, but spend time with papa and mama during and after suppertime before returning to their dormitories. Soon the harvest will come, we will make money out of our peppermint, our sugar beets, our wheat, our corn. In nearby Saginaw there are unemployment and bread lines. In Sunrise there is work for us, and food on our table. And we love one another.

There are meetings at least once a week after supper. A problem arises which causes wide consternation. We pay the fieldworkers we have hired twelve and one-half cents an hour. That is what is recommended as the going wage in the area by our professional superintendent. Are we exploiting them? Are we underpaying them? The going wage is most likely an exploitative wage. We do not like the idea of being employers—more, exploiters of labor. We decide, after long, anguished discussion, that it is fair compensation. There are those who say, Of course; it is to our interest to think it is fair. If we were the exploited we would say it is not nearly enough, because we are class conscious and those who work for us are hardly so. No one knows what they think because they are close-mouthed. We have no idea what they say among themselves. We make a decision that fits our pockets, and we know that. We feel guilty and uneasy.

While we have taken to wearing shorts and short-sleeved shirts, or even no shirts, those who work for us wear winter longies under their denim shirts and pants. When I ask the man who teaches me how to drive a Farmall tractor why he doesn't dress as I do in the summer heat, he smiles and says that way he keeps clean to the ankles and wrists all week until his Saturday night bath. I realize it saves using fuel for the hot water boiler. We use our hot water profligately. Those who work for us think we are rich.

I am one of the honored young; I am assigned to driving a tractor. I have become an aristocrat and have left the laboring herd. No longer do I have to crawl all day weeding peppermint. I learn how to plow a field, and to disk it. As usual, I am happiest when I am alone. I sit atop a powerful machine all day. I daydream, embroider heroic patterns. I will lead the proletariat to victory. I plan the seduction of a young woman with whom I have already reached the handholding stage. I am fastidious, and learn to make my furrows neat and straight. I do not have to listen to the grunting and gasping of the elderly people in their fifties and sixties. Some of my peers begin to stare at me. Are they jealous? No one dares say that, but you cannot stop them from thinking. Have I been given the honor because I am the nephew of J. J's brother, Dave, who is also on the farm board?

I ask no questions. I love plowing all day, alone, fighting the elements, the world, leading my red army to victory, angry at the goddamn tractor which keeps stalling and I have to walk five miles to the shop. I learn to clean the carburetor, and the gas line, which clogs from the dust. J. J. arrives one day with the superintendent and I am complimented on the neatness of my field. It is a forty-acre field. Plowed, it is beautiful.

Mondrian would have been proud. I am sent to disk an already plowed field, one done by one of the hired hands, and I find it no straighter than the one I have just finished. I gloat, pat myself on the back.

Every day at noon, a truck arrives to chauffeur me to the messhall in Alicia, the main town of the two which make up Prairie Farm. The hired help bring their lunch and eat it in the field, but it is believed I should eat with my brothers and sisters so I don't, I suppose, have to be alone all day without my mother's breast, my family, my siblings. I am glad. At one, I am driven back to my field. I raise my chin, I am a nobleman. Mid-afternoon, the truck returns with a pail of ice water and a ladle. I drink, have a smoke, return to my work. All summer I plow and disk the fields. After supper, there are meetings, we make plans to construct a sewer; and after the meetings my girl friend, Nadia, and I walk along the irri-gation canal. We hold hands, smooch, and still she resists, my strategies go for naught.

Sunrise Farm has settled into a routine. Some people work in the cow barn, others take care of the chickens and the horses. Still others weed all day. Our employed workers cultivate the corn and sugar beet fields. Before and after supper we gather in groups and talk. We are hardly aware of the outside world. There are meetings once or twice a week. As usual, there are certain people who talk because they are talkers, but most of us sit and listen because we are listeners. When there is a vote, it is usually J. J.'s ideas which prevail. But it is soon apparent that there are divisions. The Yiddishists speak Yiddish only, even when they are ad-vised that we have among us several who do not understand Yiddish. It is also apparent that there are several Communists, those who speak the loudest and most vociferously, but we have no Party line. Mostly the talk is about the way the kitchen is run; it needs to be better organized, the food is boring. There are several who think we should slaughter all the pigs and serve pork chops for breakfast to give us strength for the day's work. The hired farmers say they eat meat for breakfast, why shouldn't we? Others gag at the idea. Still, why must we just slaughter the old sheep; mutton is dry, why not some lambs on occasion? Because it is not good farm practice, that's why. Should we or should we not begin the construction of the sewer for Alicia, where most of the houses form a settlement? Angelo di Vito, who can repair motors and is a mason and has worked on sewer construction, says he is willing to undertake the job with Sid Greenberg, who graduated from Cooper Union with a mechanical engineering degree. But the peppermint distillery, which has lain idle for years and has accumulated lots of rust, has to be put in order in time for the peppermint harvest, and Greenberg is going to have to do that job. We distill our peppermint into crude and that is sent to a distillery in St. Johns for final processing. A pound of crude goes for about $1.16, someone says out loud. It is rumored that in time of war the price of peppermint oil goes up to $16 or more because it is used for medication. A few of us whistle. An old Anarchist in the back says in a very strong voice, "I oppose war!"

I am assigned to the repair of the distillery. Jake DeGus, the son of our superintendent, who ran the distillery in years past, will assist Greenberg. While they work on the machinery, I am to clean the six huge vats. I let myself down into a vat with a pail of gasoline and a brush. I begin to scrub away, and before I know it am overcome by gasoline vapors and cry out just before I faint and have to be carried out by Sid and Jake. They lay me down out in the sun and I am prepared to let the sun heal me as I sleep forever.

Get back to work, Bill, Greenberg calls. I have never been called Bill before, it had always been Willie. I like Bill, I am now grown up, and Bill it's been forever since.

I tie a large bandanna around my face and return to the vat. I work slowly. As soon as I feel woozy, I climb out. I learn to work in four- or five-minute shifts. It takes me two days. Meanwhile, Greenberg, a tall, contentious half-Turk, half-Jew who has become my friend, constantly argues with Jake, who never went to college but knows the intricacies of the distillery far better. Once the argument becomes so heated they resort to fists. I am tired of both of them. I just sit down and watch as they cuff each other about ineffectually, two clumsy bears. One summer when I'd been sent to a charity camp in Cold Springs, New York, I'd been instructed by a retired, battle-scarred pugilist. As I observe Sid and Jake fighting, I begin to laugh. They both swing wildly, lead with their right, leave their jaws wide open, and neither can take advantage of the other's openings. It ends up a draw, both exhausted. I tell them they are palookas and that I can take both of them. They are embarrassed and resume working on the large generator.

Summer ended and harvest time arrived with a thunderclap, literally. We had to get the hay in fast, because wet hay heats up as it rots in the barn and starts fires. The distillery was ready for the peppermint, which had to be reaped carefully—every leaf was money—and it must be brought in dry, or it will be diluted as it distills. We worked long, exhausting hours. The vacation was over.

We became a little less generous with those who couldn't, or wouldn't, work as hard as we did. There were two and three meetings a week. Quiet voices raised their pitch, gentle voices toughened. Several affairs started between someone's wife and someone else's husband. One of the young men had been seen with one of the older men's wives. There was talk. But every individual has his or her own rights; besides, husbands and wives are not each other's property. In any event, it was not the collective's problem.

I and my roommate, Ben Dvosin, have girl friends who are roommates, which makes it convenient. Ben is a talker. Eighteen years old, he speaks at meetings as an equal with the older brothers and sisters. He is one of the Communists. He is blond, blue-eyed, slender, very handsome, articulate, and I am jealous of him. We have become close friends.

Neither of us is a virgin, but our girl friends are, and that is hard work, too, though much more pleasurable than weeding: getting them to yield up that breathtakingly lovely cherry. The sweetness of it.

We manage, with the enormous help of our paid farmers, to reap our harvest; wheat, sugar beets, peppermint, vegetables for table. At Greenberg's urgings—and rantings—pigs have been slaughtered for those of us who want meat for breakfast. Our appetites are enormous, but we are satisfied. There is no money for distribution, but we have done well and look healthy. We have acquired a young physician from Detroit as a new member of the collective. All the women fall in love with him, he's so cute. Yes, we are satisfied. Still, the meetings are becoming more rancorous. Someone has called J. J. a dictator, a Stalin. The Yiddishists demand that the meetings be in Yiddish. Why doesn't J. J. work in the fields? Why are new arrivals less political, less class conscious? Standards have been lowered, people are just coming to leave the depression behind, there is not enough idealism. Still, the farm is functioning. Angelo and Greenberg begin to plan the sewer. We hope to install toilets in all our houses—which, no matter what, will always remain shacks.

Farming is not for the weak, especially if you've been reared in the city; even the old tenements were more comfortable. In New York, the needle trades workers were protected by a strong union; who protects you here? Here, everyone is his or her own agent. Speak up for yourself! I am dead tired, you say. Everyone is dead tired, but the work has to be done. The harvest is in, but the barns have to be repaired and painted. Let the help do it. We can't afford that. And so-and-so is fucking so-and-so. Everyone knows when you have to pee. You get crabs, they know that too. There are no secrets. What's happening to our individuality?

Where are the glory days of June and July? Where is the idealism? The adrenalin has stopped flowing. The hard work is just hard work; bones ache, muscles burn, the body yearns for rest. On a farm there is no rest. The other young men and I are carrying the place. At first, our idealism did the work for us. Now we are tired, too. We're just a bunch of dudes. We notice every malingerer, every lazybones, every wrinkle on the elderly. Well, some day when we are old, we will be carried, too—if the farm lasts that long.

In the dead of winter an old tonsil regrew and I had a continual sore throat. Our doctor decided to cut it out in his office with the help of his nurse, one of three Canadian sisters, Anarchists all. He used a local.

First he began to cut with surgical scissors, then asked for his scalpel. The nurse didn't have it. With the scissors dangling in my throat, the local wearing off, they went in search of a scalpel. Found one, it was rusty. Searched for and found another. There I sat, gasping, hurting, the scissors dangling, waiting for the goddamned scalpel to sterilize. Finally, the job was concluded.

It took what seemed endless time for my throat to heal. A family with their own car was going to New York, and I asked to go along. My Tante Golda gave me five bucks to eat with on the road, and something extra for a night in an inn.

When I arrived in New York, my mother was living on East 22nd Street, off Second Avenue. When I walked into the apartment she could not conceal her despair before she embraced and kissed me. There was almost nothing to eat, and all I had on me was about a buck fifty.

My sister didn't look skinny, so somehow my mother was feeding her. Our favorite meal was stale bread, soaked in a single egg and fried with a spot of butter. My mother was still going out with Goldstein, her drama critic lover, so on the nights they went out she ate in a restaurant. In those days there wasn't anything as formal as a doggie bag, but she would manage to wrap her leftovers in a napkin and bring them home in her capacious handbag.

One morning I woke up and found it impossible to raise my right arm over my head, and decided to go to the Bellevue hospital outpatient clinic. As I waited in line to pay my quarter and have a doctor assigned, I fainted. When I awoke I was in an immense ward, every bed filled, and a doctor was examining me. When he saw I was awake, he asked, When was the last time you had a full meal, kid? I couldn't remember when was the last time I'd left the table satisfied. You're still a growing boy, you need to be fed, he said.

My mother, the fool, had refused to concede and had not asked for home relief. The social service department in Bellevue sent over bags of food; my mother bit her lip and accepted them. I stayed at home a month, having to attend Bellevue's clinic for work on my shoulder. It turned out the infected tonsil had infected the long thoracic nerve to my shoulder, and the muscle had atrophied. I went daily for heat treatment and a massage. Since I couldn't afford a quarter a day, it was done for nothing. When the muscle had more or less healed, they gave me a series of exercises to do, I kissed my mother and sister goodbye, and jumped the line.

It took me almost a month to reach Sunrise. I was in no hurry. I wanted to be on my own for a while, be my own man, have privacy. On the road, it's up to you alone. Mostly I plied the corridor between Baltimore, Maryland, and Gary, Indiana. Usually I walked and/or hitched. There weren't that many cars on the road in those days. Truck drivers were forbidden by their bosses to give lifts, but some did anyway. They liked company, especially at night, or were just plain decent. Many a time a driver would tell me to get some sleep in the cot behind the front seats; often they gave me a dime for a cup of coffee and a couple of donuts when we parked in a truck stop. Sometimes they'd share what they had in their lunch pail. We talked baseball—politics brought silence, especially my leftwing politics. They were interested in making a living, putting food on the table, and taking care of their families. They liked Roosevelt, and that was as far as they'd go.

Other times, I would stop over in a Hooverville near a big city, or in a temporary hobo camp. We'd pitch in whatever food we'd cadged or stolen and eat a communal stew. Farmers' wives yielded up a meal for cleaning the yard around the house or chopping wood. They didn't like for you to come into the house, though a couple of times there were amatory adventures with lonely wives married to men who worked so hard they didn't have enough energy to give more than a quick embrace while emitting their semen.

Once a kid I met on the road induced me to hop a freight with him. It was in Ohio someplace, and we jumped out before we reached Gary— right into the middle of a herd of yard bulls. We ran like hell and I avoided getting my butt whacked. It was not for me. You had shelter, but the floor was hard, and you had to be alert; with no place to run, you didn't want to be gang raped. With fake bravado I told the other kid that if I got whacked by a bull I would kill the bastard. The kid, wise, just smiled.

I liked hitching. You could be alone, go your own way, stop at your own pleasure. I always had a book on the road, forgive me, stolen from a library. I read *Moby Dick* on the road, begun in the Cleveland library, finished in Philadelphia. Eating an apple, or a burnt spud from a hobo fire, I hunted the white whale. I read *War and Peace* the second time while on the bum. I loved Natasha in Wilkes Barre, and died with André in a hay loft outside Oswego. I skipped Tolstoy's lectures; spare me the bullshit, Lev. After a tenth reading, I still skip them. In the Academy Street library in Trenton, my hometown, I found *Notes from Underground,* and read it in one sitting, half-starved, and swore that Part I was the greatest piece of prose I'd ever read. I still swear it. Goddamn sonofabitch, you knew the score, didn't you, Feodor, you anti-semitic bastard? You reached into my heart and tore it to shreds. (I love Céline, too. You figure it.)

Most people who give you a lift want no chatter. Where you going? I'm not going that far, I'll let you off before I turn at so-and-so. If they did want to talk, you bullshitted them about your adventures on the road, or, if they looked very respectable, told them you were going to Akron or Toledo or Gary because you heard there was work opening up there. If it was a really fancy car, an Olds or up, they usually made snarling noises about Roosevelt. Once, unable to button my lip, I said to one of this sort that if not for Roosevelt, you'd get Earl Browder, and how would you like that? Earl who? he said. In fact, jobs were opening up a tiny bit, and the more that did, the more strikes hit headlines. The American working man was waking up. He wanted his share. Steel, auto, oil, meatpackers. There were Party organizers, Socialist organizers, Trotskyist organizers, Lovestoneite organizers, just plain trade unionists. I joined a picket line in Youngstown, Ohio, got beat up on one in Gary, Indiana. I didn't care whose picket line I joined, I was non-sectarian. The demands of my conscience paid, I returned to the road. After a month of it I became too bored, found it too lonely even for me who enjoyed the misery of loneliness.

The road was not very romantic. Hungry, cold, and dirty, too, even in an overpopulated Hooverville. Your hunger is personal, and so is the cold. You envied the men who had women to sleep with. A warm body. Sex. Bonfires helped, and the potatoes roasting made the saliva flow. In a city you'd steal a carrot or a bunch of celery, or dig them out of a garbage can put out by the vegetable store for the rotten stock, and that would be your share of the soup boiling over a fire. On a rare occasion someone would add a piece of meat or a meat bone. You were thankful. You talked. Where you from, kid? You hated to say New York, because if you did next they'd say, You a Jew? It seemed New York meant Jewtown. On occasion someone would say, You a kike? You fought, sometimes you just turned away. Once, tired, weak, sorry for yourself you smiled, joined in, Yeah, I'm a kike from Noo Yawk. Where you from? Scranton. You must be a Polack. Yeah. We became buddies for a day. It was easier to join in. America.

I'd been brought up never to say wop, nigger, Polack. On the road I was most often a minority of one. I had also been brought up to believe that I was part of the vanguard of the proletariat and it was my duty to educate the masses. When I tried, the response generally was one of indifference. Or, You a bolshie, kid? Naw.

In a Hooverville outside Akron I met an Irish kid from Chicago. It turned out he was a bolshie, too. We enjoyed a few hours together condemning capitalism, the Republicans, fascism. Then he started in on Stalin, what a murdering bastard he was. I stopped him cold. You a Commie? he said. A Communist, yes. My old man's a Wobbly and so am I, he said. You're being taken for a ride, kid. Alone again.

In the seventies I met a forty-year-old, over-moneyed, underdressed hippie who, when he learned I had been on the road in the thirties, breathlessly asked me what songs we had sung. He was certain every hobo camp, every Hooverville, sported at least one Woody Guthrie. When I told him that not once had I encountered a wandering minstrel, his face deflated. How terribly disappointing. There were no choral societies, barbershop quartets, or wandering minstrels like Guthrie singing working class songs on the road. Once in a while you'd see a guy playing a uke or banjo on some street corner, his hat at his feet, hoping for a couple pennies. Buddy can you spare a dime? Life is just a bowl of cherries. Three little words, I love you. Later you might run into him at the Hooverville out of town.

You were hungry, cold, and lonely. You only fought if you had to; a bully tried to steal the bread some sympathetic baker had given you in town, or a meanly intended ethnic epithet was hurled at you. People would shout, A fight! a fight! and a circle would form and you fought until you couldn't stand any more. Later you had to shake hands with the son-of-a-bitch because that was the sporting thing to do. America.

I turned up at Sunrise as spring began. They were happy to see me, Tante Golda giving me a great big hug and many kisses. I was her adored brother's orphan son. Her love assuaged my hunger, my anger. Her name fit her perfectly. I was put right to work on my trusty old Farmall, plowing and disking. Then I was assigned to help the hired shepherd during the ramming season. The ram's underbelly was painted with a red dye bought through a dealer in Casper, Wyoming. Then some fifty ewes in heat were run into a pen and the ram let loose among them. When we saw a ewe with a red behind, we knew she'd been serviced and removed her from the pen. On the ram galloped. Red behind, out. The horny bastard serviced some thirty ewes in a couple of hours. We had two rams, and they humped furiously. They seemed to get stronger as they went along; the more sex, the better. At nineteen I was proud of my masculinity; after observing those rams, my pride was put in its proper place. I was a mere man.

We started weeding the peppermint fields, the bellies of the ewes began to blossom, shoots of wheat, soy bean, and sugar beets began to sprout. There was a drought, but our irrigation ditches functioned quite efficiently, pumping water from the nearby Flint River. I walked into the horse barn one morning and saw one of our hired hands, an old guy, standing on a box behind a mare in heat and was astonished to see him humping the horse. I left in a hurry; the man had a right to his secret pleasure.

A husband beat his wife at breakfast; he thought she was sleeping with another man. One of the younger men cursed a plump man who he thought was malingering during weeding. There were more meetings during the week. J. J. was beginning to take verbal beatings. The farm was producing, but the work, relatively easy for real farmers, was hardly so for needle trades workers. What were they arguing about? Things like, Cohen should step down and let someone else run the place. He acts like an aristocrat. (He *was* an aristocrat.) Why shouldn't I be given the duty of running the cow barn, since so-and-so can't seem to get up early enough? Mostly it was personalities clashing over a smidgeon of power, over a little respect, sensitive souls that we all were. Everyone was just plain tired. My peers were doing the overwhelming amount of work. We worked hardest, said the least at meetings, were the most idealistic. Another husband and wife had a fight in public. Who was he fucking? Who was she seen walking down the road into the night with? Letters began to come from New York, Philadelphia, Cleveland, Chicago, Detroit, that shops were opening up. It made people think. Still, the farm was magnificent, the rich muck soil did not betray us. The soil was so rich, forty acres could support a family for life.

But we do not live by bread alone. Our muscles have something to say about it, and our pride, our jealousies, our envies, our nervous twitches. There was really nothing to fight about, so we made things up. Still, the work went on. The sewer system under the aegis of Angelo di Vito and Sid Greenberg was finished. (Shortly after its grand opening, an outflow main jammed. Volunteers were needed to enter the already khaki-colored slime to unplug it. Greenberg volunteered for himself, and without asking me volunteered for me as well. Infuriated, I let him lead the way down the iron ladder into the sludge. Following quickly, I placed my foot on his head and pushed once, twice, thrice. He almost drowned, urine-impregnated shit squirting out of his ears, his nose, his mouth. The operation was successful.) A bakery was built with a perfect oven. (Convalescing from the flu, I worked with the baker for a month.) Peppermint was distilled (I worked there, too) and sold. Sugar beets were harvested and sold in Owosso. We had enough; no one went hungry, everyone was adequately sheltered. We held dances, we sang, we played ball. Still, the arguments were endless. A large opposition built up against J. J. He was a proud man, and he knew little about infighting. He didn't like to stoop to debasement or vilification. But he was able to maintain a majority, and that majority was the majority of those who worked hard.

One evening after supper, it was early summer, as I left the messhall I was confronted by an irate father carrying a shotgun. His daughter and I were innocent; we had merely taken a walk together. He was taking out on me what he wanted to take out on another, the man who was sleeping with his wife. To take it out on his wife's lover would have been acknowledgment of his wife's betrayal, so he transferred his anger to me. I didn't take him seriously. As I walked towards him with the idea of disarming him, Sid Greenberg, older and wiser, knew better. He grabbed me from behind and threw me aside. Beat it, he said. I beat it. The irate man with the gun left as well. J. J. and Uncle Dave decided that I should take a short leave of absence. I was happy to do so. The place had begun to bore me; not the work, I loved nothing better than sitting atop my Farmall turning the rich soil under a broiling sun, smoking a homemade cigarette, daydreaming about a new world as I made perfectly straight furrows.

Manny, J. J.'s son, drove me to the outskirts of Detroit. I hit the road again, jumped the line, joined the unemployed looking for work from town to town, joined the hoboes to whom being on the road was a way of life, joined the bums who didn't give a shit. Things were a little better than a year before, and made to seem even better than reality by FDR's fireside chats and the endless alphabetical legislation flowing from Congress. An effort was being made by a society that had lost its ability to feed the hungry and give work to a populace anxious to work and to make a living. I went to a demonstration of unemployed workers in Detroit organized by the Socialist Party; I thought of them as my comrades, too. We all wanted the same thing, didn't we? A new world, a better world. I did my duty, resumed my travels, my thumb my ticket to somewhere. No Erewhon for me. Summer on the road is of course much easier on you than winter. In winter you spend most of your time seeking out warmth. In summer there is always a stream to plunge into, clothes and all. Farmers need help, even poor ones; farmers' wives want your help to clean up the yard, do a paint job. You get a pork chop, a piece of pie.

I returned to Sunrise in time for the harvest. Rain threatened, and the entire population turned out to load the horsedrawn wagons with bales of hay, until every field was emptied. Next came the wheat fields. We had an old stationary harvester, which we moved from field to field by tractor. Old Angelo kept the engine going, and I fed the maw of the machine as each wagon emptied its load on the platform where I stood, then left to get another load as a new team drew up. The gold seed poured out at the other end into burlap sacks held by two men. From the stack on the side, gold straw flew like gold rain into a huge, ever-increasing gold pile. The dust was gold, too, and we had to wear goggles before the gold blinded us. It was all teamwork; everyone, even the horses, moved in rhythm, the harvester sang a sweet song under Angelo's magic fingers, the magnificent tawny drays moved from sheaves of wheat to sheaves of wheat, all gold, communards bent, clutched a sheaf, turned and heaved it onto the wagon where loaders stood, like heroic giants, and stacked the sheaves in place. Somehow the rhythm, the flying gold, the broiling gold sun, and the smoothly running engine cheered the heart of the most reluctant of us. For a few days everyone smiled, and was kind and courteous.

Then the drought worsened. The Flint River, which flowed past one end of the farm, was low and our pumps could hardly dredge up enough water to fill the irrigation ditches. Beneath the crust of the soil the earth began to burn from the scorching sun. Crops failed. One evening during supper, after I had already left the farm, the big horse barn began to burn and my old comrades had to run into the furnace and throw wet sacks over the heads of those gloriously beautiful horses and lead the frightened animals out to safety. J. J. stood on the porch of his office across the way and observed. What else could he do? But of course someone said he was like Nero fiddling as Rome burned. Fist fights broke out. Idealistic communards lost their idealism and their fight, and left for the city where they hoped jobs awaited them.

The farmers who worked for us thought we were crazy. Of course we were.

I'd had enough and said my goodbyes. Tante Golda gave me five bucks and I hit the road again, this time my destination New York.

I stopped in Detroit to walk a picket line outside a Ford factory. The auto workers were really getting serious. Ford was arming itself for war. We were attacked by Harry Bennett's club-carrying goons and fought back as best we could. I wrapped rags around my fists and beat the shit out of one guy before he could nail me; it was one of the grandest moments of my life. Then we got out of there. The following year the sit-ins began, and soon Ford was beaten. Socialists, Lovestoneites, Trotskyists, and Communists did it, and just plain workers to whom Marx and Lenin meant absolutely zero.

I headed home. A truck driver dropped me outside Cleveland. I walked into town, hungry and beat. In the center of the city I stopped near a jewelry store which bore the name Schreibman. My mother's sister's family, very bourgeois. I'd never stopped to say hello in the past, but this time I was too hungry. It was Sunday. I found a cop, and asked him to lend me a nickel so I could phone my family, the Schreibmans. He gave it to me and waited with me until my cousin Willie—named after the same great-grandfather I was—arrived. He repaid my loan, and the cop and I said our goodbyes. It was only on the picket line or during demonstrations that I thought of cops as my enemy. On the bum, a few times a cop would respond to my plea and take me to the jailhouse so I could get out of the cold and get a night's sleep in a warm cell. In the morning I'd receive a cup of hot coffee and a warmed-up roll.

The Schreibmans treated me royally. Fed me, coddled me, asked me to stay in Cleveland; they would give me work in one of their stores, it turned out they now had two. My aunt and uncle had come to America, gone to Cleveland because a *landsman* had recommended it. My uncle rented space in the front window of a barbershop, set up a small table and repaired watches in full view of the world. Saved his money, sent for his oldest son living with grandparents, then for his next, and then his daughter. They bought a store, and in the depression thrived, selling jewelry on the installment plan. They offered me work, offered to teach me their trade. To repair watches, a regular trade, was below my dignity as a proletarian, one of the avant-garde, too bourgeois. I thanked my aunt and uncle and cousins. They gave me money to take the bus. I saved it and hitched home.

Sunrise lasted two more years. Fistfights, lawsuits. Just as in the bourgeois world. Feodor was right: two plus two does not equal four. But, of course. Look around you.

J. J. and his comrades had bought the farm for $195,000 in 1933. In 1994, as I write this, the ten thousand acres are owned by several farmers and the value is around $15 million for the finest muck soil in the middle west. After liquidation, Uncle Dave sent me, as I recall, $12.23 as my share.

11

My mother kissed me, then said, You are Velveleh, yes?

Yes, Mom, I'm Willie.

Glad to see you.

But from the pursing of her lips and sag of her shoulders I assumed she was no more happy to see me return than she had been to see me leave. Now she had to feed me again. Still, she loved me. I was an anxiety she had to endure.

I told her what I knew would make her—and every mama, I suppose—happy, that as soon as I got a job I would begin to save money to go to college. She smiled at that, and made me happy as well.

With my sister, everything was as usual. She went to high school, played the piano, attended modern dance class, wrote short stories, and never once asked me what my life had been like since I had left. Still, I must say I never volunteered much about myself, to her or anyone else. It was not that I was secretive; it was more a belief that no one, not my family, or even Natie, my best friend, could possibly be interested in anything I did. So I said nothing. I came and went. If asked, I gave a brief answer; then, afraid I would bore whoever it was, I asked him or her about what it was he or she was doing.

My brother was now the father of a daughter, and he paid me to babysit once in a while. Then he got me a job selling rotgut booze at fifty cents a pint for his father-in-law. I spent twelve hours a day in a dark, rat-infested cockroach of a room in the East Bronx waiting for a knock on the door. Once the half a buck was in my fist, I'd turn and open a trap-door in the floor and fetch up the booze for the poor bastard. For this I received two dollars a day. I lasted a week.

Prosperity was just around the corner, but it was to wait there until World War II began. Still not much food in the house, I copped a beat, hit the road again. After about a month, dirty, hungry, cold, I returned home and hit pay dirt: through a friend's friend I was hired on as a busboy in the Old Roumanian cabaret on Allen Street for the Christmas holidays and New Year's Eve. They fed me goulash and strudel, and one big fat cigar. On New Year's Eve a two-bit hood thought the drummer was flirting with his girl as they waltzed to *The Blue Danube,* and pulled a knife. I was standing behind him and pinned his arms to his side until one of the bouncers relieved me. I was a hero, and for reward received a cigar from my employer, and a permanent job as a busboy at the new cabaret opening in the area, The Roumanian Paradise. I was recommended for this job by the hood's boss, one of the Ash brothers who ran the Lower East Side for the Jewish mob.

That little cocksucker was gonna ruin my New Year's Eve, it's too bad you dint beat the shit outta him. He also gave me a newly minted silver dollar. It turned out to be a very profitable night. Later, when he patronized the new cabaret he always left me a half dollar, which was exactly what he left the waiter. This financial equality infuriated the latter, who quieted down only when I advised him if he didn't, I would have Ash take him for a ride.

Louie Anzelowitz, the owner of the Paradise, was a kindly man who made sure I was given more food to eat than even I could manage. The

Natalie at twenty

tips were generous—who but sporty types and hoods could afford to eat in cabarets?—and the hat-check girl paid me off under the arch for serving her dinner. I was the waiter for the three-man band, and at the end of the week they left me a buck fifty. I was able to give my mother money, and I put some aside because I began to think seriously about going to college.

I hadn't renewed my membership in the Young Communist League and thus avoided the boredom of meetings, but one never needed to hold a membership book to be a YCL or Party member. I was a Communist, that was my creed, my religion, my blood. And though I continued frequently to see my friend Natie Shlechter, who now lived around the corner on Second Avenue between 22nd and 23rd Streets, and ingested his blasphemies about Stalin and Russia without too much demurral—I didn't think it mattered, because after the world revolution it would all straighten out—I continued to maintain close contact with Party friends and affairs. Since I worked nights I had free days, and a picket line here and there could always use another body to carry a sign and a voice to holler the slogan du jour. At one of these demonstrations, things got out of hand and a cop bopped me on the head, leaving a welted scar that I still have today.

The Roumanian Paradise was doing poorly, and Louie said I'd make more money working as a waiter or bellhop in the Catskills during the summer. He found a job for me as a bellhop in a hotel outside Liberty, New York. The Hotel Leona was a small, decent, middle-class inn, but one of the several bosses insisted on assigning us—waiters and bellhops—to different women who wanted male company during the week, since their husbands only came up for the weekend. I resisted and had a run-in with the pimp. He was ready to fire me, but his wife intervened on my behalf because I lay chickie for her while she went up to her room with the band leader when her husband went out afternoons to play golf. There must be some sort of moral to this tale.

In the fall, back in the city, Louie informed me that he was thinking of closing down, and if I didn't mind leaving the city he knew the steward in a large kosher hotel in Miami Beach, where I could make good money either bussing or waiting on tables. He said he would phone the man for me, and I said okay, and thanked him. He was a rare one. I didn't see him again for perhaps ten years, when my wife and I went to a very successful restaurant he was running on Second Avenue downtown. Louie barely acknowledged my hello, and didn't even wait long enough to be introduced to my wife before running off to seat another couple. The meal was excellent, but I left terribly disappointed that my former employer hadn't stopped long enough to acknowledge the affluence that allowed me to afford his fancy prices. Louie was one of those people who was kind only to the poor; his contempt he reserved for the affluent.

Before heading south—the season in Miami didn't begin until late December in those days—I walked a picket line for the Furriers Joint Council. The Party was consolidating its leadership of the union after an alliance of all the leftwing parties had defeated the gangsters who had run it. After victory over the gangsters, the Party used its united front with the Socialists and Lovestoneites to get the Trotskyists out of the way. Then it used its alliance with the rightwing Socialists to slice off the Lovestoneites and leftwing Socialists. Finally, it settled on an alliance with pliable rightwing Socialists, and ran the union as it saw fit. One of the things it saw fit to do was see to it that the opposition could receive only temporary work cards, and so never have a permanent job in the industry. Smart.

The Party used the same tactic in civil war Spain—a tactic which helped lead to the destruction of the Republic—and after World War II they were successful with the same slicing technique in eastern Europe, fooling nobody but simps (short for sympathizers) by naming Stalinist dictatorships People's Democratic Republics, they being neither the people's republics, nor democratic. This technique, incidentally, was called the Rakosi salami tactic, Rakosi being the leader of the Hungarian Party who gave the strategy its name.

While walking a picket line in front of a fur factory, my old Young Pioneer leader, who had once chastized the Aces Social and Athletic Club for being overexposed politically, seduced me into joining some fur union strongarms on a foray to Astor Place to break up a Trotskyist open air meeting. We beat up a few of the Trotskyists, broke up their meeting, and then triumphantly marched off to the familiar Willow Cafeteria on East 14th Street to celebrate our great victory with coffee and Danish. I knew what I did was contemptible, but that did not stop me, as I repeated it several times. The Trotskyists were as much devoted to the revolution as we were, and though I adored Stalin I could only admire Trotsky, the organizer and commander of the victorious Red Army. When I was a little boy, it was never just Lenin, it was always LeninTrotsky. Till this day, though I have not seen Natie Shlechter in forty years or more, I am grateful to him for never allowing me to rewrite history. Every time I tried, he threw it back in my face. His love was Bukharin, but he was never less than honest about Trotsky's contribution to the Russian revolution. It was Stalin he held in contempt. It took a long time to place V. I. Lenin in his proper niche as Stalin's true progenitor, and Sergei Nechaev as Lenin's—and ours, too.

Sergei Nechaev, born 1847, died 1882.

"The revolutionist," Nechaev wrote, "is a doomed man . . . has broken every connection with the social order and with the whole educated world, with all the laws, appearances . . . and moralities of the world. . . . To him whatever aids the triumph of the revolution is ethical. . . ."

He lied, blackmailed friends, killed a comrade, died a heroic death in a tsarist prison. (Because he was heroic, are we to forgive him?) He could be said to be the most important person in modern history. He as much as anyone was responsible for the countless millions murdered by Hitler, Stalin, Mao, Idi Amin; we can go on and on. He was the actor who put it all together. Uniquely unique. Numero Uno. There was a time when if one put it all together in one's own little bailiwick, that was that. Now no space is impenetrable. Say *mother*, and thirteen thousand miles away someone finishes it for you in two seconds flat, *fucker*. Nechaev rules. "Be my brother or I will kill you." Slip a bomb into his anus and blow him sky high. His shit will plaster the earth. Organic fertilizer. The best.

Of course, I never told Natie about the contemptible acts I committed as a Communist. I dissembled with him, feared losing his respect. In the end, not wanting to lose his respect is what saved my life. It is not that difficult to see myself defending the slaughter of twenty or thirty or forty—pick a card, choose any number—million people, not a few whom I could call comrade. Necessary murders, of course. Weren't we going to remake man?. Which of course includes women, just in case you think I am discriminating. I had that discussion with a man named Leonard once. A sweet, intelligent man, a good father and husband, a man who not only talked Marx, but read him. He lived in a comfortable home, made a fine living. It was worth it, he said; say twenty-five million people are murdered for the cause and in the end we remake man, build a just world that will endure forever, isn't that worth it?

What could I say to that? I could have said, Let's start with your two sons, your wife and you. But that would have been a subjective response, personal, very bourgeois, so I couldn't.

Now, I'm quite a bit older and know a little more. I would have told him that that's the reasoning which led directly to Treblinka, Auschwitz, Kolyma, Magadan. I would have told him that we are a bunch of bloody savages. We are a disgusting species. I would have told him to see the daily news reports about Rwanda and Bosnia and Yeman and Sudan and, and, and, just for the first few months of 1994. Everybody has a good cause for necessary murders. And I was going to start right on him.

Still, still. On the evening of the morning I read that a half million Rwandans had been murdered by other Rwandans in one month, Jeannette and I went to see *32 Short Films About Glenn Gould,* one of our true geniuses. I cried. Wouldn't you? Our ugliness and our beauty. We're nuts. Yet, I must say, I am hopeful. (Strict toilet training is what does it. I love neatness. Turdy is my name.) I truly believe that ten thousand years after God tested Abraham, He will amputate our hands, tear out our tongues, gouge out our eyes, perforate our ear drums, perform a lobotomy, and we will at last be at peace. What bloody scum we are. Yes, it is true, in our time we have had a Martin Luther King, a Sakharov, a Vaclav Havel.

As I said, politics, I hate it. You start off on politics and soon it takes over. Power. I'm an anarchist, I abhor power. I also dislike hurricanes.

12

It was in some stranger's Studebaker that I crossed the line from South Carolina into Georgia and saw that most welcoming of billboards, "Conviction in this State means the Chain Gang." And it was not too long afterward that the sight of a working chain gang and police bearing rifles convinced me that, unlike most billboards, this one told the truth. I vowed to myself that I would uphold the law while in the South. I wanted neither the chain gang, the noose, nor tar and feathers, my images of what the South really was. I was going to Miami Beach to work, save money, and go to college either the following fall or the next, according to how much money I amassed. I was going to be twenty years old in January, the next month. I finally had to decide what my life was going to be. Several times I had been asked if I wanted to go to Party school and become a functionary. I did not want to be a functionary. What would my good friend Natie say? I would go to college and become a doctor. It would make my mother happy. I would make money. I would find a girl like Miss Veronica to be my wife. I would live a decent life.

As Louis Anzelowitz had promised, he had phoned the steward of Seiden's Floridian Hotel on Biscayne Bay and I had no difficulty obtaining a job as busboy in the hotel's kosher restaurant. I was given one of the best stations, eight tables up front. A few of my customers were horse players and they tipped well. Another was a man named Weinstock, the money man behind the Minsky burlesque chain, and he tipped me passes to the Miami link of the chain which I in turn sold at half price. I didn't like to go to the burlesque, not because of any moral principle, but because all you got out of it was an erection with no surcease. Since most of the young women in those days insisted that their virginity was sacrosanct, a young man either had to masturbate or go to a whorehouse. Abstinence was not an alternative. There were enough bordellos in Miami to service an army. Some of my co-workers at the hotel and I would go, pay our two dollars, conclude our mission, and peacefully depart—never fully satisfied, of course.

The hotel served two meals: breakfast—over four hours—and dinner. In between I had ample time to sun and swim. I made good money and ate the finest food served at the Floridian. I learned to love caviar, eggs benedict for breakfast, and rack of lamb for dinner. That's not what the hotel fed its help—we were fed oatmeal for breakfast and chopped meat for dinner—it's what the customers left over. I didn't have a dainty appetite and I was not too proud to eat such grand leftovers. Why shouldn't I have the best if it was right in front of my snout.

I had a friend who roomed with me at a little backwater hotel. We slept in the laundry room; it was cheap. He made his living as a gambler. He came from the section of Brooklyn run by Murder, Incorporated, and had been on his way to becoming a petty hood but somehow had escaped. Outside the hotel was a little stand where a guy ran an honest game of twenty-one. My friend taught me how to play conservatively and win. Stick at seventeen. At Flamingo Park and Hialeah racetracks he advised never to play a favorite to win, but bet to place or show, and at the end of the season you come out ahead. I tried it for a short time and discovered he was right, but I never got a kick out of gambling, even penny ante poker, and I quit while I was ahead.

Early one morning I went to Miami, the city, and saw a big cop boot a Negro boy so hard in the ass that the kid fell to the pavement curled up in excruciating pain, all because he hadn't jumped out of the cop's way in time. I didn't say a word, just stood there, a helpless coward, and tasted the bile that comes with guilt. If it had been in New York, I would have called the cop a dirty cossack and been prepared to take the consequences, but this was the South, and fear subdued my normal responses. In New York, whether true or not, you believed a cop had inhibitions, but in the South you felt he had absolutely none and your fear was greater. My guilt now prompted a promise I'd made in New York.

Before I left for Miami Beach, I ran into my young old Comrade Fox or Stone or Wilson, whatever. Every time I ran into him he wore a new name. He asked me if I had become active, which meant had I joined Party or YCL units. I told him no, that I had a good in for a job in a big, fancy hotel. I'm going to eat good, I said, and I'll save money to go to college. I dislike meetings and have come to the conclusion that I'm a bad Party risk, I'd make a lousy organizer and so the Party would lose money on me. I'm going to go to college and become a doctor. I like the idea of healing people.

You're right, he said primly, the good organizer way, you'd make a lousy functionary, you're too undisciplined, selfish, and for a class-conscious man, politically immature. You'll be eating good so you won't give a damn about the oppressed Negro masses. When you get down there, we'll be able to use your help. Now what about it?

I was sure he was going to ask me to beat someone up. I said something to that effect.

When you get there, he said, hardly listening to me—organizers have a busy obsessive engine going—get in touch with this couple on Fifth and Collins, perhaps you can help with a Negro sharecroppers' drive going on in southern Georgia. Not much, a couple of days.

Okay, I said. Sure.

So now, my guilt ripe, I kept my promise and called on the couple he told me about. (It was more than guilt: it smelled of adventure and, besides, like a boy scout, it would earn me merit points towards admission to Socialist Heaven.) We arranged that I'd be picked up by a comrade, an old pro, and driven to Savannah, I think it was. There we would meet someone named Tony Marchand—as phony a name as could be picked off an advertisement—and he would give me further instructions.

Subsequently, I got the busboy closest to my station to cover for me and I was driven by the old pro at an awful fast clip to Savannah where I met Tony Marchand. I recognized the type immediately. He never smiled. He was a very serious man of moderate height, with moderate coloration, and moderate-colored hair. He also spoke in moderate tones; he never exhorted. He was merely dogged. He was a Bolshevik man with a heart of steel. Moderately so. He was so positive he had no need to exhort. He was a true revolutionary. If he had ever taken power in the United States he would have lopped off heads—moderately.

Back in the car, we drove south for around an hour and Marchand drilled me about what I would say and how to plan for the future. He said he would introduce me to a young woman named Ella, a Negro teacher, and that he would try to stay more or less in the background. The South was his appointed district until the Party decided otherwise and I was there only temporarily, so I was expendable, I guess.

Ella turned out to be a young black woman, lovingly called Ellafat by her friends, for obvious reasons. She taught grade school in an area which, to my discomfort, she called Coontown. I was too callow to appreciate the irony and when I mentioned it later to Tony he advised me to cool it; purity was a luxury we could ill afford. The poverty was appalling, a mere cut above the Hoovervilles I had passed through.

Tony composed my little speeches, never forgetting to insert such nuggets as: the fingers of an open hand are easily broken, with a closed fist it is much more difficult. It was our aim, he said, to arrange meetings with two or three Negro sharecroppers in different homes in the area. Those meetings were set up by Ella. At the right time we would have all the small groups combine into what we hoped would be called The Sharecroppers Defense League of Southern Georgia.

The name I gave myself was Rob Redman. Later I would use Bill Harvey. Those of us who used a *nom de révolution* thought it gave us a certain tone, a cachet different from our contemporaries. We were the anointed, the chosen, if you will, who would change the world and remake man. Like Martin Luther King, we also had a dream. Though we pretended to scientific objectivity, really we were exceedingly romantic. D'Artagnan parading as V. I. Lenin.

The man chosen to head up the league was named Rafer. I don't remember his last name. We called him Rafe. He was as lean as Ella was fat, a tense coil of muscle. He suffered from colitis and his thin face showed it, deep furrows of pain. Round-faced, sweet-faced Ella was a tough customer with a tongue like sandpaper, yet tense, coiled Rafer was as sweet a man as I was ever to meet. Rafer had no grand ideas. All he wanted from life was to be left alone to live his life in peace and with justice. And the privilege of earning his fair share. *Don't you want to earn your fair share?* Tony had told me to ask. How could they answer in the negative?

In the next two months I was picked up after work several times and driven through the night as fast as possible in a Model A Ford (a Party perk, I suppose) to a site outside Coontown and dropped off. My eyes sleepy, my head overstuffed with advice, I would saunter, the hairs on the back of my neck stiff from fear, through the pre-dawn to Ellafat's shack. It smelled of fried bacon fat, and each time as I entered I thought of my childhood friend Miles. He and I had won a victory for justice and perhaps Ellafat and Rafe also would. There was, as I said, deep poverty in the area, as deep as any I had encountered during my times on the road, and yet an almost obsessive neatness. Neatness and self-respect always seem to go together. The people I encountered in this village had it; later I was to find it in the small towns of Spain.

Three, four, sometimes five black men would arrive at staggered times at either Ella's or another's place. She would introduce me as a young man interested in their plight, and I would go into my talk about the necessity of joining together, for only in that way could they obtain more justice from the landowners and increase their return for the hard and incessant labor they and their families put into the soil. I was a pretty good speaker, I meant and believed every word I uttered. As usual, only a few asked questions. Either Ella or I or Tony when he was present would respond, they would nod, and then again at staggered intervals they would leave, one by one. I'll say it as simply as I can so it doesn't sound overly dramatic, but the thought of tar and feathers, even the rope, kept us desperately alert.

In late February or early March, Marchand, who had seeded the ground long before I came on the scene, decided it was time to call all the little groups together—combined they would equal some fifty or sixty people—and hold a mass meeting in a clearing in the woods. It would, of course, be held at night, and its purpose was to let them see they were an army—without the hyperbole, a company at least. But most important, once revealed to each other (as if they didn't already know), they could no longer hide without being challenged as cowards. It was an early form of outing.

Marchand was my Party organizer and he had much greater experience than I; still, I had to express my feeling that it was too soon, it seemed to me, there weren't enough of those who came to the small meetings who were really committed. They were being nice, friendly, sympathetic to neighbors and church members; especially to Ella, whom they admired for her outspoken courage, and to Rafe, whom they loved because of his palpable decency and sweetness as a human being. Marchand barely listened to me. What did I know? I'd only been involved a few times, I was just a kid rank-and-filer who, left to his own, would probably drift away from the movement anyway.

A peculiar dichotomy ruled Marchand's life. Is it possible to be both moderate and perpetually in a hurry at the same time? He spoke slowly, as if from deep thought, and yet perpetual forward motion at a very rapid pace seemed necessary for him to continue to breathe, even to live. It was as if he were to stop for one bloody moment, all that had been gained would be totally lost. As I recall now, that seemed to be a distinctive trait of nearly all the Party organizers I was to know. Maybe it's true of all revolutionaries. Hurry up, move it, if we don't remake man this very moment he'll slide back into the ooze. What was Lenin's hurry? Hitler's? He, too, wanted to remake man, and as quickly as possible. We were all to have blond hair, blue eyes, an upturned nose, and a fully foreskinned cock. How lovely.

Marchand, like me, had a great feeling of empathy for the oppressed and the beaten down, but he was an organizer, a revolutionary, and that objective machine inside him was running like a time bomb. Revolutions don't wait, he had to get from A to B as quickly as possible. And, like me, he was winning points for entry to Lenin Heaven. We would, of course, sit at LeninStalin's right hand.

After I put my two cents in about slowing down the process, he ignored me and said, It's time now. For this occasion he added an exclamation point. Now! We were in his hotel room in a Savannah flea joint, and as he turned away from me he added, and I remember his exact words, "It seems to me, Comrade, you still suffer from residual bourgeois morality." Don't we all?

As I say, he was my Party organizer. I had been born under a tin embossment of V. I. Lenin, so what could I answer to that?

A time was set for a night ten days later. Ellafat and Rafer were informed and they broadcast it secretly to their people. At the set time, Marchand took me over the back roads to the meeting ground. If anything were to happen—the town police, the Klan, the landowners' goons, whatever—we were to run, jump the line, decamp, get the hell out of there, and he would meet me at the tin crate at this juncture. It was not to save our skin, he was quick to inform me, but that it would be best for the cause of the sharecroppers that outside agitators not be discovered and given responsibility. They, the sharecroppers, must accept their class responsibility and destiny. It was between them and the white ruling class.

I felt sick to my stomach; my residual bourgeois morality doing its customary job, no doubt. I must, like my leader the great Stalin, steel my spine and be ruthless.

The meeting was to be held in a small clearing in the pine woods behind Ella's shack. Open burlap sacks of sand with candles stuck into them were placed in a circle by Ella's young son, a boy I'd met several times. He was about fifteen or sixteen, quiet and studious-looking. It was a clean, brisk night. A sliver of moon rose, the sky was navy blue, and the candles were lit by Ella's son and me. Several guards were placed at points on the perimeter by Rafe.

Quietly, from different directions, sharecroppers, several of whom I had met, some with wives and friends filtered through the woods to gather before a small platform erected by Rafer. There were more than we expected and Ella and Marchand were elated. The cause was just. After a season of harvesting corn and cotton, a sharecropper after paying off his landowner had barely enough to feed his family. More often than not he went into debt, with the landowner holding the IOU's. Surely a more equal distribution of earnings was necessary. Nothing else was to be asked for. Neither equality, nor the overthrow of capitalism; merely just recompense for a family's hard labor. That's what Rafer told them after he opened the meeting. They were to form a league and hire a lawyer to represent them

Marchand gave a similar message. Then I, another representative of the white race, or at least that segment of it which believed in solidarity with the Negro people, brought them greetings from my Party—a Party which ruled one-sixth of the earth, a happy land with no discrimination, with true justice for all, and where everyone earned his fair share. And that's the name of the game, isn't it? A fair share?

In the woods, dogs barked. A whistle blew. Several of our guards came running. Dogs loped into the clearing, yapping wildly, followed by shots in the air. People began to scream, to run. I ran, too. I decamped, fled, got out of there fast. My escape route was clear. I followed it with the hope the tin crate would be where it was supposed to be. If I failed, I was certain tar and feathers would be my fate. I was scared shitless. I ran. El Lobo would have stood there and beat back the enemy single-handedly; he was without fear. Not me. I ran. I heard shots. Dogs yelped. Behind me, screaming and yelling. I ran and ran. Bushes tore at my shirt. I ran faster. There was the tin crate, its passenger door open. Marchand was already in the car. I fell in and slammed the door shut. The old pro gassed her and we left in a hurry. Moderately, of course. In the pit of my stomach, always the first part of me to react to tension, I felt an urgent need to vomit. It surged upward and I cranked the window down just in time to empty my gut, my residual bourgeois morality.

The old pro reached behind him and brought forth a bottle. It'll help, he said quietly.

I uncorked it, let the vile booze splash down my gullet. It burned, it scratched, it helped. Still I shivered, at first violently, then less so.

Those filthy scum, those bastards, I said. I hope no one was hurt.

The innocent are hurt and die every day, Marchand said. At least this time it would be for a good cause.

Yes, I said.

With little more said, we drove all night, the old crate hitting seventy, until we arrived in front of the Floridian. Tony Marchand was probably already plotting and planning his next campaign. Before I jumped from the car I told him we had moved too quickly, it had needed more time, and that the meeting should have been held quietly in a church—Stalin would have forgiven us—but not the way we did it. It was dead wrong. He replied, his tone moderate. They have to come out in the open, it's the only way.

All I could answer was, It happened too quick, goddammit, and you know it.

I'm certain he paid me no heed. Revolutionaries are always too much in a hurry. Energy and courage, they have lots of. Would that they had more wisdom.

George M. Fredrickson, in a review of Robin D. G. Kelley's *Hammer and Hoe: Alabama Communists During the Depression,* has this to say:

> Kelley makes a strong case that some African Americans
> were able to be Communists or accept Communist leader-
> ship without betraying their cultural heritage. But he does
> not fully succeed in absolving the Party's top leadership
> from the charge that they had a cynical and manipulative
> attitude toward Southern blacks. W.E.B. Du Bois was criti-
> cal at the time of Communist organizing among sharecrop-
> pers. He believed that it was recklessly pushing oppressed
> black people into a premature confrontation with white
> planters. The result, he feared, would be the shedding of
> black blood in a hopeless cause so that Communists could
> make propaganda from it.

Marchand was obeying orders, and I, an ignorant kid (no excuse), followed him.

The following year, when the Party line changed to the Popular Front, as Fredrickson and Kelley say, the Party abandoned its work among poor blacks and "called for an effort to make alliances with white liberals." And after the Stalin-Hitler pact, it changed back again.

The line has changed, long live the line!

13

I worked in the swanky Floridian for about four months, with time off for southern Georgia. I saved my tips, and at the beginning of April returned to New York with two hundred more dollars in my kitty, which now totaled four hundred. Another two hundred, I figured, and I would have a good start for my freshman year at Wisconsin in the fall of 1936, which gave me a year in which to make it. My mother was happy to see me, and happier still to learn that I really meant to go to college.

FDR was in his third year. The hand is quicker than the eye, they say, and in his case, the smile, the jaunty cock of the head, the aristocratic diction gave you hope, even if you were out of work. The sun rose every morning, but factories still were not hiring. There was home relief, but it made you feel ashamed. Farms overproduced, they said. Not a few times while I was on the road I had seen what was called excess milk dumped into rivers—this while people went hungry. Warehouses were crammed with inventory, but what good was it if you didn't have a buck in your wallet? Then FDR would make a speech and you'd feel better. Trade unionists, Socialists, Communists and their split-offs worked day and night, there were organizers all over the place, workers organizing by the thousands. Sit-ins, strikes, demonstrations, meetings. We want work! We want work! What's sweeter than a job? A paycheck? Food in the icebox? Two bits in your pocket for a movie or a soda with your girl? And there were the WPA, the PWA, the CCC, the Fair Labor Standards Act, the Social Security Act, the Federal Theater Project, the Writers' Project, the Artists' Project. Hope.

There were also the anti-semitic rantings of Father Coughlin— bankrolled by Henry Ford?—and the racist White Supremicists, and Mississippi Congressman Bilbo vomiting pure shit right here in the good old U.S. of A. In Europe, swaggering before millions in squares and piazzas, Adolph Hitler and Il Duce threatened war and the remaking of man in their own image.

In the movies, Charlie Chaplin made us laugh at them. Was it with tears in our eyes, as the popular song had it?

In my land of choice, the USSR, the purge of the men who had made the revolution had begun. It was necessary, we were told. We turned our eyes away, didn't want to think about it. We were too busy fighting against war and fascism—a contradiction if ever there was one, since to be against fascism necessarily meant going to war. And as Nazi Germany, Fascist Italy, and War Lord Japan rearmed, my Party spent its time and energy getting the United States and Great Britain to disarm. For what arcane reason? Did our Leader, who, using the scientific tenets of MarxLenin never made a mistake, here make a mistake? Did he fear the United States and Great Britain more than he did Nazi Germany? While we spent every waking hour fighting against war and fascism, was he already wooing Hitler?

World leaders, what a laugh.

What intelligence informed the Teutonic Wizard he could wage a successful war against the West and Russia simultaneously, and then declare war on the United States? Did he have no knowledge of American energy and industrial might?

And the Japanese Samurai? Hadn't they ever been to Detroit, or Gary, or Pittsburgh? Hadn't they ever seen the oil fields of Texas and the refineries in Louisiana? Were they nuts?

And Churchill, did he really believe he was fighting a war to save the British Empire?

Nuts; they were all nuts.

And we, the plebes, the hoi polloi, are we any less nuts, with our heads buried in the ground and our asses staring upward, farting at the sun? Did you ever attend a Congressional debate?

At that time there was a new coinage: concentration camps. They were invented, we were to learn much later, by V. I. Lenin, and appropriated by the Nazis. Left, right, a *pas de deux*. The Gulag Archipelago had not yet been sighted; it lay hidden behind a miasmic screen of intellectual jargon vulgarized by an obscene truism, you can't make an omelet without breaking heads—sorry, eggs. There were now also the *necessary murders* of, was it, W. H. Auden or Sidney and Beatrice Webb? Auden, when older, wiser, apologized. Did the Webbs? Or Walter Duranty of the *New York Times,* did he, or it, ever apologize for concealing the slaughter of millions of kulaks and the systematic starving of the Ukrainian peasantry—was it six, or was it seven million who died? Well, perhaps *only* five million. When I was a bit older and wiser, I went to a meeting chaired by Mary McCarthy, who mediated a debate between Corliss Lamont, humanist philosopher millionaire, and Sidney Hook, tough, wily professor of philosophy. Hook estimated that some ten million people had been murdered by Stalin (little did he know then by how much he underestimated) and Lamont, humanist, surmised it was *only* three million. Three million, not so much, he could live with that. (As for Mary McCarthy, like so many before and after me, I fell madly in love with her, and could only stutter when I spoke to her.)

It is my guess, based on no documents, that the number of people murdered from the beginning of time to the end of the nineteenth century does not equal the number murdered in the twentieth century alone.

Cambodian skull monument
(*David Portnoy/NYT Pictures*)

Remember, this century began with the Turks murdering one million Armenians, just a warm-up for what was to come on the grand stage of history. And there we are, of course, the stars of the show, my people, the Jews; bayonetted, hanged, gassed, cremated—but, descendants of Job, we survive. There were moments when I forgot I was a Jew, but after Hitler I have never forgotten for a second. Yes, what a century. For a day or two there was a lull, and then who should show up but Pol Pot and his Khmer Rouge—they just hate people who wear glasses and read a book, those damned bourgeois, kill 'em all. Karl Marx prophesied that by the twentieth century nationalism would be dead and buried, and with it capitalism. Wrong again. Here we are, approaching the twenty-first century, and nationalism is more virulent than ever; even tribes demand sovereignty, and capitalism is no less insatiable than in the past, repeating the endless litany of Saul Bellow's King Dahfu, I want, I want, I want, I want. . . .

If the twentieth century should have taught the human race anything, it is that the most revolutionary position one can take against the whirlwind of right and left is that of measure. How difficult this may be, I know better than most. We are a murderous yet fragile species. It takes less than an ounce of lead shot from a plastic toy gun to kill you.

Measure, goddammit!

Me, I was a lefty. I ate lefthanded, wrote lefthanded, threw lefthanded. Everything except bat; where I should have been left, I was right. That was me, askew. No matter what or where, I found myself outside the mass: on the bum, in the Party, standing at the plate. How could I possibly emulate the great Babe if I batted right instead of left? Oh, yes, I punted right as well on the gridiron, but I stiffarmed with my left. Whack! Out of my way. Although other kids who were lefthanded were called Lefty, I never was, because I batted righty. Damn! What's right and what's left? To consolidate and hold on to the best of the past, is that right? To better the lives of the poor, the dispossessed, the unfortunate, is that left? Because of who sat where in the French Chamber of Deputies at the end of the eighteenth century? Who? What?

A month or so after I returned from the South I went to see Clifford Odets' *Waiting for Lefty* with a young woman named Leah whom I had come to know at Sunrise Farm. We used to give Lindy Hop and Tango exhibitions there to amuse the tired colonists. She was a beautiful woman who didn't know it because she had what is called a Jewish nose, even if it is the shape of nose borne so proudly by Italian, Egyptian, and Native American women. Leah was fully aware, however, of her gorgeous, voluptuous body, which she had no trouble revealing even when dressed to the chin. A lovely chin, too. She wasn't my girl, she was Ben Dvosin's, my old Sunrise roommate's, and she was in mourning because he was fooling around with another woman. Besides, he had become a Party organizer in Manhattan and had little time for one woman, let alone two. Another reason, by the way, for my not wanting to become a functionary.

The audience went wild at the play, standing, clapping and bravo-ing for endless minutes. Though roused by the action, I was not similarly overcome; it was too propagandistic. The Lefty the strikers were waiting for, of course, was us, we, the movement, the Party. I was too steeped in good literature to fall for that stuff. You see, again askew, outside the compact mass. Besides, strikes were romantic only in retrospect. There weren't many in that audience who had walked a picket line for hours in a driving blizzard, or a pouring rain. For a worker, a strike is anxiety-ridden, even today when you don't have to worry about being beat up by rampaging cops as in the "old" days. Strikes and unions are necessary, otherwise what chance would a worker have when dealing with his or her employer? It takes one hundred thousand workers to equal one Ford.

The Cradle Will Rock by Marc Blitzstein, which opened almost two years after *Lefty*, was a much more appealing play, if only for the music. Orson Welles, when I worked for him, told me he had hoped to put it on in the grand style of an opera, but Blitzstein had felt that to do so would contravene its political message. It also romanticized the working class and yearned for revolution as led by, guess who? (With the talent and energy at our command, if we had been an indigenous democratic American party instead of a Russian party parading as American, I wonder how far we could have gone in changing our society.)

If I may make a diversion here, after I came to work for Welles in the fall of 1945, first as a high-speed verbatim stenographer, then as all-around amanuensis, escort, handholder, echo chamber, writer of descriptions, and antagonist, and we exchanged information about ourselves, he proclaimed (he rarely just said) to everyone he introduced me to that I was one of the two independent socialists in America, he being the second. He was boasting (and elevating me). Though a revolutionary film maker, he was one of those ill-informed Hollywood liberals, mouthing the clichés of the day, confused by the onset of what was to become known as the Cold War. When I told him I'd fought with the Lincoln battalion in Spain, he said he'd wanted to go, too. I have no idea what stopped him, he'd have been welcomed by Communist recruiters with great fanfare. He also failed to mention that in May 1937 he had recorded the narration for Joris Ivens' Spanish Civil War documentary *The Spanish Earth,* but that his orotund voice had been totally out of synch with the tone of the movie and his narration had been replaced by that of the scriptwriter, Ernest Hemingway.

Welles was a man I could never quite get hold of, not because he was so huge—although he wasn't as huge as he later became—but because he had so many hiding places in the vastness that was himself. He was Falstaff, he was Kane, he was Mr. Rochester, he was characters he had not yet played; he was a romantic hero, he was a conjurer, he was a child. I tried writing a novel about him but could get nowhere with it simply because I couldn't get at the man. Charlatan, true artist, stubborn, pliable, a liar, charming, mean bastard, generous. Four years old.

I would come in on an early Sunday morning, even the sun still asleep, and he would lie in bed naked, the covers thrown off, scratching his genitalia while he dictated something for the Sunday commentary radio show he had at one o'clock. A psychiatrist who took his Freud too seriously once told me, Don't be so naive, he was trying to seduce you. Was he? When talking about himself to me he always managed to segue into a shtick about how he had had to hold off the hands of men who had tried to seduce him when he was a boy. That he loved women, their bodies that is, there was no doubt. I found him in bed with several of great renown for just that, their bodies; Marie ("the Body") Macdonald, for one, and one in particular for her face, the most delicately beautiful woman I ever saw in person, Vivien Leigh. How Welles giggled and grinned and danced for his great victory over Laurence Olivier, his most hated rival, his peer. His fat jig was as ecstatic as that of Adolph Hitler at the rail car at Compiègne (a camera trick) when he accepted France's surrender. She was in town with Olivier, who'd come in with the Old Vic, and while her husband played one of the Henrys, she played with the very hefty Falstaff, Orson Welles, genius.

Still, to observe him as he drew out talents from individual actors that they themselves did not know they possessed was truly marvelous, and they were in awe of him, as was I. And his brain was a magnificent instrument. We were on the road with the musical *Around the World,* music by Cole Porter, book by Orson Welles, produced, directed, and co-starring his very own self as Mr. Fix. It was New Haven. He and the company were already there when I arrived after a short side trip to New York City to visit Jeannette. We'd just been in Boston and were then going to Philadelphia. It was his thirty-first birthday, I had just recently had mine, and I brought him a gift, Arthur Koestler's *The Yogi and the Commissar.* Neither/nor, of course. I arrived an hour or so before the opening night. Welles (out of just pure contrariness, I never called him Orson, always Mr. Welles) was preparing to leave his suite for the theater, which was right next door to the hotel, when I handed him his gift. He yipped like a little kid—he was a little kid—and unwrapped it, thanked me profusely, told me he had read *Darkness at Noon* and admired it greatly, and began to read the book as we left the room on the way to the elevator. I observed him closely as he scanned a page, flipped to the next, scanned it, and so on, as we waited for the lift, descended, strolled slowly through the hotel lobby, ignoring the stares, eyes closely scanning, out the door, down the alley to the stage door, scanning, flipping pages, into the theater, to his dressing room. All the time scanning and flipping. He had to be kidding. He loved to rib me, I was just a city yokel new to the business, and he at thirty-one the old veteran trouper. By the time he began to undress he had finished the book, some 250 pages, and started to discuss it with me, quoting full pages. Not only had he read every page, he had memorized them, had understood what he'd read, and incorporated it into a brain obviously as huge as he was. The same joker who jigged like a clown because he'd put horns on a hated rival and who went to Toots Shor's to duel with Damon Runyan characters in the game of "Can You Top This," the jokes outrageously vulgar, the winner getting the bosomy call girl giggling nearby for the rest of the night. Another beautiful body to fuck.

You disapprove of me, don't you, William?

Yes, Mr. Welles, I do.

You're a puritan, you must know that?

I guess so.

Yes, I disapproved of him. Not his wanting to have every beautiful woman who came within reach—after all, Miss Veronica and my mother, I suppose, had left me with the same voracious hunger which plagued him—but because it seemed to me he was wasting the miracle of his brain and talent on nonsense.

Once we had a real fight.

You don't like my acting style, do you, William? (He'd guessed, I suppose, because I never told him how great he was.)

Too bravura for me, I said. You overuse that voice of yours, always playing The Shadow. "Who knows what evil lurks in the hearts of men?" Come off it. If you stuck just to directing and made even a meager attempt at living with discipline, you'd be unmatchable and would give the world even more than you already have.

I've given the world *Kane*.

His face was white. I should have shut up, but, prig that I was, I couldn't.

And because you didn't use the brains you were born with, you left the unfinished *Ambersons* in the hands of the philistines and let them destroy your greatest masterpiece. Or at least damage it. You hardly know the world you live in. I'm not the rube, it's you—just a rube from the boondocks of Wisconsin, and you always will be. It's time you grew up, stopped lying to yourself. (I felt like his father.)

He turned away, white still, his magnificent eyes blurred. He was taking a beating. The play needed more money, and it was hard to come by. He thought he could get some from Billy Rose. I went with him and stood by as that little bastard whipsawed him for his lack of discipline, his extravagance with other people's money, revealed his contempt for the man. Rose was so cruel I had a terrible urge to kick his ass. He was sheer power, money power, talking.

Though Rose turned him down, he got lucky and was able to obtain more money for *Around the World* from Harry Cohn of Columbia

Pictures with a promise to do a movie for him for the money. Cohn got Welles cheap, $75,000, which, unfortunately for Welles, is the way it usually turned out for him. The movie he later made for Cohn was *Lady from Shanghai*. And Rose had exaggerated; Welles's movies nearly always came in within budget—or at least so Welles boasted.

As was customary after one of our spats, Welles would ask me to accompany him to dinner at Shor's. That's the way he punished me for my impudence, since he knew I disliked acting as his escort and preferred to go home. But how could I object; I was able to eat a huge succulent steak free of charge, and, since I was paid by the hour, I would also be paid for the time I spent eating it.

Someone had called a freelance verbatim reporting office Jeannette and I were connected with, asking for a high-speed stenographer to take dictation from the great Orson Welles at the Waldorf Towers. Jeannette was given the assignment. It turned out Welles was doctoring a play already running and doing badly on Broadway, and she worked late into the night. (As I waited for her in her apartment, my imagination could only be called lurid.) She reported that he walked about naked under an open robe constantly scratching his genitalia, and that she found it very embarrassing. However, there had been other people present in Welles's suite—the play's director and another writer.

The next time someone called on his behalf, I was sent. He was fully dressed and we got to work immediately. He held a copy of Jules Verne's *Around the World in 80 Days* from which he began to dictate a play script. He did not really require a high-speed stenographer, but he was Orson Welles who needed the fastest, the bestest, the mostest. I was overawed by his presence, his voice, his eyes, his quick intelligence. He worked fast, rarely stopped, seemed to know exactly what he wanted. I returned several days running as the script began to unfold. Then a public stenographer he had been using as secretary had an auto accident, and he asked me if I would take her place. It was not he directly, it was Dick Wilson, his partner in the Mercury Theater, who negotiated the job with me. I told him I would take the job, but at a high hourly rate: five dollars an hour.

Wilson whistled and went in to talk to Welles about it. Welles said okay, and so it was. Later Welles himself mentioned it was quite a high rate, and, already knowing my customer, I said, You have your racket, I have mine. As I expected, he laughed and we shook hands on it. Remember, this was 1945-46, when five dollars was a lot of money. My week turned out to run some sixty or seventy hours, so I was making between $300 and $350 weekly, which at that time was real dough.

One evening Welles asked me to have dinner with him in his suite, we were to work late, and as we talked he asked me how I had come by the scars on my neck. I told him I had fought in Spain with the International Brigades, and on the Madrid front had received a bullet in my cervical spine. An unsuccessful operation to remove the bullet had left the scars. He nodded gravely, then said only circumstances had prevented him from going to Spain to fight. If the idea had come to him, I was certain it had come and gone very quickly. I told him if he had gone his chances of survival would have been about fifty-fifty. (Over the years I don't know how many men have told me that they had also wanted to go to fight in Spain, but one thing or another had interfered. How romantic. How worthy of them.) After that evening, the invisible wall between employer and employee slowly became non-existent and we could say almost anything to each other. Almost. I continued to call him Mister Welles. You get too close to an employer, and by his very position he begins to think he owns you.

I was paid by his business management agent in Hollywood. Paid very slowly. It didn't take me very long to learn that should I quit while he still owed me a thousand or two, I'd probably have to wait months, perhaps years, to receive what I'd earned. It wasn't just I who had to wait, since Welles's earnings were hardly as high as his princely expenses. The Waldorf Towers, where he lived in a three-room suite when I first came to work for him, had to wait, everybody had to wait.

Here's the way the man lived. We'd go down in the elevator, the doorman would hail a cab, we'd be driven to Shor's or Reuben's or Lindy's. He'd tell the doorman when we arrived to pay the cabbie, enter, we'd eat a steak or two (he ate two, I ate one), sign the tab for the food, for the waiter, for the doorman, for the taxi coming, then get a cab to return to the Waldorf and have the doorman pay the cabbie. Once up in the suite, we would do some work—he was still writing the script or revising it or whatever—order a light supper from room service, a chicken sandwich for me, two for him, a huge pot of coffee, sign the tab for the food, for the tip, for the doorman's tip, for the taxi cab, et cetera. In all that time not one dime had changed hands. His management agent couldn't trust him with cash—money was just paper to him—and he was allotted $100 a week. Since I was being paid in slow motion, there were times when we were out on the street—he having decided to walk—that we would have only a quarter between us and we'd toss to see whether I could buy a pack of Chesterfields or he could buy a cheap cigar, as he'd been put on low rations by the cigar maker of the king-sized Corona-Coronas he smoked because of non-payment of bills. Toots Shor was happy for us to sign the tab, just so long as the genius spent his free time in his bistro and he could nudge a customer and point his bulldog chin toward the great Orson Welles. Everyone expected to see the one and only Joe DiMaggio, that quiet man over there sitting with the skinny Frank Sinatra, but the boy genius?

Those eyes, that voice; he could look quite handsome, sort of like a handsome pig. When he was mean, it was more like an ugly bulldog. He could charm the balls off you, or he could make you so mad you wanted to stick a knife in that blubber. A few times, seeing my fists balled, ready to smash his face, he transformed himself into a sweet, charming gentleman, like a brat who, knowing he is about to be walloped, suddenly smiles and apologizes, not with any particular word but with a slight courtier's bow, and even though you know he's wooing you again and that you're a damn fool for falling for it, you forgive him and go along.

My wife-to-be, Jeannette, was living on Morton Street in Greenwich Village, and once when I was there Welles called. He needed me right away. Please, take a cab. Hurry! As everyone who has ever lived in Manhattan knows, it takes longer to travel by cab than by subway. I took the subway, then walked. It took a good forty minutes. No sooner had I entered the room than he began to yell his bloody head off. His expectation had been that once he had hung up the phone I would walk right in. You want to strangle a man like that, except that this one was, you soon realized, only four years old.

The Old Vic was in town. Welles just could not stop talking about Laurence Olivier, putting him down. He was too soft, he was too pretty, he was queer. *Around the World* had already opened on Broadway (to just so-so reviews), and Welles told me to take an afternoon off and go to a matinee to see *Henry IV*. Watch Richardson, he said, the greatest Falstaff in the world—except for me. And Richardson was truly magnificent, a superb actor. But so was Olivier, of course. That evening, as Welles was transforming himself into Mr. Fix in the dressing room, I told him he was absolutely right, Richardson was marvelous, but, after all, I was only a rank amateur, so I couldn't discern any weakness in Olivier. In fact, I thought he was terrific. Welles wouldn't talk to me for two days. But on Friday night, nearly midnight in fact, as Jeannette and I were having a late supper—the matinee had been on Wednesday—he phoned to ask me to please come to the Stork Club. What for! Calm yourself, he said in his most charming voice. Something I've written in longhand, I'll need it typed in the morning.

I did not want to spend the rest of the night at the Stork Club—I despised its proprietor, Sherman Billingsley, because he hired scabs—so I went wearing a sport shirt and no jacket. When I arrived, the doorman, of course, would not allow me to enter. I told him what I wanted, and he sent a page to fetch Welles. When he came out, he smiled at me and asked them to allow me entry, I was his guest, but they refused. Orders from Billingsley: no entrance without jacket and tie. Welles became angry, but I told him I could live without the Stork Club, to give me his notes and I would see him at the theater at noon—Saturday. He had no notes to give me, said, Sorry, and left me standing there infuriated. You fat sonofabitch! I yelled at him, but the door had already closed after him. The doorman and the strongarm nearby laughed.

104

The following day, when I showed up at his dressing room for the matinee, Welles said, I'm sorry about last night, I just wanted to introduce you to Vivien Leigh, I was out with her. He sported a big grin. I wanted to surprise you. Not surprise, he had wanted to show off. I glared at him. He gave me a phone number on a slip of paper. Call her for me, please, tell her I'll phone in the middle of the afternoon, between acts. I did as he requested. It was she, all right, I couldn't mistake that voice. That terrible need for him to show off, for admiration; now of course I understand it, then it only infuriated me. As for Olivier, I suppose he had been off somewhere, too, the previous night. They were like little kids, still playing doctor in mama and papa's bedroom behind not-so-closed doors.

As I say, he was a child, and like a child he slipped out of his apartment one morning—he was now living in a multi-room sublet on East End Avenue—and about three hours later rushed in flushed, those famous eyes glistening. What? I asked him. He'd gone to an early show at the Paramount to see Rita Hayworth in *Gilda,* and fallen in love with her all over again. They had been separated or divorced for a year or more, and now he had fallen in love with the most beautiful Hollywood star in the world. Send her flowers, he said, a thousand dollars' worth. He was so excited, he could barely breathe. He had found love on the silver screen. My God, he moaned, I love her. Just say, Love, Orson.

I advised the man in the flower shop to send the most expensive flowers he could order through his telegraph service. I also gave him the business manager's address. The poor bastard was delighted with the order, from Orson Welles to Rita Hayworth no less. Perhaps just the thought of serving these celebrated personages made up for the fact he probably wouldn't be paid for six months.

One late spring night, after the curtain had come down, Welles and the lovely Marie MacDonald went to a club to catch Milton Berle. Welles couldn't resist; he had to dare the guillotine, and began to heckle the sharpest wit in America. Berle cut him up pretty badly, to the laughter of a full house. (I wish there'd been a tape, but of course there wasn't.) The following day, Welles walked about tight-lipped, full of anger—not at himself, at Berle. After the show that night, he just had to return to the club to seek revenge. I'll take him this time, he vowed. Disaster was a magnet he seemed unable to resist. This time Berle couldn't help but laugh at this yokel; he dismembered the poor man toe by toe, finger by finger, limb from limb, then put him out of his misery and slit his throat. The crowd roared. For days the boy genius was morose, was snappy with me, his amanuensis, but I felt sorry for him and shrugged it off. He simply, or perhaps not so simply, had a perverse need to be a victim, of himself, of Hollywood, of Billy Rose, of whoever would not or could not assuage his terrible hunger for attention. He was not, poor soul, appreciated.

He was always parading his nude body before me. It fed my curiosity. How could a thirty-two-year-old male have reached that age without the use of one muscle? If one there was, it was completely concealed by fat. He was a tall man, with big bones, and if he had ever used the incipient muscles that all bodies have, he could have been a superb specimen. The weight he carried was too much for his arches, so he had flat feet and required special shoes made to prescription. He also wore an abdominal belt. He carried himself with what I can call elephantine grace. I think the only athletic stimulation he'd ever had was that gotten through fornication. I knew personally about his fornication with women because when I came early to rouse him I saw them in his bed—at least, I assume they had fornicated. Welles made too many denials about being homosexual. Why deny what you are not, especially since I, for one, never asked him. It never occurred to me even to care. It has never bothered me with what gender anyone fornicates. Sex is a childish game which we never outgrow. One should laugh before it, laugh after it. Since its main purpose in nature is for procreation, which is, I suppose, a very serious matter, when you really get down to it you have to be very serious, almost grim. It's hard work, too, so you can hardly laugh while you are at it. If you bust out laughing, everything deflates, and you have to start all over. At least that has been my experience.

Still, when the play was on, while waiting in the wings, Welles would play boyish games, groping and goosing with Arthur Margetson, who played Phileas Fogg, and was, they said, homosexual. They would be carrying on, the two of them, giggling, shoving each other around, until one or the other heard his cue and went onstage.

I asked Welles how he could hack around that way prior to going onstage, and he said Margetson was a very nervous actor, experienced though he was, and he did what he did in the wings with the man in order to loosen him up. Margetson, by the way, was an ideal choice for Phileas Fogg, and it was a joy to observe him onstage.

Earlier, during rehearsals, when Cole Porter and retinue arrived, another form of childish play would revolve around me. A straight in the company of queers is subject to what I can only call reverse sexual harassment. Porter was then a crippled man, his legs having been crushed when a horse he was riding unseated him and then fell on him. He was to use crutches and braces on his legs for the rest of his life. Though in pain a good portion of the time, whenever I saw him he appeared in good humor. The rehearsals in New York took place in an old opera house in the Sixties, the entrance to which was approached by a steep iron staircase. I would be asked to wait at the curb when Porter was expected in his chauffeur-driven car. When he arrived, his valet-bodyguard-friend—what the guy was I never found out—and I would cross hands to make a seat, and Porter would be carried up the iron stairs, into the opera house and onto the stage. He was a small man, slender, and not too great a weight. But since my hands were occupied with helping him into the opera house, and thus unable to protect my virtue, Porter—giggling all the time, as were his man and the inevitable hangers-on, as well as Welles— would begin to heft my pectorals. It was annoying, and at first I simply ignored it, but a joke is a joke once, twice, three times, as any standup comic will tell you, and then it becomes a goddamned bore. So I finally had to tell Porter, One more time and I drop you on your fancy ass.

It was only in these adolescent sexual games that Porter showed any disrespect or crudeness. Otherwise, he was polite, decent, and when

Welles and I would visit him and his wife in their double penthouse apartments atop the Waldorf Towers, a perfect host. He and his wife lived separately in their own apartments, both splendidly furnished, no movie garishness for them. We were served grand meals by servants which I managed to eat with the various utensils at my setting without embarrassing myself. Mrs. Porter was very diffident, without pretension.

When his wife was not present, which was most of the time, Porter would sit at the piano and play and sing the songs he was writing for the show. They sounded great to my inexperienced ear, but later Welles was to moan that the only mediocre songs Porter ever wrote were for *Around the World*. It was not the music which hurt the show—they were melodious and clever—it was Orson Welles's continual tinkering, so that the cast and play were never at rest. It is true, though, one rarely hears the songs Cole Porter wrote for *Around the World*.

To twit this straight—I can only believe it was to tease me, make me perk up my straight ears—during rehearsals, Porter and the famous transvestite Barbet, then beyond middle age, bald and flabby, and teaching the female dancers how to use the trapeze for the show's circus scene, would talk queer talk in my presence. In Cocteau's movie *Blood of the Poet*, one of the most beautiful blondes you ever saw sits in a loge during a theatrical performance, and that beauty is Barbet. Now, for my edification, he and Porter discuss big cocks, and Barbet tells Porter the biggest cock he ever ingested was that of, guess who, the then light-heavyweight champion of the world, "Slapsy" Maxie Rosenbloom. I am aghast in my straighthood and they laugh. Boys will be boys.

Around the World was playing to half-empty houses. Welles begged, pleaded, and fawned before every possible publicity source, radio and newspaper—Gene Lyons, Earl Wilson, and particularly the disgusting Walter Winchell. They did toss a pitch or two. To no avail. Welles came up with the idea of playing *Lear* in repertory with *Around the World*, going so far as to make drawings of costumes and sets for the classic, and he spent hours dictating a cut script to me. As soon as he presented the idea to the Shuberts, they scotched it. Running a classic in repertory with a commercial flop was not their idea of good business practice. After some seventy performances, *Around the World* died. It seemed to me I was more distraught than he. If he felt bad for the cast, for his own loss of money and prestige, for the play's backers, it was not discernible. He blamed Porter's music for the failure—to me, at any rate. Whether he did to anyone else, I have no idea. He seemed very anxious to return to Hollywood.

He obtained a writer's contract for me with Columbia Pictures for whom he had, as I said, contracted to do a picture. He left before me, and I joined him in a week. I found him in a state of anxiety, touchy and bad-tempered. I soon discovered the reason. When he arrived in Hollywood he found a pop singer named Tony Martin was living with Rita in her house. Using every single cornball movie love story cliché—candy, flowers, jewelry, honey-voiced phone calls, and the ultimate: a starring role in his picture, *Lady from Shanghai*—Welles finally won over Hayworth with this Hollywood courtship, and, just as in a movie, she kicked out her current lover and replaced him with her former husband. The leaves rustled and the sun set in a purple orange sky.

She was every bit as beautiful off-screen as she was on. I couldn't but stare at her and she blushed, then gave me a smile which made my heart stop. She was a modest woman, with no pretentious airs. I thought for once he showed good taste.

Welles boasted that he worked twenty-four hours a day, could go without sleep for numberless days. It was an empty boast. It was I who worked twenty-four hours a day. The rewrites with him were endless. I began to fall apart and told him so. Though I was now under contract with Columbia, writing description scenes for *Lady* and being paid on a regular basis, I was really Welles's man and beholden only to him. He told me to take a couple days off, which I did, and used them to remain in bed, interrupted only by room service for my meals. Then he invited me to go to a party with him. It turned out to be an orgy. All the women strolled about naked. I recognized none of them and assumed they were either young women hoping to make it in Hollywood or call girls or both. There was a great deal of drinking and wild dancing. A number of the men I did recognize as movie actors. As soon as I stopped reeling, I had a drink, grabbed hold of the first woman who showed any interest, and retired to a bedroom. It turned out that she was as glad as I was to be out of the noise. When I awoke in the morning, she was gone. I felt strangely empty. What I remember is the silk that was her skin.

Word had gone out that Welles was preparing a picture, and soon the door of our office at Columbia seemed to be under constant siege by lovely curvaceous young women offering themselves to Welles, even to me. Some were well-known actresses. Audition by couch. I wasn't a prude, and I enjoyed sleeping with firm-bosomed young women with perfect, unblemished skin as much as any man, but I was after all a socialist, and this constant offering of human sacrifice sickened me. I turned them away, as did Welles, I think. Besides, I missed Jeannette, missed her terribly, especially since she had written to tell me she was studying at the Ogunquit Art School in Maine and while there was sitting semi-nude for Walt Kuhn, the noted painter. Talk about the double standard—I almost went berserk with jealousy. What with overwork and then this blow, I was really in a bad way. I phoned her and screamed at her for a good hour until she promised she would no longer model for the old man. I wish she hadn't conceded to my hysteria, for now her youthful glory would be lighting up a wall of the National Gallery in Washington. In any event, I'd had enough. I was tired of being owned round the clock by someone, began to feel like an indentured slave, and I told Welles I was quitting. He did everything but stamp his feet and put on the rejected child act. You can't do this to me, you just can't. I'm sorry, I must, I said. Finally, we embraced. I'd gotten to like this big fat kid. He was a lost soul.

I collected my pay at the gate, and flew back to New York and then to Portland, Maine, where in the middle of the night I taxied to Ogunquit and rushed into the passionate embrace of the woman I loved, wondering why I had stayed away so long. Perhaps it had been those Orsonian eyes and voice which had mesmerized me.

Several years later I received a phone call from Richard Wilson, who ran the business end of the Mercury Theater for Welles, asking me to meet him for a drink at Grand Central Station. There he pleaded with me to return to work for Welles, who was going to Europe, and I would be paid with coin of the realm, as Wilson put it. No, I said, I wasn't about to pick up to go off as an indentured slave to a four-year-old genius.

Intimacy does breed contempt. It took me decades to stop seeing the four-year-old when I saw Welles's work. Shakespeare's *Macbeth* done in a Scotch burr. Come on now!

"Your Obedient Servant, Orson Welles" is the way he signed responses to fan mail. I wrote the responses, he signed them. I even wrote the letters to his oldest daughter, Christopher. By wrote, I mean composed and typed. I bought the gifts for his children and sent them off as well. He was too busy. In addition to taking on the role of Mr. Fix, he played the magician in the circus act, for which he taught me how to load all the tricks: the rabbit in the hat, the bird in the wand, and so forth. Best of all, how to help the beauteous maiden into the box to be sawed in half. For the part, Welles wore a huge and dramatic white robe designed for him by David Cole, the play's costume designer. He considered himself one of the great magicians of the world. One of the greats of the world. He preceded Muhammed Ali—he was the greatest. He could from memory speak lines from Dante, Goethe, Keats, and all of Shakespeare. He loved the works of Botticelli and could discuss them as a learned connoisseur with any professional in the field. He knew and understood the drama of the Orient as well as the West. He could also talk gash with the basest of Damon Runyon characters who hung out at Toots Shor's. A man with a superior talent, he yearned to be one of the boys. He directed two cinematic masterpieces, *Citizen Kane* and *The Magnificent Ambersons*. He had the discipline of a four-year-old who wants what he wants when he wants it. There were times when he suddenly would stare into space and from his lips would escape the saddest of sighs. Deep in his obesity lurked an unspoken pain. In life there was one role he felt belonged to him: that of the master creator. He was God. A terribly sad man.

"Your Obedient Servant, Orson Welles."

14

When I returned from the South, the Party section which ran the Furriers Union obtained a job for me as a sorter in a small store that sold fur pieces—bellies, rumps, sides of anything from rabbit to mink—to what was known as the Greek fur trade. The pieces were sewn into a plate, from which fur coats were fabricated. You could buy a superior mink coat at a good discount if it was made from a plate instead of individual pelts.

Most of the fur piece stores were located off Seventh Avenue, between 26th and 33rd Streets. I did much of my organizing during lunch hour, when most of the errand boys and sorters gathered in the local cafeteria on Seventh Avenue. The ruler of the cash register at this busy eatery was a lovely young woman who modeled fur coats in the evenings. We called her The Virgin because not only did she turn down our requests for a date but also those of salesmen, buyers, and bosses. She was a good girl.

I was paid ten dollars a week by the store I worked for, and love and gratitude by the union. It satisfied me. Most of my evenings during the week were taken with Young Communist League and union meetings. Saturday nights were my own, and I spent a good number of them at the Savoy Ballroom in Harlem, dancing with ten-cent-a-dance taxi dancers. After the South, I felt a terrible need to submerge myself in blackness, brownness, in color. Be a Negro! After giving my mother money for the house, I began to spend more than I was earning, thus having to dip into my college fund. I never did develop the rich man's aversion to spending capital; I simply put it out of my mind. Harlem took all the available space.

So when Bill Lawrence, now Party organizer for the needle trades section in New York, met me at a meeting, asked what I was doing, and said he'd like for me and another comrade to attend meetings of a small group that was forming in Harlem, I was very pleased. We were just to lend our support he said, add a word or two when necessary. Sure, of course, be glad to, I said. Now I had two reasons for going up to Harlem.

Every couple of weeks, this other comrade—a shy kid whose name I'll be damned if I remember—and I would go to one or another Harlem flat to attend meetings of a small unit of young Communists. We talked about racism, carving out a Black Republic in the South (a Party idea given little credence and mention of which always brought a giggle), about fascism, Father Coughlin, Father Divine, the Party, the Soviet Union: the only country in the world where racism was a crime punishable by prison or even death, even though it did not believe in capital punishment; and please, do your best to interest your family and friends in joining the Party; and look, come to the *New Masses* Ball on New Year's Eve. Every time a new face appeared at one of these meetings, we fell all over ourselves greeting our new comrade. Our self-congratulations lasted weeks.

Once, after we left a meeting, my comrade and I were jumped by two black men who wanted our wallets. Between us we didn't have more than two bucks. We fought back, and I could hear my comrade beating on one of the muggers—to keep fit for the Cause, he did calisthenics every morning—and saying, Look, I'm not hitting you because you are a Negro, try to remember that, I'm just as poor as you are. At the next meeting of the group we spent the whole night apologizing for beating these guys up.

How condescending we were, how patronizing. Small wonder that the Left, and the Communist Party in particular, failed so miserably in its membership drives among the colored peoples, despite an expenditure of huge quantities of energy and time.

That little mugging notwithstanding, Harlem was safe for whites. Whites crisscrossed from east to west and north to south—to City College, to the Cotton Club, in summer to Lewisohn Stadium to hear concerts under the stars, to take the train at 125th Street. I was not the only white man to dance with taxi dancers in the Savoy or Renaissance Ballrooms. Unlike those times when I had been on the road in white Christian America, where I had felt like the only Jew in Torquemada's Spain, in Harlem I walked unafraid. I, a Jew, was one with the Negroes against our common enemy. I was certain it could be read on my face. There were plenty of Jewish bigots, but many Jews—Anarchists, Socialists, Trotskyists, Lovestoneites, Stalinists, and just plain decent people—gave their time, their thought, their passion, and their money to the cause of equal rights and equal justice for all men and women, no matter what their color. Of the white men I knew who risked their lives to work in the south to change its racial laws and the white power structure, most were Jews. So why should I be afraid? I wasn't, and every Saturday night for months I went to Harlem to dance. Then I fell in love.

At the end of the night, the Savoy Ballroom in darkness except for the revolving crystal ball reflecting a myriad of fluttering colors, taxidancer Sarah Walton and I did the old Georgia grind. Socked it in, heart pumping.

I went overboard for her. I thought about her all week. I couldn't wait to smell her; she washed with Ivory soap, must have scrubbed with Ivory soap, a clean healthy smell. I couldn't wait to touch her, too, feel her sturdy body against mine when we danced. We did the double-Lindy, the triple-Lindy, the Stomp, the Strut, and on rare occasions the Peabody, that fast, elegant transplant from Italian Harlem.

Not bad for a white boy, she once said.

Yeah, got natural rhythm.

She didn't smile. It was an irony she didn't understand. To her I was an alien from an alien country, an unsophisticated greenhorn, lacking totally in hip. I was too sincere, she once told me.

Dolled up in new suit, new shoes, starched white shirt, and the inevitable red tie, I would get to the Savoy about ten o'clock at night, buy fifty tickets for five dollars, and hand them all to Sarah. She was chocolate brown with the face of one of Gauguin's Tahitian women. Her magnificent shoulders and bosom were pedestal to her stately head. Everyone in the ballroom got to know me and thought I was a crazy rich kid, trying to buy himself a piece of black ass. Sarah thought so, too.

I wanted to tell her how I had recently taken the chance of being tarred and feathered to help Negro sharecroppers in Georgia, but would I then have to tell her how I had led them to disaster, and how guilty I felt? I was madly in love with the Negro people, sort of over-compensating for Rafe, Ellafat, and the rest. Of course, I did not understand that until I became an adult, several decades later.

Whenever I told Sarah how infatuated I was with her, she merely shrugged those great shoulders of hers, took the five ten-ticket strips and stuffed them in the little pocketbook which always hung from her right wrist. When we danced, it bumped her shoulder to the rhythm of the music played by wondrous little Chick Webb and his band. "The Savoy Stomp." "The Harlem Stomp." "The Darktown Strutters' Ball." A very young Ella Fitzgerald, said to be Webb's girl friend, did the singing then.

Ten cents a dance
That's what they pay me.
Gosh, how they weigh me down. . . .

Man, did we move! Sweat dripped from our foreheads. The chocolate brown skin on her naked arms glistened. My tanned white face shone. I wanted her right there on the semi-darkened dance floor, as the slow-spinning crystal ball overhead alternately striped us with the colors of the spectrum. I wanted to mix my whiteness with her blackness. I was bugs about her.

We met several times after work, about three in the morning, when she led me to a place called Rose's Tea Shop that had rooms upstairs. Sarah knew her way about. For her, every dime counted. Twice, on her nights off, we went to the Apollo and then to a Harlem restaurant for supper. We weren't very comfortable in public; people stared and stared, black and white, what freaks. She refused to go to midtown, to the Paramount where Duke Ellington and band were playing. "You crazy?" Once, after Rose's Tea Shop, she asked me for money. I stared at her, stricken. It was then she said, "You're too sincere. I'm not your girl friend." In the end, it wasn't our colors that refused to mix, it was our cultures. We never knew what to say to each other. Whenever I broached the subject of racism or politics, her eyes glazed over. She wanted none of it. We never said goodbye; I just stopped going to the Savoy. I went to Spain, instead.

Irving Howe called it a "brilliant masquerade." I prefer to call it an ingenious scam. The Popular Front. The League for Peace and Democracy. Against War and Fascism. My friend Natie laughed at me. Whatever happened to Lenin's *State and Revolution?* he asked. The Soviet Union, under constant propagandistic attack from a rampant Hitler, ordered a change in line. Simultaneously the Communist parties of the world announced a desire to form a popular front against fascism with anyone and everyone. The little red Party dues book became, literally, a little pink book. A few years before, we had called FDR a fascist; now we loved him, and Eleanor, too. We pleaded with Norman Thomas, the Socialist leader, to become our ally; two years before, we had named him social fascist number one. Where before we had tried to split every union in America, now we opposed the organizing of industrial unions by John L. Lewis, the mine workers' president, as union-splitting. (Flexible for once, we changed our mind when we saw that his success was imminent). Overnight, our folk singers produced songs that thrilled to the Stars and Stripes; This land is our land, tra la. Karl Marx's brilliant critique of reformism, *The 18th Brumaire of Louis Bonaparte,* could not be found on the open shelves of the Party's bookstore on 13th Street; like a pornographic rag, it had been sent underground. At Yuletide, the Party put up a large Christmas tree with flashing colored lights outside its headquarters. Christmas cards could now be bought at every Party bookstore throughout the United States. We just loved Santa. Is there a greater ally? We sang Christmas carols, and went to church on New Year's Eve to hear Handel's *Messiah.*

It worked. Despite FDR's magic the depression still lingered. Hitler loomed, and he was not just a Charlie Chaplin imitation. Anti-semitism was on the increase. The need for a pink patriotic alternative to Tweedledee and Tweedledum was great. People signed up by the tens of thousands. All that energy, ingenuity, and sheer commitment transformed the Communist Party, USA, overnight into a party as American as Johnny Appleseed and P. T. Barnum. The bullshit oozed. Actors, painters, writers, lawyers, doctors, priests, rabbis, the rich and the poor, active trade unionists, even an occasional Negro, joined up. Workers, too. Madison Square Garden wasn't large enough to hold the crowds coming to hear Earl Browder, the Kansas Twang, aver our patriotism and our love for America. Our hootenannies outdid Hamlin's Pied Piper. Twenty-four-hour folk songs echoed from the sky. America, America. We were Jeffersonians, Jacksonians, Lincolnians, Washingtonians. We even ran baseball box scores in the *Daily Worker.* We were for collective security against Hitler. We were the Popular Front. And we won a great victory: FDR recognized the USSR.

It was the first time since Eugene V. Debs that an American leftwing party spoke in our native tongue. Would that it had been genuine; our country has always needed a decent, honest alternative to the parties of the status quo.

But it was a scam, of course. False. The Popular Front's motivation, culture, art, folk songs were as fake as an exploding cigar. Pouf!

When my friend Natie quoted from the *18th Brumaire,* from Lenin's *What Is To Be Done?,* from Leon Trotsky and his American disciples

James Cannon and Max Shachtman, from Jay Lovestone and Bertram Wolfe, I blushed, stuttered replies. I developed my own theory. A very original theory. The Trojan horse. We were lulling the ruling class into a comforting sleep. When night fell, we would emerge and take over. Or, to put it another way, in the class war for power, purity falls by the wayside, a victim of rape. And when Stalin began his purge of Lenin's closest comrades, I reinforced my theory with fantasy: they weren't really shot, they were concealing themselves in deepest Siberia, biding their time, plotting the world revolution.

Yes, it was foolish, infantile, and sad. But I was a believer; the Party was my home, and I needed it. I didn't want to go on the bum again. I wanted an anchor. The Party was my anchor. I needed a hundred siblings, a thousand; I needed a place. The Party was my place, my family, my tribe, my country. I fended Natie off, knowing he was right. You can't be both a revolutionary Marxist-Leninist and stand at FDR's right hand. I detested the Party's new line and pretended not to, went gung ho for it, screamed at Natie, told him he was too pure. It's only a tactic, a strategy; look how successful we are, you and the Trotskyites are just grouplets, we're a party, a mass party. You're just jealous of our success. He shrugged and shook his head.

And successful we were. We became more than a political party, we became a world now peopled with men and women from every class; the sons and daughters of *Mayflower* families, of bankers, of the nouveau riche; from the middle class, educated, talented. You know, we'd whisper to one another, so-and-so is one of ours. Frederic Vanderbilt Field, no less. Harry Bridges. Julie Garfield—the whole Group Theater, for God's sake. They were joining by the thousands. As Yogi Berra would have said if he'd been one of ours, the more there are, the more there are.

All of a sudden there were a million things to do. Concerts, plays, dance recitals, lectures—the singers, players, actors, and dancers were all ours. Popular Front culture blossomed. Patriotic kitsch: its faded fake flowers—and some not so faded—still bloom, sixty years later. So I went to hear our folk singers sing folk songs they had made up the night before. I called Ben Shahn and Moses and Raphael Soyer the greatest painters in the world; they were ours. I cried for the Negro people when I heard Paul Robeson sing. At meetings we gave up on Lenin; anti-fascism was our name, our game. And then, in July 1936, the Spanish Civil War exploded.

If you are looking for pap, mashed sweet banana, nostalgia, myth, what Rebecca West called the smell of skunk, skip a few pages. There are still those who love to bullshit about what a passionate, romantic adventure it was. It was a war. Men died by the hundreds of thousands, splintered limbs overflowed the trash cans outside hospitals. War. Like all wars, the most stupid, obscene adventure men can embark upon. Still—contradictions, contradictions—it was a just war; it had to be fought, the enemy was supernationalism, a Church whose hatred of freedom had long ago already poisoned its love, if ever it had any, of gentle Jesus. It was also a war against elements of fascism. The enemy's slogan, shouted in church nave and university assembly hall, was Long Live Death! Yes, death. The enemy reeked of corpses. It was just and necessary to give up your job, to leave those you loved, to take up arms against the enemy. War is obscene, but sometimes it is necessary. The task of living, of upholding life, has never been an easy one. Let me remind you also that it was principally a war between Spaniards, millions of Spaniards on each side of the line. Hitler and Mussolini sent arms, men, and planes; and the Irish sent O'Duffy's battalion, which fought valiantly and sang songs whose words were written by W. B. Yeats. The Russians sent the Republic enough arms to keep it going, but never enough to win; they also sent the International Brigades and the NKVD. The Brigades were a mere pittance, though at times, especially in early 1937, this pittance did yeoman service in repelling the Franco onslaught against Madrid. We were very brave, exceedingly brave—but perhaps our wisdom can be questioned. We sang songs written by Hans Eisler, with words by Berthold Brecht. They were ours.

The war had another aspect, a very important one. It was much more than a civil war between Spanish democracy and Spanish fascism; it was also a social revolution, one that had been fermenting for hundreds of years in Spain, an uprising of the revolutionary working class and peasantry against a ruling class that had never learned how to ameliorate the arduous task of life for those born to labor. And it was this working class and peasantry, led by the revolutionary Anarchists and the revolutionary Marxists, the POUM—POUM, POUM, as Hemingway, beating his fist on the table, ridiculed them at the very time they were being persecuted by the NKVD, their leaders murdered and imprisoned—that rose and defeated the Franco forces in every city in Spain but five. The POUM and the Anarchists socialized factories and formed voluntary communes. The word *señor* was made taboo and replaced by *compañero*, friend. Was the universal city of man finally at hand? And then they had to face the double-whammy of the twentieth century, the feral fascists on one side and the duplicitous Stalinists on the other, the two most counter-revolutionary forces of our unhappy century. The word "comrade" soon became anathema to most decent Spaniards. Who was it destroyed the great ideal of universal brotherhood, of comradeship, of individual dignity and freedom?

Some forty thousand books, I've been told by a historian, have been written on the Spanish Civil War. Burnett Bolloten, Stanley Payne, Paul Preston, Alba/Schwartz, Cecil Eby; I can go on and on, books and papers by former combatants, Anarchists, POUMists, Stalinists, Falangists, so-called right- and left-wingers. There are lies and there are truths, and some day after we are all dead, some history professor will write the definitive history of the war and get it all wrong. Is it really possible to get at historical truth? History is lived by the multitudes, not by a compact mass; and the multitudes are myriad.

When I read how the revolutionary working class and peasantry took to the streets with exemplary courage and stopped the Franco alliance cold, like Delacroix's *Liberty Leading the People*, I saw myself, red flag aloft in one hand, rifle in the other, challenging the enemy, exultant. And when Der Führer and Il Duce began sending arms, planes, and even men to Franco and his allies, I wondered: would the revolution be lost, would the enemy win again?

I followed every battle, every political maneuver. The Anarchists and the Workers Party of Marxist Unification (POUM), which my Party called Trotskyite and which Natie, right again, said was Bukharinist, called for socialist revolution as the only way to defeat Franco and fascism in Spain. The red flag was held high. My Party called for bourgeois democracy, and lowered the red flag. I couldn't understand it. Ah, yes, the tactic of the unity of opposites. We really were for the revolution, but not yet; only when *we,* the vanguard of the proletariat, were prepared to take power ourselves. We held all the aces: the USSR, the Red Army, the GPU, and the International Brigades.

In November, we were just about ready to conclude our organizing drive in the fur piece trade. We pulled out every worker in the trade, and within a week had a contract. I was exultant. I had organized and successfully led my first strike.

FDR's electoral victory by a landslide that November surprised no one, but the sudden appearance of a column of Internationals at the Manzanares River outside besieged Madrid did. And on the anniversary date of the Russian revolution, too. Willi Münzenberg, genius propagandist, never missed a trick. It was called the Thälmann column after the imprisoned leader of the German Communist Party, Ernst Thälmann. As the press had it, they had halted the approaching Franco army practically by themselves.

Thermopylae. Two thousand German Communists had stopped thirty-five thousand fascists! I believed it. Everyone believed it. We Communists were unbeatable. Answer that, my dear Natie. We had the energy! We had the will! We believed! We were prepared to give our lives! (When you're twenty-one, exclamation marks are weapons on the barricades of history).

Ah, history. The truth is harsh, but the fact is that the Franco army had stopped its approach to Madrid in order to relieve the besieged Alcazar in Toledo, held by its forces (see *The Siege of the Alcazar,* by Cecil Eby, considered by both socialist and conservative Spanish historians to be a classic), and thus gave time to the Anarchist, Socialist, and POUMist forces to strengthen their positions around Madrid—together, of course, with the sturdy citizens thereof.

But wily Willi Münzenberg, or, as the Germans pronounce it, vily Villi, had done his work well. The Communist Thälmann column were the heroes. Is there a time when we do not need heroes? They besiege the mind; you don't have to think too hard, their deeds do it for you. For those who required predigested thought, a very complex social revolution became a simple anti-fascist war.

15

Serendipity. How much is the direction of our lives governed by that splendid word? On the day the *New York Times* ran the story about Madrid being saved by the Thälmann column, Ben Dvosin, Party organizer and a friend from Sunrise, met me for lunch. On our way to the cafeteria ruled by The Virgin, the object of our mutual lust, we talked about the heroism of the Thälmanns. In my excitement, out of comradely solidarity and pure bravado, I exclaimed, Boy, would I love to be there! Forgotten all my promises to my mother to go to college, forgotten the University of Wisconsin's acceptance of my application, forgotten that nagging, unspoken thought that I had to do something with my life. At last—the Paris Commune! The Winter Palace of Petrograd! The Red Flag high!

Two weeks later, Dvosin phoned me and asked me to meet him at six that evening, he had something to tell me.

We met in the Fur Union office and immediately after we shook hands he said, "When you said you wanted to go to Spain, did you mean it?"

I replied, "Yes, of course." The "of course" was, again, pure bravado. I hadn't stopped to think what going to Spain entailed: fighting with a gun in my hand, being shot at, suffering a wound, possibly being killed. Could I now back out? Of course not.

Ben said, "Good. Then come with me."

We walked downtown from the union office on West 26th Street to a shoddy two-story building, and went up the creaking stairs to the Lower East Side Party offices. The place was empty except for a middle-aged woman, the section organizer, in a sparsely furnished, beat-up office.

We were introduced, and, without further ado, she asked, Do you mean it?

Yes, I mean it.

What unit do you belong to?

YCL branch of the Fur Floor Boys local of the Furriers Union.

Good, she said.

After I gave her my home address, we said goodbye with raised fist salutes. The Popular Front line hadn't changed that. That was it.

A week or so later I received a note on onionskin paper, Report to the fifth floor on such and such a date and time, period.

The fifth floor was the offices of the State Party in the East 13th Street building. Excited, scared, lips dry, already feeling the hero, right on time I was shaking hands with Comrade Bidarian, the State org-sec. We knew each other. Good to see you, Willie. You, too, Comrade Bidarian. He spoke quietly, as did I. We were in the inner sanctum, a holy place. Take a seat, he said, it won't be long.

I sat. Across from me a burly blond man with the inset eyes and high cheekbones of a Tatar tribesman smiled at me. His name was Bob Gladnick. He worked on the waterfront, I in the fur market, both locations renowned for their Party militancy. We did not say much. He, incidentally, spoke with a slight Russian accent. It must have been difficult for him to remain quiet, for he turned out to be a very garrulous man.

An unseen door opened and closed, and Bidarian appeared and nodded at Gladnick. Fifteen minutes later the unseen door opened and closed again, and Bidarian appeared and nodded. I followed him into a large room. Four men greeted me. One was Charles Krombein, member of the political bureau, heavyset, stern, a man who looked perpetually angry. The second was a pleasant-faced short man named Crosby, routinely our candidate for New York governor. The third was ramrod stiff, also stern and soldierly, with a supercilious narrowing of his nose, introduced as Major Johnson. (Every time Mickey Mickenberg mentioned him in Spain he would add, "Major Prick.") The fourth was one of the men who used to meet with Earl Browder at our apartment on Second Avenue. We nodded to each other. He was introduced as Comrade Fred Brown; he was a Swiss Italian named Alpi, the Comintern rep to the American Party.

Krombein asked the questions. I belonged to the Young Communist League, was a member of the Fur Floor Boys local of the Furriers Joint Council. Yes, I had shot rifles while hunting in the Michigan woods, and I drove Farmall tractors and Caterpillars when I worked on a large farm. Right now we were organizing a section of the fur market, and I was on strike. They all nodded, they all smiled, even Krombein. I shook hands all around, gave the Red Front salute, and Bidarian ushered me out. You'll be hearing from me, he said.

At about the time we were negotiating a contract for the fur sorters, I received another onionskin message to appear at the Ukrainian Hall on East Third Street in Manhattan. There were guards at the door. I, and I daresay the other volunteers, had been cautioned to keep our mouths shut about the operation. It would be revealed to the world when we were already in Spain.

There were thirty to forty of us to start, Gladnick among them. Bidarian introduced Phil Bard, the *New Masses* cartoonist, a decent, sweet-tempered man I recognized from the Commie Coops, as our political commissar; and a thin, nervous man named Jim Harris, from the waterfront, as our military commander. We looked each other over—a young, poorly dressed bunch of proles, faces recognized from demonstrations, picket lines, mass meetings. There was a collective tension, a nervousness, an electric quietude. We heard some inconsequential remarks from Bard, Harris, and Bidarian. So far as I could tell, everyone in the place was Party. We formed squads, did some military exercises—about-face, left-face, right-face—and were told when to return to the Ukrainian Hall.

Each time we returned, our number increased. We learned to march in squads, led by a Comrade Doug Seacord, a very clean-cut, handsome man from Cape Cod. He turned out to be a close friend of Doug Roach, who appeared in Spain shortly after our group arrived. Seacord's skin was the color of ivory. Thirty years later I learned that he was a Negro. This idiotic business of color; I've known scores of white men who were darker than Doug Seacord. He was an ex-Army man who spoke in a quiet, authoritative voice. We immediately had complete confidence in him. He led us in bayonet drill; without bayonets, of course, or even broomsticks.

There was no hacking around, very little laughter. Grave, dead serious, were they all as scared as I was? You didn't mention your fear, you were too scared even to think it. There were many moments when I asked myself, what am I doing here? Later, at the front outside Madrid, lying in a trench hearing the thumping of artillery shells searching us out, naked, sunning myself to avoid trench rot, eyes open, then squeezed tight as the planes unloaded their silver-glinting bombs, I asked myself the same question: what the hell am I doing here? I was wounded too early to stop asking myself that question. Joe Gordon and Doug Roach told me they stopped after the second or third battle. Somehow, they said, you just thought of the moment, how to get where you were going, inch by inch. They were honest men, neither boastful nor reticent about their feelings. Doug was the terser of the two, a stereotypical Cape Codder who spoke Hahvid Yaad. He had a sweet smile, and understood what you were saying before you finished saying it. Built close to the ground, and fearless. There, you see, even I want to believe in fearless heroes. He was not fearless; no one is fearless unless he is brain dead. He was brave, knew himself, made sure of every move. No bravado for him. He was a black man from P'town, Cape Cod. Doug

The admirable Doug Seacord

Doug Roach and Steve Nelson

Seacord, his townsman, loved him; so did Joe Gordon. So did I. You could not help but love him. He went about his business of soldiering with no bullshit. Strong as an ox; on the march he shouldered your load as well as his own. At war, he learned to hate.

One day, an old man in his late thirties named Akalaitis led my squad to an Army & Navy store on Canal Street. Akalaitis bought us World War I doughboy outfits: puttees, pants, shirt, socks, shoes, and sheepskin coats. (Idiot that I was, on the march from our camions to the front line under a broiling Madrid sun I dropped my sheepskin, and was too tired and hot to pick it up. Late that afternoon, after the sun went down it was so cold I thought I'd freeze to death.) We also all bought the same boxy, cardboard suitcases. I hid the suitcase and clothes in an overstocked storage closet before my mother came home from work.

Another day, Bidarian gave me ten bucks for my passport. Don't tell them you're going to Spain, he said, make something up. So I told them I was going to visit my grandmother in Poland, and then I was going to the Sorbonne. The passport was in my original family name, William Horvitz.

One afternoon shortly before we left, Ralph Bates, the novelist and Comintern rep in Spain, talked to us. He had come directly from the front lines, where he was a brigade political commissar. He looked about ten feet tall. He told us about the heroism and bravery of the International Brigades, and how cowardly the enemy was. We are anti-fascists, he said with a smile, and winked. Why, I wondered, should we conceal the fact that we are Communists? We should proclaim it proudly. Why should we lie to the Spanish people? I couldn't understand it.

Goodbyes had to be said. We were to leave on December 26, 1936, on the French liner *Normandie*. I told my mother I was being sent by the Party to school in Russia. She looked hard at me, her eyes trying to penetrate my skull. To Party school? Yes, to school. I thought you were going to college in the fall. I changed my mind. The Party thinks I should go to school in Russia to be trained as a Party leader. Don't forget to write me. Of course, Mom. Take care of yourself. Sure. She didn't quite believe me, I could see. Perhaps she was afraid to acknowledge to herself what she thought. We hugged, we kissed; she held on very tight before I could separate myself from her.

I was not supposed to tell anyone, but I told my friend Natie. He was furious. Your Party is acting the counter-revolutionary in Spain, it is trying to destroy the most legitimate democratic socialist revolution of our time. It is not a Leninist coup d'état, this is the real thing. I wasn't sure, but I said the defeat of fascism came first, what was most needed was a popular front. You read the *18th Brumaire*, he said, you know better. Let's not argue; I'm going to Spain to fight the enemy, not the Socialists or the Anarchists, or even your POUM. What if you're asked to shoot revolutionaries? Don't be ridiculous. You're politically illiterate. Oh, shut up, I'm going off to war, and you're trying to give me a political lecture. Try not to be a big hero, he said. It won't be like catching a forward pass. I'll try, I said, smiling at him now; he still was jealous that I'd been called Dick for Dick Merriwell. This is very serious, he said. If you have any doubts when you're there, pretend you're stupid and express them in the form of a question; they'll accuse you of being politically immature, not of treason. Okay, sure, I'll make an effort. It was very good advice, intelligent insight, except it did not quite work.

I told one other person I was going to Spain, a young woman I have not yet mentioned and who became my first wife, Evelyn. A lovely girl, graceful and pretty. On one of my leaves from Sunrise I met her at a dance near the Communist Coops. She was about sixteen, seventeen then, and a very good dancer. We saw each other a few times, and she told me that she and her best friend wanted to run away from home. I convinced them if they did run away to come to Sunrise, where they could work, be helpful, be fed and safe. I gave them the address of a friend in Stelton, New Jersey, a good intermediate stop. Sure enough, one morning Uncle Joe called me into his office. He had received a wire from the New York police; Evelyn's parents had found a letter from me. Was their daughter in Sunrise? I told J. J. their daughter was in Stelton.

When I left Sunrise for good, I looked Evelyn up in New York, but her parents refused to let her see me. Her running away had been my fault, I was a bum, a no-goodnik, et cetera, probably all true. So Evelyn and I fell in love, just like Romeo and Juliet. We saw each other surreptitiously a few times. Her mother found out and threatened to commit suicide, or whatever. Evelyn told me not to wait for her any more, as I had a way of doing at one street corner or another near where she lived in the Bronx. It was so romantic, so frustrating, so infuriating. I would wake up one morning with this hunger, this need for a sight of my beloved Juliet, my forbidden love; no matter what I was doing I'd run to the corner of her block and wait for her, hour after hour, rain, snow, ice, until she appeared. Please, she would say, and Please, I would say. To no avail. This went on for several years. Now I was going off to Spain and I wanted to see her, to kiss her goodbye, to feel her breast one time before I went off to die for the cause. She was working in the office of one of the ILGWU locals on West 33rd Street. We met for lunch and I told her I was leaving for Spain. I wanted her tears. She didn't cry, merely told me I was crazy. Still, she yielded and met me after work at my mother's apartment on West 22nd Street. We did kiss, and I did get to caress her breast, and she did come to the *Normandie* to kiss me again and give me two cartons of Chesterfields and the latest issue of *Esquire* magazine. Phil Bard, our political commissar, gave me a bawling out for this breach of secrecy, but without too much steam in his voice. All my love for Evelyn hadn't stopped me from desiring women before I went to Spain, and didn't stop me from wanting to have sex with a Folies Bergère dancer on the *Normandie*. Bob Gladnick had discovered the troupe as he perambulated freely about the boat. Gladnick was not an American citizen and couldn't obtain a passport; he was a stowaway helped aboard by the French Party cell, which seemed to run the vessel. Joe Gordon, a deserter from the American army, had also been secretly stashed on board by the Party.

Joe I had met the night before we left at a Christmas party given by the stenographer-secretary of the Fur Floor Boys local. She and her husband were new Party people, fruit of the Popular Front. Goldie was her name, the name of my beloved aunt, and perhaps it was that which had made for the quick sympathetic bond between us. In any event, Gordon was at the Christmas party, a square-shouldered, stocky man who moved like a graceful middleweight—and actually was—and who slurped when he spoke. One look, and you knew you had better not kid him about that slurp. He, too, was going to Spain, with an odious man named Ruby. Both had done strongarm work for the Party furriers during the fight against the gangsters. Joe had been at Fort Meade in Maryland, in horsedrawn artillery where he was trying to organize a Party cell, when the Party instructed him to desert for the fight in Spain. He was, of course, happy to volunteer. We liked each other, and for amusement

Joe Gordon in Spain
(*Courtesy of the Abraham Lincoln Brigade
Archives, Brandeis University Libraries*)

played craps. I had a run of luck and cleaned Joe and Ruby out—a couple of dollars each. I gave Goldie the winnings to give to the fund for medical supplies for Spain. That night I slept in an unknown actor's apartment on Broadway, found for me by Goldie, since I had already said goodbye to my mother and sister. Goldie's mother, who had been at the Christmas party, gave me a bon voyage gift of fifteen dollars.

On the morning of our departure, we were to go to the Second Avenue

Yiddish theater across the street from where my family had once lived, and there in the lobby was our leader, the Kansas Twang, Earl Browder, who proffered a limp handshake. Since we already knew each other, he also gifted me with a mustached smile and the words Good luck.

Our voyage tickets had been supplied by Intourist, the Soviet agency. Evelyn met me in the tourist cabin to give me her gifts and, best of all, a long kiss. You're crazy for going, she said again, but this time, to my pleasure, she cried.

My roommate turned out to be the man who was to become our meat butcher at Villanueva de la Jara. His face is as clear as if it were just yesterday, but his name is long forgotten. He died in Spain.

No sooner were we aweigh, when Gladnick appeared to co-opt one carton of my cigarettes, and Joe my issue of *Esquire*. We had the run of the great vessel, thanks to the French Party cell on board. I don't know where Gladnick and Joe slept, but I wouldn't have been surprised if it turned out to be the cabins of the Folies Bergère dancers. We ate what were probably the best meals of our lives, though many did not appear in the dining room due to *mal de mer* (just to show that I do remember some of my high school French). We were not supposed to know each other, our mission secret, but one lovely day nearly all ninety-six of us appeared on deck wearing our brand-new Army shoes, the unanimous idea being to break them in that morning. On another day a notice appeared on deck announcing that the United States Congress had declared Spain off-limits to American citizens. We laughed.

At Le Havre, customs was a farce. When we opened our identical new suitcases before the inspectors to reveal our doughboy O.D.'s, they nodded and banged the valises shut. Non-interventionist France was still looking the other way.

Gray Le Havre was, gray the night. We deployed to different lodgings in the working class district near the harbor. It was New Year's Eve. My group, led by Akalaitis, ate in a port restaurant, and then decided to bring in the New Year in a bordello. There were several merchant mariners in our group who seemed to know their way around. There we drank beer, smoked, and spoke with the nude and semi-nude women via sign language and high school French. They quickly found out who we were and where we were going, and were happy not only to display their charms but their tricks as well, picking up coins we placed on the tables before us with their labia. We whistled, we cheered, we danced. At midnight, the small band which had been serenading us played the "Internationale." We stood at attention, stirred, sang along, cheered, got laid. I treated with the fifteen dollars given me by Goldie's mother. Akalaitis and Joe, who'd walked off the *Normandie* with the ship's crew, declined. When I looked at Joe with a question, he shrugged. Don't feel like it. Joe was not one to follow the mob. He was a believer; he loved the Party and its ruthlessness in politics, he loved Joe Stalin, he just barely adhered to discipline because the Party demanded it. He was, however, strict about the Party line. There he was immovable. Most of the leaders he found despicable, however; he couldn't help himself.

The following morning I and several others were sent to a local doctor for tetanus and cholera shots. Most of the others had had theirs in New York; I'd missed mine because of union work.

In the early evening all of us met at the railroad station for the Paris train. This entire operation had been organized and was being run by an almost invisible hand, and very efficient it was. In Paris we were met by stern-faced French Party people who ordered us to shut up since we were a noisy group—Americans, you know. We boarded buses which dropped us off at a French Party cooperative restaurant for supper, and then took us to the railroad station where we got on a train known to many as *le chemin de fer des Brigades Internationales*. Our group had several coaches to itself. I occupied a compartment with Joe, Ruby, and a fellow named Raven. We tried to sleep as the train headed south, but our excitement was too great, especially since every time the train stopped at another station it was met by shouts of Popular Front slogans by what seemed like thousands of French comrades and our coaches were invaded by French, German, Belgian, and Irish volunteers on their way to Spain. We hugged, slapped backs, shared wine from canteens. We were soon pretty damned drunk. We were part of an army, a red army. We were going to make a revolution. We were going to make a new world, a much better world; poverty would be abolished, there would be jobs for all, war would be outlawed, fascism destroyed, men and women would be free, free, free; liberty, fraternity, solidarity, long live life, long live the revolution, long live Stalin, long live Dimitrov, long live Browder for he shall not be moved, long live, long live. . . .

As the train approached Perpignan the night broke, the sun began its ascent; the railroad ran along a strip of sea, an inlet, and the uniting of land, sun and sea was magical. It gave us a feeling of immortality; the very forces of nature saluted us. Our cause was the most just ever advanced by the human race. Twenty-year-olds, most of us, we believed that as Communists we knew for a certainty the solution to every problem the world faced.

Upon disembarking, every national group went in a different direction. As I say, the organization was magnificent. We gathered in a wooded glen not far from town. After we ate the food prepared and ready for us, a doctor appeared for, believe it or not, short arm inspection. We were immortal, what the hell were they worrying about? Sure enough, one guy, a merchant seaman, turned out to have a dose. Hypocrites that we were, we despised him. Dumb son-of-a-bitch, how could he do that to us? We were human after all. He would join us later. Months later, in the hospital in Murcia I was bedded near the VD treatment room, and he was there being medicated. He soon left for the front. He managed to survive.

16

Before us, looming purple in the descending sun, were the Pyrenees. They stood, a majestic wall, between Europe and Spain, that exotic mix of Christ, Mohammed, and Moses. My people may have been expelled, but were not forgotten. It was we, Unamuno had written, who had introduced the use of olive oil in Spain, and no one in Spain cooked a meal without olive oil. Laugh if you will, but what you eat determines in large measure who you are. The Christians had made sex prurient, the Moors had produced the *canto hondo* of Andalucia, and we had pressed the olive.

As the sun descended, the mountain crests shadowing mysteriously, several ancient buses appeared. We were not to march over the mountains as we had assumed; France still cast a blind eye. My heart beat faster, and I could hear its every thump. We were suddenly deathly quiet. We rolled; we were on our way into Spain. Don't forget, our leader, Phil Bard, said, if anyone asks, we're not Communists, we're anti-fascists. On entering Spain, we were to lie, and on leaving Spain, we were also to lie. Sorry, history is just not romantic and pure; it is real, very real, very, very real. It has that sickly sweet odor of decaying rat.

High in the mountains, we crossed the French border. The guards saluted us and waved us through. We were in Spain, and greeting us were Anarchist border guards with rifles held high shouting, "¡Viva la revolución! ¡Viva la revolución!" And we responded as previously instructed, "Long live the Frente Popular!" We were just plain, anti-fascist democrats. We fooled no one except, to use Lenin's term, the useful fools, the sympathizers who rallied round our cause.

We were in Spain. And now one of the boy scouts, as Joe Gordon called them, began to sing, Browder is our leader and he shall not be moved. I had to join in, even Joe did. This was our group, our compact mass.

Late at night we reached Figueras, a mountain town dominated by an immense heap of stone called a fortress. In what seemed to be a dungeon cell, I and the lone vaquerro, a Cuban named Cardenas—we had already become good friends, muy simpatico with barely a word said between us (he spoke English, no problem there)—shared a hard stone floor. Excited as we were, two would-be heroes, we slept.

After a breakfast of strong black chicory coffee and a large chunk of hard Spanish bread, we were excused for several hours. I sneaked off by myself; I didn't want the hindrance of Party discipline. The town seemed on holiday. Flags flew everywhere, every color imaginable. People smiled at me. There was much laughter. We said comrade, the populace here said *compañero*, friend, companion; it was the term used by the Anarchists. By the time I left Spain, some ten months later, comrade was a term of disparagement, accompanied by spit.

Not speaking or understanding the language was hellish. I ran into Gladnick, but told him to get lost. He was already speaking Spanish. He picked up languages the way an infant does, naturally. He spoke Russian, his native tongue, and English, of course. In the twenty-four hours we were in Le Havre he was already speaking French. In Spain, among the International Brigades, he would speak Polish with the

Poles, Italian with the Italians, and Spanish, too, of course. He was totally without inhibition; he just waded in.

I stopped in the Party office. In Catalonia it was called PSUC, United Socialist Party of Catalonia. There were red flags, pictures of Stalin, and of La Pasionaria. The young women and men there were all over me. I smiled broadly. They grinned back. *¿Norte Americano? Sí sí. ¿Frente Popular? Sí sí. ¡Arriba democracia! ¡Abajo Franco! Sí sí. ¡Me cago en Franco! Sí sí sí sí.* Laughter. On the way down from the fort—which, incidentally, was run by the French Party—I had passed the office of the POUM. Off limits. Lousy Trotskyites. In *Pravda,* Stalin had said they were to be exterminated. Natie's crowd. I stopped at the bottom of the hill for dough dipped in boiling oil, powdered with sugar—better than any donut—and a cup of hot chocolate. Delicious. Nodded to comrades, but hurried along by myself. Ran into Joe. Call me José, he said. José can you see? He joined my laughter. We were already very close. He was with Ruby, also known as Uriah Heep. I left them. Inhaled the mountain air, this exotic foreign air with its smell of olive oil. Flags all over. Red flags. Red and black flags. Red, gold, purple. Red and green. Offices of what seemed to be dozens of different political parties. A big smile pasted on my face. Elation, strangeness, fear all mixed in one. Nodded to armed Spanish militia, bandoliers strung from shoulder to belt, each wearing his own inimitable uniform. A motley crowd. Tough. It was they who had stopped the Franco rebellion cold. Without them there would have been no civil war, Franco would have won almost immediately. I smiled at them. They smiled back.

It was time to go back up the hill to the fort. Past the Party offices. Past the POUM offices, the party that my best friend believed told the truth. As far as I knew he had never lied to me, though I had—if only by omission—lied to him many times. Looked around once, twice; no one I knew in sight. Slipped in. Red flags. Hammer and sickle. Pictures of Marx, Lenin, Bukharin, Trotsky. Pictures of their leaders, Andreu Nin and Joaquin Maurin. Maurin had been captured by the Nationalist forces and was still alive because his brother was an archbishop; proof, the Party said, that he was in the pay of Franco, a spy, a traitor, a Trotskyite. *¡Viva la revolución! ¡Viva la revolución! ¿Brigadas Internationales?*

Sí sí. ¿Norte Americano? Sí sí. They couldn't believe it. Asked again, *¿Norte Americano?* *Sí, Americano.* They pushed leaflets, pamphlets in my hand. They were me, they were my twin. *Salud, compañero. Sí, salud.* I ditched the criminal evidence as I sneaked out, looking first this way and that.

The fort was in turmoil, new volunteers arriving constantly: refugee Germans, Italians, Belgians, Poles, Hollanders, French; anti-fascists all. The word "Communist" was not spoken. If you didn't know their language, you tried Yiddish and as often as not were answered with a smile and a stream of Yiddish. Most of them spoke it much better than I. The Europeans still wore their civilian clothes, and were a ragged lot. Alongside them, we felt like millionaires. Then we donned our dough-boy olive drabs for the first time. The puttees were difficult. We were helped by Joe and a man named Royce, an American army veteran who had fought in Nicaragua against Sandino. Now he was a Communist. In our uniforms, we felt very dressed up, very military. Our international comrades stared at us in astonishment. We looked so superior. Little did they know. Most of them had had their year in their country's military. Most of us had never held a gun.

I tried, but I can't say it better than I did in my novel *¡Hermanos!* It is in a letter from Joe Garms to Jake Starr, the novel's protagonist.

> . . . We get off the train in Barcelona and there are these
> catalans with armbands CNT FAI AIT POUM PSU PSUC
> UGT USC IR (left republicans what the hell they doin'
> here) and a million people are out lining the streets to
> meet us. These guys with the armbands they line us up by
> country, the Irish, the Germans, the Belgians, us, and we
> march up the Barcelona boulevards and pass a statue of
> Columbus banners flying red gold purple black red white
> blue the works and a million people on each side of the
> street and its real quiet as we march you can just hear our
> heavy army shoes pounding the cobblestones quiet like I
> never heard it in my life a million people crowding the

sides of the streets their mouths a little open just looking at us and its so quiet you can hear the guy next to you breathing and your own heart too, . . . and the banners are flying red purple gold CNT UGT FAI AIT PSUC USC IR POUM hammers and sickles fists hammers big posters real beautiful too. Dead quiet. A million people and they're looking at us as we march up the boulevards the Irish and the German exiles in their old raggedy clothes and us in our 1917 doughboy uniforms and dead quiet and I don't know what it is. I snuck a look at this redheaded bignosed kid who come to meet us at the station an American who fought already in Madrid wearing dirty coveralls and straw sandals and he all most split a gut laughing at us in our uniforms but who marched with us. I see him sneaking a look at me a strange look on his face as we march under the colored banners and these million people crowding there dead quiet with their mouths a little open. This kid got a strange look on his puss, a tough bastard too, and its quiet all around us and then like the sky opened up and began to let go with a hundred thousand cannon the million people begin to yell and it sounds like the whole world's yellin' hermanos hermanos hermanos brothers brothers brothers Oo! Er! Pay! Unios Hermanos Proletarios and it sweeps over us, takes us in its arms, a million people yelling and this kid who fought in Madrid without any guns he begins to cry and I begin to cry too and other guys too are crying. A million people loving us up and we're loving them up too.

And we all feel like dancing and singing and crying. We're going to make a new world, a great new world, . . . where there'll be no poor and no wise bastards who think they own the whole goddam place. We all own it . . . and we're goin' to fight for it. . . .

The way of Unity is the road to Victory!

An International Brigades poster

That's the way it was, I swear it. Yes, I cried, and Joe cried, and lots of others. We cried.

This is what I had lived for. And when I say I cried, it was also with a pang of sadness. It was not my party that was in ascendance here, it was the POUM and the Anarchists. They had defeated the army and its fascist allies and taken the city and the province. They had formed voluntary collectives in town and country, in the fields and the factories. They were not mere grouplets, they were large parties. The Anarchist union, the CNT, was said to have over two million members; the POUM in alliance with revolutionary peasants was a mass party. In this city, my Party was the grouplet. I can hear Natie laughing at me. And we called them the enemy. Soon we would prove their treason with forged documents. It was the indomitable Ortega y Gasset, among others, who fought the lie and proved the lie. To no avail; my comrades from the imported NKVD prevailed and hounded them to prison, and some to death. Long live Ortega. Long live Orwell, who revealed the lie as well. Still, after some forty thousand books, there are those who prefer the smell of skunk, as Rebecca West called it, to the truth.

So we marched through the din, the flags and banners furling and unfurling in the Mediterranean breeze, the gold sun soaring, and the populace roaring its cannonading welcome. They would be betrayed but never beaten. And as we of the International Brigades marched, each group would be led off to the barracks of one or another political party, one to the Karl Marx barracks of the Party, another to the barracks of the CNT, another to that of the FAI, the Federation of Iberian Anarchists. Half of us were led, where I don't know; and the rest, unlucky us, we were led into the Lenin barracks of the POUM! Phil Bard, our political commissar, must have shit in his pants. An asthmatic, he paled so whitely I thought he would die then and there. I am sure it was held against him the rest of his life. Bravely, he smiled. Their leaders smiled. We had come to help them in their revolution. So they thought. They hailed us, *¡Viva los Norte Americanos!* They fed us cold potato soup and garbanzos and mountains of bread and fruit and jugs of red wine, and then they all rose and we with them and we sang the International Soviet shall be the human race, and then we got the hell out of there alive and marched back to the railroad station and left that fucking city that didn't know yet that Stalin had ordered it not to be a revolution but only a fight for democracy so that England and France and perhaps even the United States would think that he had given up on such foolishness as socialist revolution. And just to make sure his back was covered, he was already dealing with Adolph Hitler.

The train was crowded with peasants carrying livestock, chickens, lambs, one a piglet. They were friendly and gave us huge slabs of pork and bread, and taught us how to drink wine from leather botas that everyone seemed to have. We had a hilarious time learning to drink from them. You placed it on your elbow, put its mouth just above your open lips and raised your elbow high over your head, then squeezed the pouch. Until we learned to aim, squeeze, and swallow simultaneously, we wasted an awful lot of wine. The Cubans among us had an easy time of it. Instead of having done bayonet drill without bayonets or broomsticks, we should have had Spanish lessons. The train was very slow, very bumpy, and it took us many hours to reach Albacete, the I.B. headquarters base. It looked like a town in a cowboy movie, flat, stucco instead of clapboard, yellowish, dusty. As we marched through the cobblestone streets we passed groups of ambulatory wounded, and stopped once in awe as a company of German Internationals marched past us in machinelike precision, singing Berthold Brecht's and Hans Eisler's "Song of the United Front." It was more than real, it was right out of a movie in a movieland town. They were heroes and soon I would join them. My, how much I wanted to be a hero, wanted to be taller than tall. At the end of the movie, that dark-skinned nurse we passed and I would kiss and clinch.

We stood at attention in the middle of a bullring, and standing before us was the great man himself, the supreme commissar of the International Brigades, the mythic leader of the Black Sea mutiny, executive committee member of the Communist International, politburo member of the French Communist Party, André Marty. Unlike us, he wore an I.B. uniform, khaki ski pants and jacket, and on his head was what had to be the largest navy blue beret in the entire world. He was, as I recall, a large man, or perhaps it was his reputation. He spoke to us in French English. We were, he said, like the Yanks of 1917, come to save Europe from the barbaric Hun. I recoiled. Lenin had called the First World War an imperialist war and had opposed it. It had been one of the most senseless wars in history. Millions of men had died to satisfy the ego and pride of their rulers. How far, I wondered, would the Popular Front line take us? Since a goodly number of my comrades there were Popular Front Communists, they probably took little cognizance of what Marty had said.

At rest, we were given what was now our customary bitter coffee and a large chunk of bread. Wine-filled leather botas were passed around, and we did much better than we had the first time with them.

During the break, Joe and I went on an exploration of the underside of the bullring stands, looking for the dressing rooms, the pens for the bulls, and so on. We discovered a room, the whitewashed wall of which was streaked with blood and pocked with bullet holes. For a long quiet moment we stood there in awe. Was it here the town's fascists had been executed? For days after the beginning of the Franco rebellion, in city, town, and village the so-called right had murdered republicans, socialists, and communists or those they just plain hated, and the so-called left had murdered rightists, priests, nuns, falangistas, retired military officers, and, again, those they just plain hated. Who murdered more has been a subject of great debate. As if it matters which side killed more. Both right and left murdered tens and tens of thousands. It is what I have called the left/right *pas de deux*. Joe and I looked at the wall, looked at one another, and returned to our comrades.

We boarded trucks, and as we wound our way through the narrow streets of this Spanish cowboy town, the sight of the many wounded I.B. men stilled our usual ebullience. The boy scouts even failed to rouse us with Browder is our leader and he shall not be moved.

144

History books tell us that four thousand or so people were herded together in the environs of Badajoz and machine-gunned to death by rightwing murderers. Some twelve to fifteen hundred prisoners of war held by the Communists in the town of Paracuellos were shot down by order of Santiago Carillo, a Party leader, and Mikhael Koltsov, the famous Soviet journalist and intimate of Ernest Hemingway. It was "done Soviet-style," writes Stanley Payne, the eminent historian, "with large trenches prepared ahead of time and the executions done at the edge of the trenches."

In Granada and environs, some forty-five hundred republicans and socialists were murdered in several days by the rightwing enemy. One of the murdered was the great Federico García Lorca.

My dear Anarchists, those derived from the violent Bakunin and our old friend Nechaev, were as trigger-happy as the rest.

The history books say seventy-five thousand nuns and priests were killed at the beginning of the civil war by the left.

This sort of insensate murder filtered down even to our American battalion, and the rest of the I.B., I assume. In the diary notes found on the body of Harry Hynes, killed in battle (he was an Australian in the Comintern underground on the West Coast, the man who "organized" Harry Bridges and was a company political commissar), the following entries were found: "Heard later about an execution in which N.S. [?] was involved which sickened me." And then, "I do not want to be part of the setup here. My heart is against so much that it represents. I saw the bodies of twenty officers, their heads cut open, riddled with bullets. Such a savage bloody execution after such a beautiful victory."

André Marty, political commissar of the International Brigades, saw non-existent Trotskyites everywhere. His goons roamed the front as well as the rear and left many dead. In his autobiography, written long after the civil war, he modestly claims to have ordered the executions of *only* five hundred men. I daresay his memory was failing.

17

Entering Villanueva de la Jara, in the province of Cuenca, we passed a mammoth, fortresslike church. We had already noticed the many huge thick-walled churches of Spain, every one of them closed, with sandbags barring entrance. We had also not seen one priest or nun. Some had been murdered, some driven out, some had fled in time. The Church stood at Franco's right hand. Marxist priests were not yet even on the horizon: disaffected with one dictatorship, they would seek out another.

We were barracked in a convent left filthy by its previous occupants, a French battalion. It had six-seater outhouse-type toilets and we soon found bags of lime to empty into the pits. I slept in a nun's cot and thought often of her. What had she been like, this little nun whose bed I filled? From what village had she come? Had she been a daughter of the religious rich, or the pious poor? Had she exulted in her marriage to Jesus Christ? Had she ever committed carnal sin? Rumors about the nuns flew among us, originating where, I know not. The nuns' little bastards were buried in the courtyard where, to add to the six-seaters, we dug a long latrine trench. The monks from the two or three monasteries in this tiny village of one street had used our nunnery as a house of assignation. In such manner we titillated each other.

It wasn't long before we learned why the inhabitants shunned us and lived behind shuttered windows. As we paraded through the narrow cobbled street we could see one or another of them peeking through a raised shutter slat. The French battalion training here before us had been an undisciplined lot, drinking heavily, fighting among themselves, discourteous and arrogant to the peasant folk who lived here. The French Party, in its rush to fullfil the Comintern resolution to form an international army, had scoured the streets of Paris, careless about whom it recruited. Our behavior, on the other hand, was exemplary. No one had to tell us. Most of us, as were those Americans who came after us, were idealistic young men. We had come to help the Spanish people defeat fascism— with the hope, of course, that the Party itself would take power. As Communists it was our desire to be an example of discipline and decency. On arrival, we were ninety-six men; by the time we left some four weeks later, we were a battalion of four hundred, and there had not been one incident to upset the people of this peasant village. One man did get drunk publicly, but he was quickly hauled in and placed in the brig for a night. His name was Ray Steele, a merchant mariner who called himself a Wobbly. He was one of the few non-Communists in the Lincoln battalion. Though Ray had a club foot, he could outrun anyone in the battalion. I thought I was fast, but he beat me by yards in a hundred-yard dash. We had a football that we passed around and punted to each other. Ray could kick beautiful spirals forty, fifty yards. He became one of the finest machine-gunners and soldiers at the front.

Phil Bard, our battalion commissar, we saw rarely. He was not well, and was off in Albacete a good part of the time. Then he was gone for good, sent back to the States because his asthma attacks increased. We were sorry to lose this sweet man. His place was taken by one of the other three commissars, Marvin Stern; he was intelligent and young, with a carping axelike voice. We did not like him. The two remaining commissars were Phil Cooperman, an obese, cold-faced operative, and Bernard Walsh, a sculptor, slender, taciturn, serious. They did not participate in maneuvers or training, even though they were going to the front with us.

We trained with only two guns, very old World War I French rifles for which we had no bullets, and an old Russian Vickers-Maxim machine gun, for which we also had no bullets.

Through Joe's conniving, I was transferred from an infantry squad to the machine gun company and was assigned as runner for Doug Seacord, the company commander. I rarely left Seacord's side. His commands were confidently given in a gentle, soft-spoken voice. He was very handsome, and we all loved him. He also was a secret drinker, as was Jim Harris, our battalion commander. Seacord was said to have served a hitch in the American army. Of Jim Harris it was rumored that he had trained Chinese Red Army units, and had earlier been a soldier in the Polish army before he came to the United States. He had come to us from the Party waterfront unit of the Maritime Union. Seacord came from P'town on Cape Cod, where he had been an active Party member. When Doug Roach's group came through from the States, Seacord immediately had him assigned to our company. Within a couple of days Joe and I took him into our circle; he was tough, terse, even-tempered. We all laughed a lot. When I was alone with Seacord, he told me that Roach was A-1, topgrade, the best. It wasn't long before I agreed.

Doug and I soon had a competition going to see who could strip and reassemble the old Vickers-Maxim faster blindfolded. We were just about even. One day, much to our joy, bullets arrived. Enough, at least, to enable each rifleman and each member of the machine gun company to fire three or four shots. Doug's score surpassed mine and I had to suffer his superiority with a bow. There were to be no more bullets until we left for the front.

A Comrade Vidal, André Marty's deputy, came to tell us how cowardly the fascist soldiers were; according to him they ran away when faced with heavy fire. The boy scouts cheered. Joe, Doug, and I looked at one another. Though we had not received much news from the war fronts, we hadn't heard of any great victories from our side, either. Then G. Marion, correspondent for the American *Daily Worker,* came to visit. We got another silly speech about how the fascists would run when we shot at them.

One morning, Jim Harris introduced a tall, bespectacled, beaming man at an assembly in the former convent hall. He had just come from the Soviet Union. An American. He was to be our adjutant commander. It was rumored that he had come directly from the Soviet Frunze Military Academy, which was of course very impressive. Then there was another rumor that he had come from the Lenin school in Moscow. How nice.

Where Jim Harris was a thin, slight, very shy man, Robert Merriman, our new adjutant commander, was tall, square-shouldered, and spoke with a ringing voice. Blond and blue-eyed, he was an ideal picture of the Popular Front man. There were bets that Jim Harris' days as commander were limited. The winners never lived long enough to collect their bets, a direct result of their having won them.

A new group arrived one day, this one not from the States but from the British battalion training camp—an Irish company. Though so far as we knew no bullets had been fired, the Irish troubles had broken out among the British, and the Irish company was transferred to us. We were warned the evening before their arrival to watch our tongues; we were being joined by Irish Catholics, and we were to clean the prayer-books we had been using for toilet paper out of the six-seaters and latrines. Within a few days after the Irish joined us, they had found the books and were themselves using them.

We were approaching battalion strength. A meeting was held at which it was decided to name our battalion after Abraham Lincoln. Who suggested the name, I no longer remember. Earl Browder claimed credit for it. It was unanimous, of course. Someone suggested Tom Mooney, of Mooney and Billings fame, as the name for the machine gun company. It was unanimously chosen. Then it was suggested that Comrade Kavorkian be chosen as machine gun company commissar. Again unanimously, and this time heartily, agreed to. He was one of the strong silent type. In my time with the company, he never disciplined anyone. When I became an officer, he was in one of my squads.

The villagers invited us to a dance. We had won their full trust. Mamas, papas, grandmas, grandpas, aunts, uncles, babes in arms, nubile young women in old-fashioned long dresses, all came, but no young men, they were off to war. The fiddlers played unknown tunes. We danced. How pleasant to hold a girl, a woman, in one's arms again. Modestly. No double-Lindy here. We smiled. Essayed a Spanish word or two. The Cubans had no problem, of course. Even the lone vaquerro, Cardenas, was voluble. Gladnick's laugh was loud and his voice louder still as he rampaged through the Spanish language almost as if he owned it. Some guys are lucky. We were very polite. We had wine and cakes (tasting of olive oil). And were very proud of ourselves because of our exemplary behavior. Within a week, Rodolfo Armas, a handsome bull of a boy, the Cuban commander, and a lovely young woman became affianced. After a day's maneuvers, she and he could be seen hand in hand strolling down the main (and only) street of the village. Rodolfo was killed during the battalion's first battle at Jarama, on February 23, 1937.

Peripatetic, curious, Joe had found and made friends with the Party leader in Villanueva de la Jara. He was the village school teacher and now with his family occupied the priest's quarters in the huge fortress church at the entrance to the village. He was also the village mayor. Joe got himself, along with me and Cardenas, invited to the mayor's for supper. Huge hams and sausages hung above the charred hearth, and hot soup and sausages are what we ate with gigantic slabs of hard bread. And vino rojo, dry and harsh to the throat. We spoke in Spanish monosyllables, helped out by Cardenas when we got stuck. Cardenas told us the mayor said that a marquis had owned nearly all the land in the area and had run it as an absentee landlord. The marquis' *cacique,* the boss foreman, had absconded at the beginning of the civil war, and the mayor and the Party had taken control of the village and that now the land was run more or less cooperatively. There were several who wanted a collective formed, but the Party said this was not a revolution but a bourgeois republic, and he and the Party had fought off the opposition.

Several nights later, we heard what the opposition had to say. Our convent chapel was to be used for a village meeting and the battalion was invited. The mayor, whom in my novel *¡Hermanos!* I called Espartico, chaired the meeting. Cardenas and I sat together, I made sure of that. His translation of the proceedings would, I was certain, be helpful. It was the sort of meeting run by Communists all over the world—well orchestrated. They were discussing daily business and whenever Espartico proposed something, there was great applause; when anyone spoke in opposition, bedlam. Then Espartico gave a report on how the war was going, optimistic and rah rah. There were great cheers. Next a skinny little guy stood up to speak, and before he uttered a word the heckling began. The opposition leader, no doubt. A large shawl was wrapped around his thin shoulders and he carried a spotted handkerchief in his hand. He coughed and brought the handkerchief to his lips. He was tubercular and spitting blood. They were yelling at him, sit down, shut up. He merely stood quietly, staring from face to face. An old man stood, faced the jeering crowd and said something about being ashamed before their American guests. The little skinny guy just stood there, facing them down, his black eyes like knife points. One had to admire his guts. Espartico finally raised his hands, and they shut up.

He spoke quietly, yet firmly. The only victories against the army, against the Church, against the falangistas had been won by the workers and peasants, while the democratic government had sat on its hands. We can run the factories and we can run the fields as brothers, they belong to us who do the work. We can manufacture our own arms, what we must do is take over all the factories of Spain. We must give Morocco its freedom and so stop the flow of Moorish mercenaries by Franco. You Communists have given up the fight for socialism, we of the POUM who are free of foreign influence, Stalin is not our leader, we govern ourselves. He coughed blood. Cardenas looked me square in the eye and I returned his stare. I was certain he was with the POUMist, as was I, but of course we dared not say a word. We were outside the compact mass. The POUMist sat down and hell broke loose. Marvin Stern, our commissar, gave us a sign and we all rose and left. Inside the hall POUM POUM was bombarding the place.

Two days later I was ordered by Seacord to observe a machine gun squad during maneuvers—without a gun, of course. We were guarding ingress to the village at the narrow point where the road passed the fortress church. As we chatted and smoked, we saw a donkey pulling a two-wheel open wagon laden with bedding, pots, household goods, and a young woman holding an infant. The donkey was led by the tubercular POUMist. He was leaving the village with his young family. He was a kid, really, as young as we were. Without a word, we watched them as they moved slowly down the road. I realized I was with him all the way.

Joe told us that night that Espartico had said the man was a Trotskyite fascist trouble-maker and had been expelled from the village by majority democratic vote. Joe added an expletive. He, of course, was a red hot. I loved him and barely listened to him when he issued political dicta parroting the Party line. He detested leaders—except Stalin. He would always say, If only Stalin knew what a bunch of jerks we are led by, petit bourgeois bastards. Doug Roach rarely if ever made any political remarks. He was a Party member, period. Cardenas, who was one of our gang, also kept his mouth shut. Gladnick, the most voluble man in the battalion, managed not to talk politics in Spain. When he returned to the States, he vomited it all out. But of course by that time he had spent twelve months as an interpreter and tank driver with the Russian Tank Corps. He had learned about the Russians firsthand.

Our time was fast approaching. We were becoming nervous, tense, anxious to get into the ring. Bring on the enemy. Let's get this thing over with. Several fights broke out. Seacord was drinking more, as was, Gladnick said, Jim Harris, our commander. Adjutant Commander Merriman was partial to the infantry commander, Scott, two WASPs on a hot tin roof. Scott was much liked by his men, as was Seacord by his. We of the machine gun company thought of ourselves as the royalty. We sneered at the infantry companies and disliked Merriman. We were probably prejudiced against him from the start, and were most vociferous in our criticism after he had led the battalion into disaster at Jarama. He had, of course, followed the orders of the XVth Brigade commander, Colonel Copic, Yugoslav and Red Army officer, later recalled and purged. Not because of his disdain for the lives of his troops, but simply because of Stalin's blood thirst.

One morning several days before we left the village, as we stood at attention outside our barracks, Commissar Stern introduced a plump, middle-aged, unprepossessing man named Sam Stember as our new battalion political commissar. Then Stern, to our utter astonishment, strode white-faced to an infantry squad and just like that became a simple rank-and-filer. Our heads whirled. There were no explanations. The Party leadership and its mystical ways.

The narrow cobbled street outside the convent was filled to overflowing with villagers, old men and women, children, lovely young women. As we boarded the camions, they cheered and wept. We were going off to war. To fight. To die.

18

In the Albacete bullring, André Marty, the beret looking larger than ever, sent us off to war. The enemy was cowardly, we were brave, our cause was just, we would win. Again that spiel about how you Americans have come as those before you came to save Europe from the Boche. The moment was serious; we were going off to the front, yet this man, the way he moved his hands, the words he spoke, that idiotic beret on his big head—this man was a cartoon.

As he spoke we could see large wooden crates stacked beside him. He ordered them opened. Brand new rifles, still covered with cosmoline. Russian carbines. (Some later said they were Mexican; I don't know.) We yipped in glee. We cheered. We laughed. We waved our hands against the sky. Long live the Soviet Union. Long live Comrade Stalin. Long live the Frente Popular. Long live Comrade Marty. Thank God, we're gonna have guns. Each had a long, slender tri-bladed bayonet. They were frightening—the thought of one entering your body, the thought of slamming one into the body of an enemy. We were given helmets, gas masks, cartridge belts with bullets. Now we were real soldiers. We cheered again.

We were called to attention, our leader wished us luck; but before we left, if we handed in our passports, they would be held in safety until it was time for us to return home. Good idea, I thought. I handed mine in. Some men, less stupid than I, did not.

We boarded the camions.

It was dark now. The truck I was on bumped along. We smoked, spoke an occasional word, that was all. Each man seemed holed in on himself. I was scared; still, I hoped to be a hero, to do brave deeds. Dick Merriwell. Jack Armstrong of the U.S. Marines. If I were hit, I hoped that I would die fast, with little pain. Were the others as scared as I was? None of my close friends were on the truck with me. I wished Joe and Doug were. Joe would be talking away, describing war strategy, Doug would be his quiet self, calm, terse. I would feel safer with them nearby.

The trucks stuttered along in the dark, lights out. Going, stopping for long periods. We must be approaching the front. We listened for rifle shots, artillery. It was dead quiet. I slept some, as did the others.

The morning was clear, the air fresh, cool; it seemed everything on earth was dead still. It also seemed I was living a strange, surreal dream. We jumped off our trucks and sought out our friends, our squads, our companies. Seacord reorganized the machine gun company and I was made adjutant commander of Section 2, with three squads. Joe, Doug, Kavorkian, and Pete Shimrak, a Chetnik, were in my squads. I was exhilarated. I was on my way to hero, first class.

Seacord ordered us to spread out and fire five shots from our new rifles at some distant rocks. Joe was at my ear. Don't pull, squeeze, Dummy. Everyone was shooting, suddenly there was dead quiet. Two trucks with comrades were missing. Where? What? We would wait. What lousy luck. The rumor factory was at work, soon confirmed by Comrade Stember, our new battalion commissar. Trotskyite fascists had infiltrated the truck unit and had driven the trucks into fascist lines. In addition to the comrades, the trucks had carried all the battalion records. We kept hoping our comrades would turn up. Cardenas, I think, was among them. I never saw him again.

Years later, Bob Gladnick, in correspondence with a Spanish historian, learned of a document held by the Spanish army which noted that two trucks carrying Americans had entered their lines near Chinchon, had been ordered to stop and disembark, had refused, and had fought until every last one of them had died. The drivers, too, who were not Trotskyite fascists, of course. On a trip to Spain, Gladnick was led to a mass grave where those on the trucks had been buried. Gladnick, who had rediscovered Judaism by this time, said a kaddish for the dead. Spaniards who had gathered to observe this strange American later told him that they too were descended from Jews; oddly enough, not unusual in Spain. What one can conclude from this I don't know. There was, incidentally, a high proportion of Jews in the Lincoln battalion, over 50 percent, as there was in the International Brigades.

Single file, led by Jim Harris and his staff, we marched over the romantic magical hills and dales of Spain. An olive grove here and there; in the distance, peasants working in the fields. The sky was cloudless. It had been briskly cool when we started but, as the morning waned, that huge simmering copper pot they call the sun in Spain began to boil and overflow. Men began to shed their overcoats, drop them, leave them behind. The heat began to overwhelm us. Soon I dropped my beloved sheepskin coat; I hoped some peasant would find it. Our new rifles made us feel like real soldiers. We marched in silence, each step, we knew, taking us closer to the war front. It was not only we who were silent; the world itself was silent—the vast sky, the rolling hills, the olive groves. We marched.

I have no recollection that we ever stopped to eat. Perhaps we required no food. We were sustained by our beliefs, our hopes; we would conquer the enemy. Others might die, we would not. I would guess that by now our comrades on the two lost trucks had already fought and died. Was the mass grave already dug as well?

As we passed over the rounded peak of a hill, we suddenly heard the snap snap of rifle fire. We were in sight of a narrow road, saw toy trucks and ambulances. Men moved like ants. Our steps, our heart beats quickened.

And then, and then we were at war, for the ambulances themselves dripped blood. Dog-tired soldiers in I.B. uniforms lay about the shoulders of the road. An enemy plane suddenly swooped low and amid hysterical shouts of Down! Down! we heard the whistle of a falling bomb and threw ourselves to the ground. My mouth was dry, I couldn't swallow.

As we were ordered up a hill to our right, two men helping a wounded comrade toward an ambulance asked if we were Yanks. They were Englishmen. They presented us with encouraging words. They had been a full battalion several days before and now were but few. Our battalion commanders hurried us along. Somewhere ahead there were sporadic shots. It didn't sound serious at all.

It was now dark. The battalion was sprawled about the hill and the order went out to dig in. With what? We had no trench shovels, had never been issued any. We dug with our bayonets and helmets. I remembered my duties as adjutant commander of Section 2 of the Tom Mooney Machine Gun Company. I went searching for my three squads. They and infantry company squads were intertwined. No one seemed to know where they were. Everyone was digging just where they stopped. I found Joe Gordon and his squad working away. Then I found Doug Roach and his squad, also digging vigorously. The third squad, with Kavorkian and Pete Shimrak, was with me. Sudden shouts in Spanish, a couple of shots. It was dark. Joe's voice. I ran over. We ain't got no passwords and these guys loom up. What the hell are we supposed to do? Two Spanish soldiers stood cursing, their fury unchained. A Cuban comrade came over and straightened it out.

We, I, returned to our digging. I was cold. I was scared. I dug and I yawned. I fell asleep.

Everyone reacts differently to fear. Some panic. Some become brave. I yawn. I fall asleep. Lucky.

Ever since the sun had gone down, the cold had been horrendous. Somehow, somewhere I found a thin gray poncho. It didn't help very much. I hugged myself within its folds and cursed myself for having thrown my sheepskin coat away. Fortunately I still had the windbreaker my mother had made. I was to have it until it was cut off me in the front-line hospital.

When I awoke it was dawn. The entire battalion was asleep, many well dug in. My trench was so shallow it could not have protected an ant. I commenced digging again, using bayonet and helmet. I was not much good at it and seemed to tire easily. That was fear again, it cut my lung capacity. On one side of me was a deep, beautifully cut trench in which its proprietor slept peacefully. He was a Negro named White, a powerfully built man. There was another White, a white man, who was to be shot for alleged desertion months later.

As the copper pot in the sky began to rise, Gladnick turned up carrying a huge urn with hot coffee and chunks of bread. No one had ordered him to do it, he just did it. I suppose he had followed his nose to the cookhouse somewhere behind our position. My squad, enjoying every sip and every crumb, expanded right before my eyes, began to smile, even to laugh. I ordered the other squads to send someone for coffee and bread. Joe was his usual self. If he was scared no one could discern it. The fact is he was now in his natural element. He was talkative, full of know-it-allness; how he garnered the information he was more than willing to dispense to anyone who would listen could only be attributed to his peripatetic ways. We were, he said, in the second lines. The enemy was over there. The St. Martin road below led to the Jarama River bridge to Madrid. The enemy was trying to cut the road in half; there had been terrible battles and both sides had lost many men, but the Republican lines had held. The enemy, he said with a shake of his head and a little sneer, did not run away. They fought like hell. Madrid was still open to Valencia. The I.B. was heavily involved here. The British had taken a terrible beating. If we stay in a defensive position, we'll be okay. His use of colorful expletives made my efforts look pale and puny.

He made us laugh. When he was in a hurry, his slurp was more pronounced, but as I said, no one ever dared mention it. He had fought as a middleweight for his unit in the U.S. Army and had won the championship, which earned him many perks. He had surreptitiously spread Party leaflets about. He was allowed into the officers' library and was astonished to find Marxist literature. That shows yuh how smart the capitalist enemy is, they wanna know everything we have to say the better to fight us. We're gonna beat 'em anyway. To Joe there were just two kinds of people, good guys and shits. Anyone he considered a shit, he ignored. When you were with him, somehow you felt more alive.

Doug's trench was a marvel to behold. Deep, the walls perfectly perpendicular, with shelves dug into the earth which held the many objects he had managed to garner over time. A can of condensed milk was among them and he gave me a swig. The sweetness brought renewed energy and immediate contentment. He smiled broadly. Somethin' sweet's like a gal's kiss. He had helped everyone in his squad with his portion of trench and was still looking for more work. I wished I had the nerve to ask him to help me dig mine deeper. Right next to him was an infantryman named Oscar Hunter, who was to become my commissar in Murcia, the I.B. hospital base. Oscar was a powerful man, and as I remember had played football for Morgan State University, a black college. A black man, he said he was part Seminole Indian. He was well-spoken, a literate man who hoped to be a novelist. He came from Chicago originally, but was living in New York, I think, before he came to Spain. Intelligent, quick-witted, witty, as a Negro he was on an upward track in the Party. Later, we were to have our cots side by side in the hospital and were to become close friends.

Seacord's new runner arrived with an order to come to the company headquarters. It was below us, to the left, on the other side of a narrow gauge railroad track which traversed the hill we were on. Seacord was there with a man named Tomlinson, his adjutant commander. We are in the second lines, the enemy is over there, they've been trying to take the road below (just as Joe had said). Have your squads designate someone to get the food in the cookhouse, and he pointed to a low-slung, white-washed stucco building on the other side of the road. On the wall facing us was printed in large letters, MADRID 32 kms. Don't hold me to the 32. When the sun is high, Seacord said, have your men take off their shoes and socks, give their feet an airing, we don't want anyone getting trench rot.

It was a gorgeous sunny Spanish day, the frigid night air soon forgotten. We could hear firing in the distance, but only sporadic; the residue, Seacord explained, of the battles earlier that month. It was now the middle of February. I talked with my trench buddies, went to visit Joe and then Doug, got to know Oscar better. He was one of those marvelous raconteurs—Mickey Mickenberg was another—who kept you wide-eyed, open-mouthed and laughing, if possible, simultaneously. I liked him, and was jealous of his story-telling ability.

For lunch, a mess of beans, a slab of bread, and vino rojo. Earlier, men from each section were sent to dig a latrine down below the battalion's perch on this lovely round hill. The sun high, hot as all hell, we removed our shoes, our socks, some all their clothes, and enjoyed our siesta hour. Out of the western sky, a throb, closer, a flight of what Joe told me were Italian Caproni bombers headed our way. Seacord's voice, loud and clear, Stay down! Make sure you put your helmet on. I was on my back, stark naked. I couldn't keep my eyes off those approaching huge black crows. From under their bellies, silver sticks floated down towards us. What a horrible shriek they made, what a howl. Put the helmet over your balls! Keep it on your head! Your balls! Your head! I was in a panic. The whistling, the whining shriek, closer and closer, filling your head until you thought it would explode. I couldn't watch them any longer and shut my eyes tight. Ear-splitting explosions as each bomb hit the earth. There was a terrible odor—gas! Everyone started yelling, Put your gasmasks on, put your gasmasks on! The bombers were now directly over us, and away. Not gas, merely the odor of explosives. We sat up. Hurriedly dressed. I inspected my three squads, everyone was okay. No one in the entire battalion had been hurt. They had missed. Joe merely grinned, but I noticed he said not a word. Later, however, he said the statistics showed they hit the periphery more frequently than the bullseye. Certainly that was not so for cities, as we were shortly to learn about Guernica. In the ten days we lay on that hill, what Joe had said proved to be the case. The bombers came every afternoon at about the same time, dropped their load, and clumsily hurried away. Not one man was wounded from the shrapnel, but one day during the raid, two men side by side, infantrymen—thank God, not the machine gun company—shot a couple of their toes off and were carted away by the medics. Our disgust was palpable and very noisy. Dirty cowards. It was difficult to forgive. Each person has her or his own threshold of fear. Those boys had encouraged each other's fear. If they had been able to hold on another day, perhaps they would have become heroes. Who the hell knows. I hope for their sake they learned to forgive themselves. Not everyone can be el Lobo.

The second or third night on the hill, we came under artillery fire. It was a horror. Seacord came to sit with me in my trench, now a reasonable depth, as the shells whistled terrifyingly overhead to burst somewhere behind us, alternating with those that burst somewhere before us. A searching fire, Seacord called it. We pressed close together—it helped a great deal to touch—as the shells searched us out. You were certain that inevitably they would find you and blow you apart. The best thing, Seacord said, is just to lie low until the damned thing is over. The inclination was to get up and run. You can pray, he said, and we both laughed. In an interlude, he left me to give comfort to Doug and his squad. I was terribly afraid, yet I had laughed, and I wondered how that was possible.

It became a regular pattern. Every afternoon during the siesta hour, the Capronis as we cowered under them came to lay their lethal eggs, and though they did come closer, so far no one was hurt. During the night the terrifying artillery shells searched us out. Hour after hour the earth trembled fore and aft, your teeth chattered, and yet you did not get up and run.

And then we had our second casualty. Our first had been the battalion scout named Edwards, who had been killed the first or second day of our arrival at the front. None of us had seen it, and I for one hardly knew him, so we sort of passed it by with a quick, painful shrug. I suppose for his friends it had been not so quick, and much more painful. During the second or third night of artillery fire, an elderly comrade named Chelebian was killed. A piece of shrapnel had torn off a chunk of his head. His trenchmate had found him in the morning and had screamed. I forced myself to look. There he lay, dead, cold, rigid, his brains splattered inside his helmet, which had been thrown off by the collision of hot iron and brittle skull. We thought of him as a sweet old man—probably in his forties—whose wife had died shortly before he came to Spain. Many believed he'd joined up to forget.

And the twenty or so men on the lost camions. Were they so quickly forgotten? Now I realize I have not counted as casualties the two men who shot off their toes. They were, of course. Have I not yet forgiven them? Like most of us, they had volunteered to give their lives for the Party, for the cause, and had been wounded by their fear. They were casualties of war.

About the third or fourth afternoon during an air raid, improbable as it may sound, the entire battalion laughed. That morning when I went for daily instruction to Seacord's h.q. he introduced me to a tall, well-built Negro who he said was now part of his staff, a man named Oliver Law. Just arrived in the lines and already on the company staff; must come well-connected, I thought. During siesta hour, when the Capronis made their daily run, as the bombs glinting silver off the sun began their descent, we could hear Law's voice from Seacord's headquarters call over the rumble of bomber engines, "Look, they're dropping leaflets." "Shut up!" Seacord yelled, "they're bombs." Old veterans now, three days in the lines, we laughed. Thereafter some of the men referred to him as Leaflets Law.

One night we left the artillery bombardment behind for a starlight maneuver. Captain Jim Harris wanted his troops to experience a night march at the front. He was taking the opportunity to train us under war conditions. We gathered somewhere to the flank of the hill, the enemy fire desultory, and with him leading the way we marched through the night. As we assembled, my section commander, a man named McCarthy, received a flesh wound and was left behind under the care of a medic.

I distinguished myself. By sheer happenstance my section led the battalion as it marched single file behind us. In front of me as we marched through the night, bullets sporadically whistling overhead—Seacord had explained that it is the one you don't hear that hits you—were Jim Harris, Doug Seacord and Bob Merriman. It was, but for the occasional bullet overhead, a very quiet night. Jim Harris, usually a very laconic man, that night seemed to be very voluble as he spoke to Seacord and Merriman. I have no idea what he was saying. Every once in a while Seacord would hand signal me to stop and get down. Since I led the entire battalion lined up behind me, in my best Victor McLaglen, tough-sarge, *What Price Glory?* voice, I passed on the order. Down on your bellies, you sons-of-bitches! or some such, and the battalion threw itself to the ground. The entire front, friend, enemy, and God Himself must have heard me. When Seacord signalled me to rise and proceed forward, I stood, and, repeating myself in an even louder voice, ordered my comrades to their fucking feet and forward. I must surely have been overwhelmed with my sudden rise to power. I was in a movie and I wanted to be a hero, or sound like one at least. There in front of me within easy earshot were my top commanders, and not one told me to shut up. The enemy, which was entrenched only four or five hundred yards away, must have been dead asleep. Perhaps they were simply astounded at the sheer idiocy of their opponents. Perhaps they were just laughing at us.

Thus, with Bill Harvey's loud voice echoing through the night in much the same way, we made a large circular movement, returned to our positions on the hill above the road, and retired for the night. One of the guys in my trench stumbled, shrugged, lay down and went to sleep. In the morning he complained of a stomach ache and I sent him to the medics. They found drops of blood at his belt buckle and on his back. He had been shot without knowing it, the bullet having gone right through him, not hitting anything vital. He survived, believe it or not.

I think it was that morning, when I made my duty call to headquarters, that Seacord informed me Jim Harris had flipped and Bob Merriman was now our battalion commander. What many of us had long suspected had finally happened.

From Lenin on, our Party had basically thought of itself as an educational and propaganda tool. It was our main task to teach the masses that we were the leaders of the proletariat who would spearhead the revolution. We were the revolution, no matter what the line. If the Abraham Lincoln battalion was to serve its revolutionary purpose as an education and propaganda tool, it should have a commander who looked like a commander, an American commander, tall, handsome, and well-spoken, as later it would have to have a black man to command a battalion named after the Great Emancipator. But first it was Robert Merriman. Jim Harris was pale-faced, slight, spoke with a Polish accent, was hardly prepossessing. Merriman could and would become friends with Hemingway, Dos Passos, the correspondent for the *New York Times,* Martha Gellhorn, Louis Fischer. With whom could Jim Harris become friends? His friends were his merchant marine buddies from the waterfront who could probably drink and fight the great Hemingway under the table.

Secrets breed rumors. What rumor do you believe? Our leaders, and I mean the Comintern Commission that ruled the International Brigades, of which the Lincoln battalion was but a small part, seemed to prefer secrets and rumors to facts.

Everything about both men was alleged, rumored, sent off on flight into thin air by whom we shall never know. Wife, friend, agitpropnik. Guess. It was rumored, as I've previously said, that Merriman had been a student at both the prestigious Lenin school and Frunze Military Academy. In truth, it seems he had spent a year or two in the ROTC while at the University of Nevada at Reno. It was also alleged he was not a Communist—supposedly further proof that we who went to Spain were not Communists but pure, 100 percent, anti-fascist democrats. But if Merriman was not a Communist, then why did John Gates, an honest man so far as I know, and also the most able commissar/commander the Americans were to have in Spain, relate how Merriman and the brigade commissar, Dandy Dave Doran, gasbag non-pareil, had constantly boasted that as former students of the Lenin school they would never permit themselves to be taken alive by the enemy? Were they simply braggarts? Unfortunately for them, the enemy did take them alive and did shoot them, or so it has been believed for many years. Now Cecil Eby writes that he has received a manuscript from a Spaniard who'd fought with the Americans at that time, and who says Merriman was killed by enemy machine gun fire as they lay next to each other on the battlefield. What happened to Commissar Doran he does not say.

Was Jim Harris an instructor for the famed Chinese Red Army on its Long March, or wasn't he? We felt fortunate. We did know he was a Polish American, a merchant seaman, a member of the waterfront Communist Party. After his dismissal, was he or was he not seen in the International Brigades prison in Albacete? Had he or had he not flipped? Did he really shit in his pants, as Merriman reports? Where had this taken place? In his headquarters behind the second lines? Was he so scared that he would shit in his pants out of sight or sound of the first lines? Oscar Hunter and I ran into him in Murcia. He recognized us and spoke to us in what seemed a garbled tongue. Polish? Is it or is it not true that Harris later fought with the Polish Dombrowski battalion, considered among the best in the International Brigades, became its captain, and died in battle?

Every day now the Comintern archives in Moscow reveal their nasty information about the infamous way the Communist parties of the world treated their volunteers who went to Spain, brave men all. Perhaps one day they will rectify the rumors, secrets, allegations, and undo the lies. The dead cannot be disinterred. Yes, we went to Spain to fight fascism, but democracy was not our aim.

To understand and reach into the very heart and soul of the volunteers in the International Brigades you must know who we were. We were Communists, the overwhelming number of us—80 percent of the Americans, John Gates said—and believers in Lenin.

Lenin demanded of his followers that they give "all of their lives." And what Lenin demanded, we gave. Everything said after that is pure adornment, rationalization, line. A lie.

Yes, we gave all of our lives. That was our greatest strength and our greatest weakness. For in giving all of your life, you fight to the death, but you also yield up all of your brain and your heart and your morality. You are not a free man.

So I reported to my squads, and anyone else who would listen, that Jim Harris had been deposed and Merriman was now our commander-in-chief. Joe Gordon said "It figured." Doug Roach shrugged. Oscar Hunter kept a poker face.

The Capronis appeared during siesta hour, their bombs terrorizing the earth and us, but today, for the first time, Moscas, Russian pursuit planes, buzzed the bombers. We cheered. We screamed. The Soviet Union, our savior, how we loved it.

As I remember, the Lincoln battalion left for the front around February 12, Lincoln's birthday. At pre-dawn on February 22, Washington's birthday, after the artillery shelling had long ceased its nightly horror, scared, asleep, I was awakened by a gentle pulling at my shoulder. It was Captain Seacord. Come along, he said. He had hand-picked two squads and, with a Captain Wattis, a Brit who was an officer in the XVth Brigade, leading, we wound our silent way over stone and mesquite. Joe and Ray Steele were in the other squad, some nine men, and my squad included Kavorkian, company commissar, and Pete Shimrak, among others.

As dawn reared its coltish roseate head, one by one, led by Seacord and Wattis, we ran, flopped, ran, flopped—at one point I hesitated, hated to rise again; Seacord looked at me quizzically, I blushed, rose—

until we reached a battalion of men who crouched, slept, smoked long stogies behind a long battlement of stones. They were the Franco-Belges battalion led by Captain van den Berghe. Joe and I were introduced to him. Seacord hung a pair of binoculars around my neck, patted me on the shoulder, and, with the Brit at his heels, departed, running, flopping, running, flopping, until they disappeared.

Van den Berghe positioned Joe's squad at the extreme right of the Belgians' line, and then led my squad to a rise farther to the right, behind another wall of stones. There is, he said, a battalion of Moors facing us. They have tried to break our position several times. He spoke English well with an accent. He also pointed out two Christy tanks, ours, at the right flank. You will not fire, he said, unless they attack and I give the order. He returned to a position slightly behind his troops.

Morning was now in the saddle, the copper pot beginning to simmer. The nine of us sat behind our stone wall and looked at each other. Kavorkian had been given a gunny sack filled with hand grenades. What do we do with these? he asked me. I looked at him. I hefted the gunny sack in my hands. I didn't know what to do with it. I suppose we should each have one, I said. Pete Shimrak suggested it might be best to bury the sack in the middle, so if we were attacked we could get at them quickly. No one seemed to want to hold one. They looked so lethal. What if you had one on your person and it was hit by a bullet? Since I was in command, I made the decision that we bury the gunny sack and its burden behind us where we could easily get at it.

I made a map of our position for whoever might relieve us. It showed our position, the position of the Franco-Belges with our comrades, and our tanks on our right flank.

The sky was clear of clouds, very blue. The sun was spun copper. In the distance behind us, peasants could be seen tending their fields. The front was not quite dead, still punctuated on occasion by a rifle shot. Earlier, someone had brought us coffee and bread. We babied the coffee along and smoked. We had been issued Gauloises. We talked, some of the men napped. At noon, several men separated themselves from a

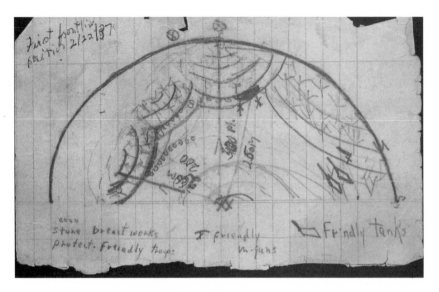

Sketch of a battle position

pine wood on our extreme left, heading in the direction of our positions. Halfway, they flopped to their stomachs. As they rose, one fell, hit before we even heard the rifle shots. The other fell on top of him. One of them began to scream with pain. The whole line stared in their direction. I kept looking at van den Berghe wondering what he would order. I saw him point to someone, ordering him down. It was Joe Gordon, no doubt preparing to go get the guys. We stared at one another. Kavorkian said something about the captain being a professional. We felt good about that. Shortly, two men left the pine wood, crawling, rising, running, crawling, until they reached the two men, who, it turned out, had been bringing us something to eat. We watched, barely breathing, as they hauled one man back to the woods, returned and got the second.

We could see our old friends, the squadron of Capronis, approaching what we assumed was the battalion's position on the hill, and then the Moscas harrying them. We could see the glint of the bombs as they dropped lackadaisically, and then heard the rumble as they burst. With a suddenness that veritably shook the earth we came under heavy machine gun fire. It was not necessary to give an order, we were all hugging the ground, pressing into it, biting our lips. I kept my eyes on the captain; he and his men were down as well. To my astonishment, some of the Franco-Belges were lighting up stogies and puffing away. I tried to slow down my breathing. Our Christy tanks on the right began to fire at the enemy positions. A runner from the captain slithered into view. The enemy will soon be attacking. Do not shoot until the captain gives the order. Swiveling on his belly, he slithered away. My lips were very dry and I kept wetting them with my tongue.

The enemy fire was high over our heads, to keep us down, I supposed. If the enemy troops were to attack, their machine gun fire would have to be high. Kavorkian and I discussed it, and felt better. I neglected to mention that Kavorkian was a man older than the rest of us, and someone who had fought in World War I. The Christys never stopped pounding the enemy positions. Then, to our astonishment we saw enemy soldiers rise in the perfect unison of the Roxy Rockettes and fling themselves from their trenches. Some looked as if they had white towels wrapped around their heads. With awe and astonishment, both frightened and curious, like spectators at a colorful war movie, we watched as these men, their capes flying, winged they seemed, came at us, running, falling, rising, running, falling. From us only the Christys fired their guns. The enemy was still distant but approaching, their capes flowing behind them. The captain, his back straight as a rule, knelt on one knee behind his troops. The Christys kept pounding. We lay there deathly pale, our mouths dry, in our first battle, as the enemy seemed to fly at us in slow motion. The captain held his fire. Now the enemy were so close we could hear them yelling, bloodcurdling it was, and at last the captain gave his order. Our machine gun shot one bullet and stopped dead. But we were firing our carbines at last, just shooting, the carbines becoming hotter and hotter in our hands, and the enemy was falling, still coming at us, still falling. The Franco-Belges were bringing dynamite cans to their lit stogies and flinging them at the enemy. We were firing, just shooting our guns. And then the enemy turned tail and fled, our fire whipping at them. At our left, below us, Joe was sitting atop his parapet, soon joined by others in his squad, laughing and firing at the retreating Moors. None of the men in my squad had been hit, but one man whose name I no longer remember in Joe's squad had had the tip of his ear shot off. Captain van den Berghe came by to congratulate us. It warmed us, but not enough to ward off the cold as the sun began quickly to descend. We huddled close to each other. We had been in our first battle and had survived, and we were suddenly very frightened as we clung to each other and one of the men began to cry. Kavorkian gave him shelter. We had, by the way, totally forgotten the buried gunny sack and its hand grenades. Fortunately, we had not needed them.

Under cover of darkness, we were brought beans, bread, vino. We spoke little, ate quietly and quickly. Drank our vino, smoked our cigarettes as we reclined low behind the stone breastworks. Wondered aloud what in hell we were doing here, trying to kill the men who were trying to kill us. We discussed that and concluded that men in all wars, no matter the cause, had their moments when they wondered at the sheer idiocy of war. Kavorkian, our political commissar, eschewed giving us an agitprop lecture, and I for one was thankful.

We began to hear the enemy taking their dead and wounded in and we sat there quietly and sad. As we set up a guard and prepared to take our turns sleeping, Captain Wattis appeared with another American squad, this one led by a man named Wohl. Many weeks later, after I became ambulatory in the Murcian hospital where I was bedded, Wohl's body lay in state in the lobby under red flags, and I stood before him as honor guard.

Through a night so quiet that the occasional rifle shot echoed, led again by Wattis we rejoined the battalion, now resting in a gully off the road. Seacord greeted us, gave us all an embrace, and then there was Joe, anxious to recount every detail of the battle we had participated in that afternoon. He was very explicit and full of beans and I fell asleep.

19

The following afternoon, February 23, 1937, as the battalion readied itself to leave the gully and enter the front-line trenches before going over the top, Seacord informed me the machine gun company would remain in reserve, but asked if I would take Kavorkian and Pete Shimrak and set up our machine gun at the left flank of the battalion's position. I told him that the gun had fired only one shot and then quit. He said there was enough time for us to take the gun to the armorer down the road, have it repaired, and then return to set up our position.

The road was under heavy artillery fire, but we managed to find the armorer, a man named Sugrue, if I recall correctly, who worked on the gun for a few minutes, oiled a few parts—it was an old 1918 Vickers-Maxim which the Russians had shipped to Spain; later they would send a lighter and better machine gun—and the three of us found our way to the position Seacord had pointed out. It was now deep into the afternoon; the battalion had moved into trenches to our right, and as we began to set the heavy gun in place a sledge hammer hit me in the back of the head. As I fell, I wondered who could have hit me. I must have been unconscious for a few minutes, but as I came out of it I heard Kavorkian say, "Poor Bill, he must be dead."

I tried desperately to move, to speak, to let him know I wasn't dead, don't bury me, but I was paralyzed head to toe and could not utter a word. I also felt no pain. Soon Pete Shimrak appeared with two medics carrying a litter. By then I had found my voice, and as they placed me on the canvas I uttered the memorable words, "Long live the Communist International," for one must die bravely, and I was positive I was dying. It was not as frightening as I had always believed it would be. I remember it distinctly. The best word to describe it is peace. I felt at peace, and very fatigued. I would be very grateful for the rest. I did not feel the needle as one of the medics gave me a shot.

When I came to I was in an ambulance on the way to a front-line hospital, half in and half out, paralysis receding, the oncoming pain in the back of my neck so agonizing I did not stop screaming the length of what seemed an endless ride through hell as above me a dead man leaked blood, piss, and shit into my face, and a Frenchman at my side cried, "Merde, merde, merde" in counterpoint to my screams of "Mama, mama, mama." War—very romantic. A great adventure.

I received another morphine shot when I was carried into a front-line hospital reeking with the smell of hot blood. There was much screaming. As through a haze I saw bandaged men moving about, and then felt the soft touch of Spanish nurses as they whispered soothing words. I woke again to hear the words, "Poor Bill, he's dying." This time it was ex-commissar Marvin Stern, leaning over me, one hand wrapped in bandages; then there was Walter Garland, his plump belly dappled with iodine—a case of bullets he was carrying had been hit and exploded—and Paul Burns, one of the infantry commanders, also with a flesh wound, and several other American comrades. The battalion had in clear daylight gone over the top in idiotic World War I fashion and been repulsed, with some twenty dead and sixty wounded. They shushed and whispered encouraging words as a soft-faced Spanish nurse began to feed me pitted dates. I can still remember how sweet the meat tasted, how pleasant and soothing it was to my tongue as I lay there half in, half out, believing I was dying. The morphine masked the pain, but I could not move my head or feel my hands. Soon there was another American lying nearby, an infantryman named Reinlieb, and when my morphine wore off I joined him in an endless howl of pain so loud the other comrades who were spending the night in our ward could not sleep and kept begging the nurses to give us morphine.

In the morning, my pain again masked by dope, Stern, Burns, Garland, and several others whose wounds had been slight and who were about to return to the front, whispered goodbye and wished me luck. Garland, a tall, slightly obese and light-skinned African American who was in my machine gun company, kissed me on the forehead and I asked him to give everyone my regards. I was to see Burns and Garland again, survivors of the war, but Stern became one of those rumors, allegations, mysteries.

Marvin returned to fight in the horrendous battle of February 27. He was not one of those who mutinied. He helped repel a Moorish attack early in March, and then, the front moribund, asked for a transfer to a French battalion. Shortly thereafter, Phil Cooperman approached Marvin in the line and asked him to come along.

That was the last seen of Marvin Stern by his American comrades. When Oscar Hunter was bedded next to me in the hospital late in May, he told me that Marvin had told several comrades he was keeping a journal in which he was noting the history of the Lincolns, and that he vowed to show his journal to Earl Browder upon his return to the States. Marvin, to say the least, was not being very wise.

Shortly thereafter, when Steve Nelson replaced Sam Stember, an abject figure, as battalion commissar, he held a meeting and told the assembled troops, whose morale was at nadir and for good reason, that he would answer any question they asked. Mickey Mickenberg (later Morris Maken) stood and asked Nelson, What happened to Marvin Stern? Nelson's response was quick and to the point, I don't know, and don't ever ask again!

(The second phrase of that answer doesn't seem quite to go with the first, does it?) Nelson was never, so far as I know, asked again.

In August 1937, Phil Bard, now a member of a committee of three—Max Bedacht, a Party politburo member and General Secretary of the International Workers Order, and a young man named Martin, an officer of the National Maritime Union, were the other two—appeared in Murcia. There was a party for the committee at one of the hospitals. I had recovered from an unsuccessful operation to remove the bullet from my spine and was ambulatory. I went to the party. Of course I spoke to Bard. He had brought regards from my mother and sister, whom he knew from the Communist Coops. As I've said, he was a gentle, soft-spoken man, one who could be called a sweet man. After we spoke for a few minutes, I said more or less the following: Phil, Marvin Stern was a friend of yours, a good comrade, no one seems to know what's happened to him; perhaps he's still alive, can't you look into it and do something about it?

His response was quick, and it wasn't sweet, and it wasn't soft-spoken. In Party matters, he said, friendship doesn't count, the Party comes first—and don't you forget it!

I had been in a jam with an NKVD man just before this, which is another matter, and I thought caution was called for. I nodded and left him.

In the middle 1950s, Mickey Mickenberg told me that every time he met a French I.B. man in Spain he would ask if he'd ever encountered an American named Marvin Stern. One day, during the Brunete offensive in July 1937, he connected.

"Mar—vin? Oui."

He had known an American named Marvin, he said, in one of the French penal battalions (a collection of drunks, criminals, and dissidents—Marvin?) and, as was the custom with battalions of that sort, Marvin had been sent out with a patrol to cut barbed wire before an attack, a most dangerous mission, of course. One afternoon—it was nearly always in the afternoon, the sun high, visibility clear—on just such a mission, Marvin had been killed.

Rumor? Truth? What?

20

Supine in an ambulance train, doped up, head immobile, a Spanish nurse feeding me slices of orange and the
sweet meat of pitted dates, the passage of time snail-like,
I arrived with hundreds of I.B. wounded in the rich market city of Murcia. I was deposited in a hospital named after La Pasionaria. Forgive me my latter-day bitterness;
she was an impressive figure, a great orator, who kissed
Joe Stalin's ass before breakfast, lunch, and dinner, and
once more before going to bed. She blackmailed the
Spanish government: the Soviet freighters lying outside
its harbors would not unload their cargo of arms unless
there was acceptance of the Party demands that each
army unit have political commissars (and who were they
to be?), that the voluntary collectives be demolished and
abolished, and that the POUM be outlawed. In *Mundo
Obrero,* the Communist Party newspaper, she wrote that
it is better to kill a thousand innocent people than to permit one Trotskyite to live. She was a charming woman
who affirmed her love for Joseph Stalin until the day she

herself died, long after his own people had convicted him for his massive docket of crimes. There are those who still call her a great woman. I am not among them.

I was bedded in a broad corridor of a stately municipal stone building making do as a hospital, and was soon joined by my buddy, Joe Mendelowitz Gordon—a bullet had grazed his temple and left him blind in one eye—and not a few other Americans wounded on February 23. Though the machine gun company had been held in reserve on the 23rd, it did not stop Joe from becoming a hero. The infantry commander John Scott lay out there wounded, screaming with pain. In an early evening lit up by a flaming, exploded tank, Joe and several others decided to bring him in. Two of the men with Joe were soon hit, but Joe and the first aid man, Toplianos—who was to become one of the true heroes of the battalion—running and flopping managed to reach Scott and bring him in. Then they went back under heavy fire to get one of the two men who'd started out with them. As Joe said, he ate dirt, he vomited, but somehow he and Toplianos were able to bring this second man in. Scott died, this man survived. "Killing," Joe said, "is a pleasure compared to saving of life." Darkness having fully descended, after having made an advance the infantry was ordered back to their original positions. Angry, discouraged, as the medics went out to tend the wounded and dying, himself dead tired, Joe returned to his trench, on his way kicking someone hiding under a blanket—someone he would never forgive, for he was not, after all, the forgiving kind—threw himself to the ground and fell asleep. He was found in the morning, unconscious, blood at his temple.

Within a few days we were joined by new American wounded, the battalion having gone over the top again on February 27, again senselessly, heroically, by orders of Colonel Copic, Yugoslav, Soviet Red Army man, commander of the XVth International Brigade of which the Lincoln was a battalion. Bob Gladnick has said that within minutes of going over the top, the men remaining in the trenches were protected by the heaped dead bodies of the Bronx Young Communist League. Copic's orders, almost everyone agreed, would somehow have been thwarted by Jim Harris. Merriman, amateur, didn't have the ability and courage to stop him. To everyone's sorrow, Doug Seacord had been killed, and Merriman himself wounded; in fact he now lay in another part of La Pasionaria hospital. When Joe heard about the 27th, in his anguish his slurp more pronounced than ever, he said, Twice, the dumb bastard, twice in four days. Fucking Captain Murderman. So dubbed by Joe Gordon, hero, Merriman remained forever.

I was examined by a Dr. Catellet, a French surgeon and chief doctor of La Pasionaria, a very handsome, very soft-spoken man. He found the bullet's tiny entrance hole, but could not find an exit. The bullet is still in there, he said, shaking his head. He hoped the numbness in my fingers would go away, and the pain in my neck as well.

The corridor in which we were bedded was broad and sunny. It was filled from one end to the other with I.B. wounded, some of whom never stopped screaming. One becomes accustomed to it. The guy next to my cot had lost half his face, and his head was encased in plaster with holes for eyes, nose, and mouth. I learned to distinguish between his cry and his laugh; his scream was a gurgle. Another man lay in his bed motionless, his body numb from the neck down, something I had been lucky enough to avoid. There was an Englishman who'd had a bullet enter his right ear and emerge from his left cheek, yet had not suffered major damage. Mashed faces, shoulders, arms, legs. A Pole who had lost his leg screamed the loudest. They screamed in German, English, French, Serbian, Hungarian. I screamed in New York Gutter, my very own tongue. When it hurts, you scream, and if you scream in obscenities it helps more than if you scream in the language of the tea room. If you didn't understand what a comrade said, you tried Yiddish, and as likely as not he responded in kind. How did we, always suckers for an alleged good cause, come to be the burr, the thorn, in the human promenade through this so lovely—oh, dear!—garden of life? Always looking for trouble. *Tsuris, tsuris,* as my mother used to say.

If you don't understand what I'm talking about, ask one of your best friends.

So I lay in my cot, head immovable, hands numb, having to be fed by the nurses. Joe, however, was soon ambulatory, his bad eye staring wildly, and he would come to sit at my side and together we would sing pop tunes, It ain't gonna rain no more, no more, Life's just a bowl of cherries, Yes, we have no bananas, we have no bananas todaaaay, at the top of our voices as nurses, doctors, walking wounded, men and women from the countries of the world, paraded endlessly past my cot. Joe went out every afternoon during siesta to get laid, and soon became infatuated with a pregnant neophyte whore, recently a refugee from Malaga, which had been captured but weeks before by Franco's forces. Franco also captured Cordoba; his iron ring was slowly closing, but Madrid stopped him cold.

One morning I woke to find a note pinned to my blanket: I couldn't stand it no more and got myself a lift to el frente to kill more fascists. I'll give Doug a kiss for you. José can you see?

Life burgeoned from him, and I had drunk from it to keep me alive. His energy was boundless. He was brave above and beyond, he loved war, was careless with his life, and though one-eyed he became what everyone admitted was one of the best soldiers in the line—the bester, as he himself put it, being Doug Roach.

From what guys who came from the front kept saying, it didn't take long for Doug to be admired by everyone in the battalion, what was left of it. He rarely opened his yap, unlike Joe, who never shut his, but was the man everyone turned to when in greatest despair. After the massacre of February 27, with Seacord killed and Merriman wounded and after a short-lived mutiny about which there have been 57 different stories, brigade appointed an infantry squad leader named Martin Hourihan battalion commander, and Oliver Law battalion adjutant. Law, they said, had been a sergeant in the American army. A patent lie. He'd been a buck private, and not for very long before he'd been discharged. Law never showed his face to his troops in the line, and was seen hiding in the cookhouse guzzling vino during the battle of February 27, as reported by Bob Gladnick. He was being pushed ahead simply because he was a Negro. Great agitprop for a battalion named after Lincoln. Steve Nelson, a topnotch battalion commissar—later co-opted to the central committee of the Party, and later still to courier for Stalin, and yet later still to the Soviet nuclear team organized to steal American secrets, a very competent man was he—Nelson admitted in old age that it was he who made the decision to push Law ahead. He even went so far as to say it had been a mistake. He could say that because he was no longer a Party man, so far as we know, when he said it. Just a simple mistake that was to cost many lives, and in the end Law's life as well, killed by his own men after leading them into several ambushes during the Brunete offensive. Agitprop, Lenin's great invention.

Doug comported himself with great dignity and bravery, and was considered the finest soldier in the battalion as it began to resume full strength by the arrival of fresh volunteers and the addition of young Spanish conscripts. (Soon some of the latter were sort of co-opted as buddies by the older merchant mariners in the battalion, and Brigade Major Nathan, an English officer right out of Sandhurst, took one for himself.)

When Oliver Law was appointed battalion adjutant, Doug and Oscar Hunter, another Negro, scribbled up some picket signs demanding equal rights for whites, much to the delight and laughter of our comrades, who'd said nothing for fear of being called racists. Sound familiar? Doug seemed to take Oliver's difficulty personally. He even went one day back to battalion h.q., cornered Law, and asked him to resign his command.

Law told him the truth. In the Party, Law told him, you can't resign. You don't volunteer nothing. You belong to the Party. And the Party means a lot to me. It gave me a life I never had before. Try to understand.

Doug refused to understand. With all his dignity, his self-respect, he was still a kid—we were all kids. So he refused to understand. What are yuh, a fucking Uncle Tom? Still a slave? Give it up, you're not fit to be a commander.

Leave me alone, just leave me alone. Go away. Poor Oliver, he was a hooked fish.

On another day early in March, Hourihan was away and Law was in complete command; the enemy attacked our lines, almost overran our trenches, and Law just wasn't there, did not come forward. Doug, Gladnick, Mickenberg, Bob Raven, and several others held the battalion, what there was left of it, together—the dead and wounded of February 27 had not yet been replaced—by sheer will, and managed to repel the attack. Raven, in his nervousness and lack of training, pulled the pin of a hand grenade, dropped the grenade at his feet and threw the pin at the enemy. The bursting grenade maimed him for life, blinding him.

By chance, soon after that Doug met Law one night at the latrine trench. Doug refused to acknowledge the man's presence even though Law tried talking to him. The man needed a friend, but Doug was too infuriated even to give him a crumb. Perhaps it would have been different if he had.

Doug was the obvious choice for a command position, but never got beyond corporal. He didn't care, because, like Joe, he was a born rank-and-filer; command positions meant nothing to him. He wasn't jealous of Law, he just identified with him too much; they were both black, and Law's inability to overcome the shakes in the front lines made him ashamed the way a Jew is ashamed when he reads that a Jew whom he doesn't even know has been caught with his hand in the till. Only when you grow up, say around fifty, are you able to separate yourself from the racial stereotype that the ignorant and malicious have created for you. Doug, sweet man, never had the good fortune to reach the age of fifty. Still, kid that he was, he was a man of insight, had marvelous antennae, but could not escape from himself. Those stereotypes can be the death of us.

It took a good month for the numbness to recede from my hands and for the pain in my neck to diminish, and for sex to raise its engorged head. I had fallen silently and passionately in love with a nurse to whom

I had never spoken. Twice a day, to and fro, she strode in queenly dignity past my cot, her uniform crisply white. Tall, erect, her black hair cut Nefertiti style, her eyes black as well, her skin honey-colored. She looked to me to be Egyptian. She had full dark red lips, her nose was slightly aquiline. Every time I saw her, my heart somersaulted. Looking neither right nor left, she strode regally through our corridor ward, my wounded comrades and I dazzled. I suddenly realized I was alive. It made me happy. It also made me sad. Guilty is probably the right word. So many of my comrades had been killed, and here I was, alive, and damned glad I was. Doctor Catellet took a picture with a small portable X-ray machine and there was the bullet, a sixteenth of an inch from the spinal cord. *Suerte,* he said in Spanish, *muy suerte.* Very lucky. You see, I said to myself, you are immortal. But if I was not going to die, why couldn't the goddammed bullet have waited until I'd had enough time at the front to become a hero, to have experienced war to the fullest? To have proven myself? Be glad you're alive, I kept repeating to myself. All around me were the wounded, men with half faces, with smashed legs, amputees, splintered arms. Be glad you're alive, I said again and again, feeling guilty as hell.

One morning a tall Frenchman appeared at my cot, the payroll master. Name, battalion, company? *Mitrailleuse,* he wrote. *Officier, sous-officier?* I shrugged. I was an idealist; I didn't believe in an officer caste, or that officers should receive more pay than the ordinary soldier. Besides, I had been wounded so early I hadn't earned it. He gave me seventy pesetas, seven pesetas a day for ten days. That was the first money I had received since my arrival in Spain. It surprised me; I'd never thought of receiving money for my military service. It also exhilarated me—money in my pockets. Later, when I told Joe that I hadn't asked for officer's pay, he told me I was a dumb jerk. He was right. Mostly it was guilt, sheer guilt at having been wounded so early.

Except for the continuing pain in my neck, an inability to move my neck other than stiffly, numbness at the tips of my fingers and slight tingles in my toes, I felt strong and healthy. With the help of my little

Periode		Sommes		Unité
du	au	Ptas.	Cts.	

Carte de prêt

Nom: *Harvey*
Prenom: *William*
N.º de la Carte d' identité:
Brigade: *15*   Bat: *17*
Compagnie: *C.M.*   Sec:
Unité: *Murcia*

Pay card for William Harvey, front

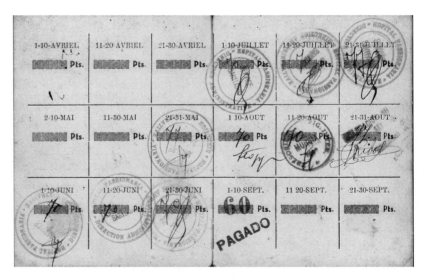

Pay card, inside

Spanish nurse I dressed in my new I.B. uniform—brown corduroy ski pants, khaki shirt, straw alpargatas—and, head held stiffly erect, I trod my way out of the hospital into a scorching sun. It was siesta hour. I was in a vast square bounded by the hospital, another stately government building alongside it, the Segura River across the way, picturesque and stinking like an outhouse, and near the river, an old obviously fancy hotel, the Regina Victoria. Wounded I.B. men stood about smoking, talking; men on crutches, men in winglike casts. Before he left, Joe had instructed me. Get a droshky and tell the driver, Muchacha, and he'll take you there. A girl, I wanted a girl. The old nag clopped through busy narrow cobbled streets and when we came to a small plaza the droshky driver pointed in the general direction of several casas where I.B. men lolled about. I went into one, smiled at the first girl in a bathrobe I encountered, and she led me into her room.

I had heard the rumor that a wounded I.B. man had died atop one of the women, and so, obviously, had she. She questioned me about the bandage around my neck, having to use her hands more than words for me to understand her. *Bueno, bueno,* I'm good, I told her. *Mucho bueno. Mas bueno.* She smiled, nodded, disrobed. I just stared at her. All of her. I wanted to bury myself in her, be ingested by her into her womb. I was alive, and so was she. I no longer remember what it cost, but I gave her my entire hoard and stayed with her until she kicked me out. She had been very accommodating. My neck hurt, but who cared? I was alive and this was one of the sweetest hours of my life.

Through narrow cobbled streets, across wide plazas, passing swarms of wounded I.B. men, talking, talking, smoking, drinking, ignoring Murcianos and they ignoring me—we seemed to have pushed them off their very own streets—I found my way back to the hospital, climbed the broad marble stairs, found the corridor, my cot, undressed, and fell asleep.

So the days went in sunny Spain. I would lie in my cot until mid-morning, be washed by my Spanish nurse, a sweet young woman who would giggle and ask me to wash my private parts myself; my commander, Robert Jordanesque in his winglike cast, would stroll past, give me a cool nod, continue on, followed by Bill Wheeler, *muy simpatico*, one of the infantry company adjutants who would stop a moment to chat. Then Frank Flaherty, a Boston Irishman who had two brothers at the front, an intelligent, literate man with his leg in a cast, would come to visit and we would talk for an hour before he went out for his daily shave. A barber who visited the hospital daily had been shaving me, but soon I would be joining Frank. It cost a peseta or so, and no tips were allowed since the beginning of the civil war. Tips lead to obsequiousness and they were forbidden, as were masturbation and prostitution, the Anarchists proclaimed in the most beautiful posters you ever saw. The Party, more realistic, merely forbade prostitution. Thus they vied for the minds of men. On occasion a man just come in from the front, either wounded or given a short furlough, would stop by and give much-wanted news of the battalion and my friends. The front, it seemed, was quiet; the boys played ball and held boxing matches, on occasion went out on patrol. How jealous I felt, and inferior, also, to those who hadn't been hit and were still at the front. Ah, to have been a dead hero.

I read *Mundo Obrero*, the Party paper, with the help of a dictionary. Also the *Daily Worker*, which arrived weeks late. I perused the pictorial magazine *Soviet Union Today*. The fronts were holding. In April we won a major victory in the Guadalajaras against one of Mussolini's divisions, our fight led by the Garibaldis, an Italian International battalion. (Where was the Spanish Republican army? one wondered. A battalion defeated a division?) The Garibaldis were led by Carlo Penchienati, a Socialist, later to write one of the bitterest condemnations of the International Brigades and the Communist Cheka in Spain. He had been harried by the commissariat until he was forced to resign so that the Party could take control of the Garibaldi battalion. He left Spain.

Though my neck was still stiff, the pain was not too bad, I became more ambulatory. My toe and finger tips were numb, but still I felt healthy, strong. When I spoke to Dr. Catellet about being released, he laughed. I drank vino with American comrades in one or another cafe on Plateria, a promenade street of silver shops and cafes, off Calle Traperia, the street of what were called rag shops, dry goods, and the like. That area was our hangout, and it teemed with young women from Malaga and Andalucia, exotic in their colorful clothes, beautiful, dark. We would buy them drinks, and later visit them in one or another bordello.

I never felt any guilt about exploiting them, and so far as I know neither did any of my International Brigades comrades, though who knows. One American, a union brother of mine, fell in love with the most beautiful woman of the lot and urged gifts upon her. I have no idea if he was jealous of her many customers. The Anarchists and the Party declaimed their opposition to prostitution, but I never discerned any attempt to prevent it. In fact, months later, in Barcelona, several American comrades and I visited a magnificent bordello which we learned was inhabited by whores who belonged to the CNT, the Anarchist union. Have you ever heard of a union that turned down an opportunity to enroll dues-paying members?

Early one afternoon, heavily involved in a tumultuous encounter with one of the whores, I heard someone laugh in the adjoining room, a booming familiar voice speaking Spanish with a Russian-American accent, and sure enough it was Bob Gladnick. He was wearing a beautiful Harris tweed suit, and carried a side arm on his hip.

Are you Cheka now? I asked.

He laughed his booming laugh. Gladnick was not a shy man. He was now, he told me, an interpreter and tankman with the Russian Tank Corps in Spain. He hobnobbed with generals and leather-jacketed political commissars. Right now he was stationed in Archena, the Russian tank base.

How come? I asked.

He had been one of the spokesmen for the ninety-some men left of the battalion after the massacre of February 27. Most of them had just picked themselves off the ground and headed for the road. They were getting the hell out of there. Before they got very far, I.B. military police rounded them up and returned them to brigade. They demanded further training and competent officers. Several Russian officers were present during this meeting. One of them asked Gladnick, who had spoken to them in Russian, "What is a nice Russian boy like you doing with these idiots?"

No, they were told, they could not be sent back for further training. It would seem the safety of Madrid depended on these ninety bedraggled, demoralized Americans. The Spanish Republic only had over two million men in arms. Could Madrid rely on them? Martin Hourihan, one of the two or three spokesmen, an infantry squad leader, was given command of the battalion, and Gladnick, a vociferous spokesman, was ordered to volunteer to be an interpreter for the Russians. I eat like a king, he said, and have lots of pesetas.

Great, I said, then take me to a restaurant and buy me a decent meal. All I've had for supper now for three weeks running is one artichoke and some vino.

Bob did have lots of money, and I ate well. I ate two plates of *huevos diablo* and four pork chops and half a pound of grapes. Later, I walked him to the railroad station where he picked up the train to Archena, which was not too far from Murcia.

A week or two later, I saw a group of Russians—they were called Mexicans, though everyone knew who they were—all wearing Harris tweed suits, going from one haberdashery store to another on Calle Traperia, and I ran over to see if Bob was among them. He wasn't, but I was astounded to see them piling up boxes of underwear, shirts, socks, and suits. They think Spain, Bob later told me, is among the richest countries in the world. Ignorance is bliss.

In the beginning of May the newspapers erupted with stories of street fighting in Barcelona. According to the Party press, the Anarchists and POUMists had staged an uprising against the forces of the Republic, and the Anarchists had attacked the *Telefónica*. I read that again. How could that be? At the very beginning of the Franco rebellion, the Anarchists had taken to the streets and seized many government buildings, one of which had been the *Telefónica* in Barcelona. Why in the world would they have staged an attack on a building they themselves held? It was a bold Party lie, and if the Party lied about that, could the rest of what it said also be a lie? Was it the Anarchists and POUMists who had staged an uprising, or had the Party provoked it? Since I did not believe the Party lie that the POUM was Trotskyist and fascist, why should I believe this lie? It is my belief today that if the Anarchists and the POUM had brought their troops in from the front to help their poorly armed forces in Barcelona, they would have won and the course of the civil war might very well have been changed. Of course, that would have left the front which they covered unprotected. (Burnett Bolloten's *The Spanish Revolution: The Left and the Struggle for Power during the Civil War* gives a minute-by-minute account of the Communist provocation.)

Soon thereafter, Largo Caballero, the leftwing Socialist who was prime minister, frequently called the Spanish Lenin, was deposed and replaced by Negrin, a pliable rightwing Socialist. Among my comrades there were secret smiles; we had broken the power of the Anarchists and the POUM, and were now in control of the Republic of Spain. Ercoli, we whispered among ourselves, Ercoli is running Spain. He was the Italian Togliatti, our very own. Natie, my nemesis, had been right—we had betrayed the revolution, we were the most counter-revolutionary party in Spain. Damn him! Why hadn't he left me alone? I wished I hadn't known what I knew. I wished I were a total, utter, complete believer. All these men in the hospital, with their smashed faces, their shattered limbs, were my comrades. Brave men who had come to Spain prepared to give their lives for the fight against fascism, for the Party, for the Soviet Union. My comrades at the front, my friends, Doug, Joe . . . I had to pretend, I had to watch what I said. I knew if I asked about the events in Barcelona, challenged the Party view, questioned it, my life would be in danger. Rumors were already floating all over Murcia about comrades, leaders, having disappeared, shot perhaps. Hans Beimler, the German Party leader, had disappeared; arrested, shot, killed by an enemy bullet? One wondered. Then General Kléber disappeared, the commander of the I.B. during its brilliant defense of Madrid. Who was he anyway? Some said a Canadian.

A Yugoslav. He was gone, disappeared off the face of the earth. (Kléber turned out to have been General Moishe Shtern of Soviet military intelligence. He had been recalled, sent to the Gulag, where he died.) Why? The same question could be asked of some scores of millions. Why? Rumors, rumors. Like snakes, they reveal themselves for a moment in the sun then suddenly disappear under a rock before you have a chance to examine them.

As a reign of terror by the NKVD began against the POUM, in the Soviet Union the magnificent Marshal Tukachevsky, the general staff, the admirals of the Soviet navy, tens of thousands of Red Army officers were being stood at the wall, murdered by order of, guess who?

Again, why?

Those of us who filled the hospitals of Murcia, the wounded of the International Brigades, the very cream of the international Communist movement, heard about it, whispered to each other about it with pained faces, then shut up about it. Perhaps it was necessary. Denial can save your life.

I spent the days drinking Spanish beer, eating Spanish peanuts, shooting the breeze on the Plateria, going to whorehouses. Why the lot of us did not come down with a nail or a spike, I'll never know. I met Gladnick again and he invited me to go with him to Archena. You'll get a topnotch meal, he said. We went by train, not too long a trip. At Archena we sat at a table with several Austrians who'd been in the ski patrol in the Pyrenees, and now were tankists. We ate a seven-course meal served by Spanish waiters wearing white gloves. (Years later, when I was a freelance verbatim reporter, I covered a luncheon meeting of big-shot bankers in the exclusive Union League Club in New York and was served by African American waiters, also wearing white gloves. Remembered with a pang.) I was impressed. My Russian comrades did not spare themselves. Smoked fish, pork chops, mashed potatoes, soup, cake, ice cream, vino.

After we ate, Gladnick approached the plump commander, and, speaking in Russian, asked if I could be enlisted as a tankist, since I had driven

Caterpillar tractors on a farm. No, the commander said, I was too skinny (I had lost some twenty pounds), but he could give me a job driving half-track trucks called Cominterns. No, I said; brave me, I wanted to go to the front. A month later, the commander, who looked like Khrushchev, was re-called to Russia and purged, along with thousands of others.

On the way back to Murcia on the train that night, my fingers felt stranger than usual, and every time I moved my head something like an electric shock ran down my spine. Tired, I thought, just tired. In the morning, when I was given my mug of chicory coffee, I dropped it.

At this particular time, internecine political warfare had broken out in the hierarchy of the International Brigades. Up to now the French Party had run the show, but suddenly the German Party was given con-trol—except, of course, for André Marty. Dr. Catellet had been dis-placed as head doctor of La Pasionaria by two German doctors named Lang, man and wife. They examined me together, using a large X-ray machine, and said they saw no bullet in my spine; it must have come out the other side of my neck, though no scar was visible. Perhaps I was imagining it, or malingering. No, I said to them, I had shit it out. Day after day it became worse. My hands were totally numb; every time I moved my head an electric shock convulsed me. I didn't know what to do. Serendipity intervened. The French, Polish, Belgian, and this American wounded mutinied, took over the corridors of the hospital, and demanded the return of Dr. Catellet as head doctor. The Germans fled—they were later replaced by Tito's Yugoslavs, who proved most ef-ficient—and Dr. Catellet resumed as head doctor of the hospital.

He examined me again, using the large X-ray machine, saw the bul-let, said it had moved, and decided to try to extract it. Frank Flaherty waited for me outside the operating room. Later he told me he had waited eight hours. In the post-operative recovery room, Dr. Catellet told me with sadness that he was unable to get to the bullet without ei-ther killing me or thoroughly paralyzing me, but that he had been able to manipulate a muscle enough to nudge it further away from the spinal cord. "Let's hope it helps," he said.

I was lucky; it did, and I have been forever thankful to the man for his kindness and his skill. A slightly stiff neck, numb finger tips, toes, and left thigh; one can live with that.

I also had a new nurse. My heart leaped, so did other parts of me. I wasn't sick, just wounded. She was my silent love, my Queen Nefertiti, Elizabeth; not Egyptian, but Hungarian, half Magyar and half Jew. We spoke in German. My German was of course half Jewish, but I had taken three years of it in high school, plus two years of French, and that helped, too. Her hands were gentle when she washed me, changed bandages, and for a time fed me. I literally spent hours observing her as she moved around the ward—a huge square room with a high ceiling and large windows through which the sun poured, magnanimously healing us—watching the way her buttocks moved, her breasts rose and fell, and when she leaned over me her fragrance overwhelmed me. I knew she was vain because even wearing her starched white nurse's uniform she managed somehow to give off the aura of Parisian chic. No, she smiled, Budapestian chic, second to none. I appreciated chicness; remember, I was the son of a woman who made chic with her fingers in a very chic dress establishment for the most modish women in the United States, and who herself was the most chic habitué of Cafe Royale on Second Avenue, New York City. I soon realized Elizabeth favored me, because whenever she became tired from her arduous labors she would come to sit on the corner of my cot and then not move when my foot under the linen coverlet would manage to find itself pressed against her lovely haunch.

It turned out she was the wife of the political commissar of the Hungarian Rakosi battalion, who alternated between the front and Albacete. He, as far as I know, was Laszlo Rajk.

So taken with Boishke, as she was called by her friends, am I even today that I have neglected to mention that next to me in my new ward was Oscar Hunter, who'd had to leave the front because of an anal fistula that required repair. He was an ebullient man, full of laughter, and we had great fun that drew Boishke to my cot as much as, if not more than, her feelings about me. Oscar spoke English only, and beautifully, a graduate of Morgan State University. I spoke my half-assed German, Yiddish, and even less French, and Boishke spoke German, French, and Spanish, so somehow we managed to make hilarious sorties into the vagaries of Magyar, Yiddish, and Negro life.

Oscar soon became ambulatory. With the finagling of Ruby Kaufman, one of the Jarama wounded, and myself, Oscar became the political commissar of the Americans and English in Murcia, replacing a man who had never been to the front. During the meeting, Ruby kept calling the man we wanted to replace a Trotskyite (a bit of overkill), and to her glory an American nurse, the wife of G. Marion, the *Daily Worker* reporter in Spain, stopped it cold. Ruby didn't even blush. That sort of talk could get a man imprisoned, if not killed.

Oscar told me he had not wanted to come to Spain, but as a Party functionary he had been ordered to volunteer. Because of his initial refusal, the Party punished him and made him remain in Spain until the last American left. He was a marvelous commissar, thoughtful, understanding, wily in his negotiations for the benefit of the men under his jurisdiction. He remained in the Party most of his life, and never advanced in its hierarchy because of his one and only demurral to a Party order.

I fell in love with Boishke, and as soon as I became ambulatory we became lovers. I sneaked into her room in the attic of the small I.B. cholera hospital near the Segura River, which curved through the city, and spent the night. Later she rented a room for us at the edge of town, on the Paseo de Malecon, where the lush huerta began. She always seemed to have lots of money. I never asked how come. I say we became lovers, though actually she never said I love you, it was I who was always saying Ich liebe dich, yo te amo, I love you, and serat lak in Hungarian. I called her Liebchen, she called me Bill. We'd meet in our hideaway four or five times a week during siesta. The straw blinds down, the heavy curtains drawn against the African sun, we would drink cool wine or limonada, talk about the progress of the war, discuss books we had read, and make love. My stiff neck was a hindrance, but as they say, love always finds a way. I was very proud of being loved by an older woman. I preened, I swaggered. I wondered how I could have loved Evelyn so much just several months ago (and before her and simultaneously Sarah Walton, my taxi-dancer sweetheart) and now love Boishke? Was I fickle, shallow, or was this something that happened to young men normally? Murcia was outside the bombing limits for Nationalist planes; still, the wounded and the medical staff seemed to be so elated to be alive that sex became an urgency. Could that have been it?

But sex was not our only amusement. The internecine politics among the high muckamucks of the I.B. was ludicrous. The Germans, as I said, fought to displace the French administration, and, after succeeding, lost out to the Yugoslavs. Great internationalists all. But it didn't really matter, of course, because no matter who ruled, the NKVD, since May, overruled.

When I first became ambulatory after the operation, Boishke decided to take me out during siesta for a short walk across the square to the outdoor cafe of the Regina Victoria. My legs were weak, my skin pale, my neck very stiff and sore, but I was so damned happy to be alive I felt no pain. And I was on the arm of this handsome older woman, and, boy, did I beam when we ran into some of my American comrades.

As we sat down in the shade of the canopy, Comrade Neumann saw us and came over to sit with us. It seemed Boishke and he were old friends. He carried a gun on his hip. Short, broad, head shaven; his head was a cannonball, his eyes bullets. I had seen him once before when I was bedded in the corridor-ward on my arrival in Murcia. He was striding through the corridor and ran into Bob Merriman, whose arm was in a winglike cast. They greeted each other in English, Neumann's accent mittel-Europish. My commander, incidentally, who had paid us but cursory attention—perhaps he was just too good for us, having been sent to us Stalin-blessed, or it could be someone had reported to him that Joe Gordon had dubbed him Captain Murderman—was gone now, arm still in a cast, and last heard of was training an American-Canadian battalion in Tarazona. Oscar, too, had mentioned Neumann to me. He told me that after he became political commissar he reported to a Comrade Neumann, and was given tasks like reading mail to and from English and Americans, and the like. Oscar said the man served a dual purpose in Murcia. He was superintendent of I.B. hospitals and also chief of security; of what Party organ he did not say, whether NKVD or SIM—Servicio de Investigación Militar, run by the Hungarian Erno Gero, also known as Pedro in Spain. There again we see the marvelous use of the unity of opposites. One half of Neumann saved men, the other half killed them. Sure enough, after the amenities, cognac glass in hand, Neumann began to boast how he and his men captured a merchant seaman who'd jumped ship in Cartagena and who, he said, turned out to be a foreign Trotskyite fascist trying to infiltrate our lines. With a smile of satisfaction, he told us they shot the poor bastard. Innocent me, I felt myself blanch, my lips become dry, and Boishke, noticing, turned Neumann off to more innocent subjects. A young, callow American. Idealistic. That was me. To Neumann, it was just plain table talk. I didn't believe that so-called Trotskyites were working for the enemy, and I didn't believe they should be shot. The more I read the newspapers and magazines that came my way, the more I was becoming divorced from my Party, my life's blood. We were duplicitous, pure and simple, without the dialectic to gussy it up. And now that we had destroyed the revolutionary forces in Spain, we were not doing any better at the fronts, either.

Another time, having earned a few days' leave, Boishke obtained a pass from Neumann for the two of us to go to Alicante for a short holiday. She was my nurse, she was taking care of me. We went by train, and it took many hours. Alicante was a beautiful old port, a resort town for the rich; she checked us into a posh hotel, a palace of a place, again for the rich, our room spacious and overlooking the sea, the bed large and comfortable, no hospital cot, and in the morning sitting on the terrace, the sea sparkling gold and green, we had a breakfast the likes of which I had not had since working in the posh Miami Beach restaurant. Boishke's Magyar father was a banker and she had grown up rich, only to become a revolutionary when in *gymnasium,* and she knew how to live it up. At the table next to us was an American seaman off one of the freighters unloading arms from Mexico. I invited him to have coffee with us, and he gave us Lucky Strikes to smoke. He couldn't keep his eyes off Boishke's bosom as we talked about the growing CIO, he was an ardent union man, and finally she nudged my arm and said we had to leave. Were you selling my breasts for American cigarettes? she asked angrily as we left. In that sweater, what would you expect? I said.

Later, as we sat in a small seashore park, two enemy planes flew over Alicante and dropped several aerial bombs. I threw her to the ground and covered her with my body, and told her I loved her, Yo te amo, Liebchen, and she muttered something about me being too young. When I asked her what she meant, she wouldn't elucidate. I guess what she meant was that for her this was simply a little affair and for me it was a very serious matter. If so, she was right. She was an older woman, about twenty-eight or twenty-nine, I was just twenty-two; she was a sophisticated European, I was a dumb American kid. What did I know?

Back in Murcia, a French fellow who suffered from a head wound and I started, at Oscar's prompting, an English and French newsletter for the wounded. Oscar also gave me a book to read and to report on whether it was fit for the troops. It was Margaret Mitchell's *Gone with the Wind.* A good read, I reported, but sympathetic to the South, and patronizing of Negroes. Good Communists, we decided it should not be read. I asked to be discharged from the hospital and sent back to the battalion. I was examined this time by an American doctor, who merely shook his head. You're lucky, he said. Don't push it.

Another day off, Boishke decided to take me on a picnic to the hills in the huerta, among the date, fig, and orange trees. We went by bus to a tiny village—a grocery store, a bakery, a bar, and a fortress church. The native women and children nodded in salute, we nodded back. All their men above the age of fifteen were at the front. We hiked up a hill under a very hot sun—I always think of the sun in Spain as African—until we found a level spot surrounded by a decent stand of scrub pine. I was happy to discover that I was recovering my strength despite what the doctor had indicated.

We unrolled our blanket, undressed. She had a magnificent body, tawny, feline. She told me to stop staring. I smiled, kept staring. She said, Be patient, Bill. I paid her no heed. She laughed at my impatience. Afterwards when I raised my head I saw a young peasant boy, maybe thirteen, standing among the trees, his mouth agape, his dark Spanish eyes as round as half dollars. He turned and ran. Startled by the noise behind her, Boishke asked what that was, and I told her it had been a dog.

We ate oranges, figs, and dates, and finished the wine in her canteen, and discovered that in my rush to get away with her I had neglected to fill mine. It made her angry and she was short with me. She turned away to read her book, a novel by the Communist author Anna Seghers, and I began to glance through the only thing in English I had been able to find on short notice in the hospital reading room, a pictorial book about the Soviet Union. It was full of palaces of culture, of labor, of justice, of this and that, and without thinking, forgetting in my bliss, I suppose, who I was and where, and with whom, I said aloud, Why do they continue to build these palaces when what they need are just simple places for people to live in? (Note it was in the form of a question.)

Boishke sat up very fast and very straight and gave me a very cold eye. I remember her exact words. "Du bist ein Opportunist, Bill." She wasn't kidding. She continued to stare at me for a good minute as I bit my lip, speechless, then she returned to her novel. I knew I had made a bad slip, just lay back and pretended to nap. Thank God, she hadn't called me a Trotskyite. Later we made love again, resumed as before, loving and laughing at my linguistic malapropisms.

Boishke did not bring my breach up again. Several days later, to my dismay, she advised me she was leaving Murcia. She had been transferred to Albacete to work in the base headquarters of the Hungarian battalion with her husband. She didn't say so, but I believed that our affair had become too public and word had gotten to her husband, who found it embarrassing. (He was one of the top Communists in Spain; later he was one of the rulers of Communist Hungary—with a different wife—and then he was purged—but of course.) I was extremely unhappy at her going; we stopped meeting at our trysting place, and then she was gone without a chance to say goodbye. I was out with some of the ambulatory wounded on the Street of Ragshops when I saw her sitting in the back of a staff car as it was leaving the curb in front of Neumann's office. I waved, I suppose you could say frantically, but there was no response from her. I was heartbroken. I left my friends and went to a very crowded bar on Plateria and drank myself silly.

I mooned about for several days under the sympathetic eyes of Oscar Hunter. On the third morning of her departure, I was wakened in my hospital cot by two I.B. men with guns on their hips and ordered to dress and to follow them. It was still pre-dawn; the night nurse was nowhere in sight, and the wounded patients were either asleep or pretending to be. Perhaps another comrade was found to be a Trotskyite and would be lost from sight. I started to ask what the hell was this about but they told me to keep quiet and dress. In the cot next to mine, Oscar Hunter continued to sleep, or at least pretended to sleep. He never once mentioned it later.

I walked between them through the silent streets of Murcia, plane trees rustling in the pre-dawn breeze, to the Calle de Traperia and thence to what everyone in Murcia knew were the offices of the Chief of Security, Comrade Neumann. I was ordered up the rickety stairs ahead of them, and then they shoved me from behind into Neumann's office.

He was sitting behind his desk, a light directed over his shoulder on to papers he was reading. When I stood before him he didn't raise that cannonball head of his, and he said nothing. Lying on the desk, staring me in the eye was the barrel end of a large black pistol, probably a German Lueger. The sight of the gun frightened me. This was serious. What the hell did he have it out there for? I had kept to myself my dismay at the betrayal of the social revolution by my Party in Spain and had never said a word about the executions of Marshal Tukachevsky and the others; I sure didn't want to be stood at the wall, and Boishke could not possibly have turned me in for that trivial remark about the Soviet Union, could she? Would she? True, she was a cool, sophisticated Party militant, but she'd been a passionate and tender lover. Of course, the Party came first, it always came first. I'd revealed a tiny crack, that's all. Neumann continued to read his papers, the light glancing off that shiny shaven skull of his. I stood erect, my eyes hypnotized by the barrel end of that German-tooled black gun. He never looked up once. I stood. He read. On occasion he scribbled a note in the margin of one or another of the papers. Who the hell was he? What did he want from me? I have no idea how much time elapsed. I suddenly needed to piss. When I was shoved into his room, it had been dark outside. Now the sun was rising, its rays beginning to spray the room. Still he read. Still the barrel end of the gun hypnotized me, held my attention. All I was aware of was my fear. Fear emits a bad odor. You sweat, you stink. My bladder was bloated and I badly needed to piss. Soon that was all I was aware of. That terrible need to piss in the morning. It began to hurt. Finally it forced me to speak. I need to urinate, Comrade Neumann. No response. The son-of-a-bitch. He read reports, the black gun, which seemed to be getting larger and larger, kept staring at me with its lethal one eye. I simply had to go piss. Again I dared. Comrade Neumann, please, I need to urinate badly. Nothing from the bastard. I tried to hold the piss in, tried hard, but finally I couldn't. Just let it run and run, my pants leg soaked with it. It smelled of sour wine. The shame of it. I hated him. Wanted to grab the gun and put a bullet through his fucking head. What had I done? Had they read my mind? I stood there immobile, stinking of sour wine and piss, keeping my face as impassive as possible. I would have to dissemble. Beat them at their own duplicitous game. We, they, us, them. I stood erect. Immobile. He read his papers. Outside, the streets were coming alive with *holas* and laughter. The gun's eye stared. I stank. Finally, the man raised his cannonball head. Stared at me with those bullet eyes.

When he spoke, it was quietly, with no threat in his voice. Elizabeth said you're an opportunist, still young.

It seemed he was not after all going to shoot me. And she . . . and she . . . Party comes first. Discipline is all. I had revealed a tiny crack in the foundation of my belief. Tiny cracks widen, become crevices, and soon the foundation crumbles. The edifice comes tumbling down. There is a purpose to the total discipline of a total party running a total state. I am a good example. The best thing to do with people like me is to shoot them.

I sighed with relief. No, he was not going to shoot me. I would not have been his first, would I?

Then he put me through the grinder about the Party line. I knew the line as well as he did, inside out, upside down. The revolution must wait, first the war has to be won. We were for democracy. The revolution and winning the war were not indivisible, as the Anarchists and the POUM said. I passed my orals with flying colors. Didn't I read *Inprecor* and *The New Masses* and the *Daily Jerker* every day, memorize every word?

Finally, he let me go, but, no, I wasn't through with him yet. How I hope he got his, the piece of scum, when Stalin began to purge his deracinated Jewish Party leaders in eastern Europe, nearly all of them veterans of the Spanish Civil War. Boishke's husband, Laszlo Rajk, too, though according to the newspapers his wife's name then was Julia. He was purged in Hungary by the hangman Erno Gero, who in Spain was known as Pedro, leader of the United Socialist Catalan Party (PSUC) as the CP was known—Gero spoke Catalan like a native—and also capo of the military intelligence service (SIM), resident address for several members of the Lincoln battalion as well as the NKVD. (There was also a Spanish SIM.) It was Gero and the Russian, Orlov, chief of the NKVD in Spain, who engineered Operation Nikolai to torture and murder the most brilliant revolutionary Marxist in Spain, Andreu Nin, the POUM leader. They also murdered Kurt Landau, a German dissident Communist; Camilio Berneri, an Italian Anarchist; the Czech Erwin Wolf and the Pole Hans Freund, two Trotskyists, as well as Mark Rein, son of the exiled Russian Menshevik leader Rafael Abramovich. It turns out that they had George Orwell on their to-be-murdered menu while he was in Spain, and little did he know how close he was to death when he left. All the above while my comrades and I were giving our lives for the Communist International as democrats and anti-fascists.

I don't know what happened to Boishke. I have often wondered if she survived World War II and the Holocaust—remember, she was half Jewish. Her Magyar father had divorced her Jewish mother, who then went to live in Paris. Perhaps he protected his daughter, though I doubt it. In any event, when Rajk became a leader of Communist Hungary after World War II, Boishke was no longer his wife.

Neumann had a job for me. He still had to test my loyalty to the cause, I suppose. He was concerned, he said, about Philippe, who was putting out the hospital newsletter with me; would I talk to him, and if he said something he shouldn't, report it? Now he was making an informer out of me. Of course, everyone knows by now that the Communist movement was also known as Informer University International. One of the first lessons you learned when you joined a Party unit was the necessity for informing your organizer if one of your comrades uttered a critical word about the Party or the Soviet Union. If you informed on yourself, something called self-criticism, you got an A+. I was now going to matriculate for my B.A. Boishke, it seemed, already had her Ph.D. The very first time I saw Philippe after Neumann's order, he began to blow off about executions of comrades in the I.B., and about the I.B. prisons overflowing, and so on. I recognized immediately what this was about. A set-up, a trap. I wasn't a total idiot. This kind of talk was verboten. Neumann was testing me, with Philippe as shill. Next time I saw Neumann, he asked me about Philippe. I smiled, then said, Oh, he's suffering from his head wound. Neumann seemed to understand that I had caught on to his petty game. He also smiled, said, Yes, you're right, and, to my relief, let it go at that. When I saw Philippe at our little office on Calle Nicolai several days later, he greeted me sort of sheepishly, embarrassed. He had no reason to be embarrassed; he had in his way let me know what was up, and we still had our heads attached to our bodies.

Neumann wasn't through with me. I was being put through Herculean labors. Another test or two. One day I was in Neumann's office, actually in a cubbyhole near the water closet, reading incoming letters addressed to American and English truck drivers located in Almeria. I was looking for enemies of the people propagandizing our dear comrades, sort of pre-censoring the war censor's work. Of the hundreds I read, one was from an English Trotskyist who not only criticized the Party, but the Anarchists and the POUM—which, despite its being labeled so by those who knew better, was not Trotskyist but Bukharinist—so I lit a stinky Gaulois with my trench lighter, a simple device of flint and lint, and put torch to the wayward letter before the English comrade to whom it was addressed was accused of heresy and burned at the stake. As I was leaving late one afternoon, on my way down the rickety stairs I encountered Neumann. Be here at eight tonight, he ordered, and passed on.

Now what? I was there, of course. Right on the dot. When was I going to be through with this bastard? Maybe I ought to make a contract with some Murciano hood to slip a dagger into him. Every week or so, one comrade or another was waylaid at night and killed in the Murcian manner. Murcianos are renowned in all of Spain for their knives and knife work. If I could only manage it. I would have loved to see his throat slit. At eight that night, he was there with several of his I.B. apparatchiks. We piled into a couple of cars. I sat with Neumann in the rear of one of them. We sped into the huerta; above us a very bright yellow moon illuminated a strange landscape of olive trees and various fruit groves. We passed Monteagudo, a black basalt natural monument. We rode for about thirty minutes, and finally stopped at a fortress-church. There were guards at the entrance.

I now discovered what this particular heap of Gothic stone was being used for. The heavy stone steps lit by lanterns, we descended into the cellar, more like a dungeon. The lanterns burned a greenish fuel and the dungeon was eerily green. We were in a large, stone-walled space.

I am standing near Neumann only because he has grabbed my arm and pulled me to him. There are a couple of Interbrigade goons standing around in addition to those who came with us. Neumann is impatient. Let's go, he says in German, and issues an order. A Belgian whom I have met at the office on Calle de Traperia, as solid as a dray horse, leaves us and shortly returns, pushing a skinny kid ahead of him. The boy has his hands tied behind his back. He is dragging his feet, is terribly scared, smells of shit. He is wearing straw *alpargatas,* and his clothes are ragged and filthy. A Spanish boy.

Yes! Neumann orders, and the Belgian raises his side arm and puts a bullet into the base of the Spanish boy's skull. The shot reverberates like thunder through the entire church.

Right there in front of me. Where is my revolutionary bravery, heroism? Why don't I step forward and cry, Stop! Stop! Why don't I ask, Why are you doing this, why? I'm a great hero. I say nothing. I stand there stiffly, biting my lip.

The boy slumps to the stone floor like a pile of bones, and one of the German comrades, a Communist who escaped from Hitler and came to Spain to fight fascism, picks the boy up and with ease throws him into a corner.

The Belgian leaves and returns pushing another kid ahead of him. This one is a girl. Skinny, all bones. Her clothes are torn, ragged, dirty. Hysterically, she screams, "¡Viva la revolución!"

Neumann is holding my elbow in a vise. Do it! he barks.

Again the shot, again the thunderous roar, again the heap of bones on the stone floor.

Neumann is still holding my elbow, but I am standing there shaking with fear, with shame—oh, the shame of it. These are my comrades who are murdering my comrades. Confusing, it's very confusing.

The German picks up the dead girl and throws her on top of the first boy.

Now the Belgian comes out with another. This one is not being pushed ahead. He walks out on his own. Straight. Older than the others.

An old man. He is about my age, twenty-two. A Spanish man. Powerfully built. Filthy. His hands are tied behind his back, but he tenses his shoulders as if trying to sunder the cord tying his hands. He spits at us once, then again, as Neumann orders, Do it! and the Belgian puts a bullet into his skull. He is a dead man. All twenty-two years of him.

Neumann issues an order, then he and his men turn to leave. I merely stand there staring at the dead. Thou art dust, and to dust shalt thou return. Neumann's fist, like a claw, grabs my arm and pulls me along.

In the car Neumann closes his eyes and nods off. A Yugo in the front seat passes his canteen of vino rojo around. I drink and drink. We are soon back on the Street of Ragshops, in front of Neumann's headquarters. I haven't said a word and neither has he, not even as I turn back toward the hospital. Before the Yugo gave me his canteen, I had puked out the window, my queasy stomach again. Do you think that if I'd had a stomach lined with steel I would have made a better bolshevik, been a man of steel like my great leader?

I ask myself now, and have asked myself for more than half a century, what, William, would you have done if he'd shoved a gun into your fist and ordered you to shoot one or even all of them? Killed them, you cowardly son-of-a-bitch! Yes, killed them.

And wouldn't you have?

Neumann never bothered me again. Had he been testing me to see if I could become one of his? Was he merely trying to scare me? I don't know. I have no idea. He never said, I never asked. I did as I was told simply because I felt my life depended on it. Just simply that. Once I ran into him on Plateria. He seemed lonely and he asked me to have a beer with him. He told me he'd seen Boishke, that she was doing well and had sent her regards. You figure it.

Neumann was not a professional agent from the NKVD or Cheka academy; he was on the pick-up team made up of European and American Communists whose zeal was so great it gave them enough of an adrenalin charge to kill. They may have been well paid, but money was not the object; their aim was to be placed on the honor roll of those who proved they had given their all for the good fight. *Vae victis.*

Tell me, I ask all those who have spent their lives studying our pitiful adventure and which some have deigned to call an Odyssey, an Iliad— Joe Stalin our Agamemnon? the likes of Erno Gero our Odysseus?— studying the Movement, Marx, Lenin, Stalin, the late USSR, you whom my mother would have called *gelehrnte menschen,* learned men, searchers for truth, do you still believe in the tactical lie, the murder which Auden in his callow youth called necessary? Do you still think the slaughter of scores of millions of people, of the horrors of the Gulag, was just an aberration, one of those things, merely another failed experiment in a Cambridge or Palo Alto laboratory? I didn't sleep for nights. My neck seemed to become stiffer, I could almost feel the fascist bullet in my spine, and it hurt terribly. The numbness at my finger tips and toes spread upward. My half-dead left thigh began to hurt even though it was numb. It was all in my head. I felt ashamed, and that was the worst of all. Should I have spoken up? What should I have done? Should I have kept a poker face? Would Joe or Doug, my brave friends, have been brave enough to have spoken up? Later I was to learn that they too had committed what they thought to be a necessary murder—life or death, and I refused to judge them. Were some murders more necessary than others? Can you answer that? I, yes, I, had murdered three Spanish revolutionaries. Real ones. Somewhere along the way, Neumann had said something about Trotskyite fascists. Who, goddammit, was the fascist? I remembered Lyovka, that love of a man, who had disappeared off the face of the earth, and how I had shrugged it off. I remembered the picket lines I had walked, demonstrations I had attended, my comrades at the front in Spain, dead, wounded, my comrades in the American South daring vigilantes, the Ku Klux Klan, tar and feathering, comrades all over the world rotting in prisons, and, yes, comrades being murdered in the Soviet Union. And these three Spanish kids. They were Natie. They were me. I was them. I had murdered them. I had murdered myself.

Crazy. I wept into my pillow so Oscar Hunter, asleep next to me, couldn't hear me. He never said a word. Perhaps he didn't know. The bodies of those kids were probably thrown in a heap at some square's edge near the Segura, which stank like a latrine. A warning, a threat.

For years a shame I couldn't quite understand stood in the way of my revealing this incident. I'd approach it, stop short. Finally, after several attempts ended in the wastepaper basket, I wrote a fictional scene in ¡Hermanos!, founded on what had happened in the church basement, and it was the protagonist himself who shot one of the young revolutionaries. Afterwards, readers, friends, even professional historians, all who should know better than to confuse a fictional character with the writer kept asking me, some even insisting, whether I had executed someone in Spain. Now I was afraid I would be called a killer. Of course not, I would respond indignantly. Don't you give me credit as a fiction writer? It never happened; I was never in a church basement in my life; I made it all up.

Of what was I ashamed, of what was I guilty? I knew, whether I admitted it or not, that if Neumann had pushed a gun into my fist and ordered me to kill one of them, the chances are very great indeed that out of fear for my own life I would have committed the crime. I was not, after all, the hero I thought I was, or hoped to be.

There is, of course, a vast space between would have and did, but in my case I have had to live with the thought that would have was as close to did as my skin is to my flesh. Up to the moment Paul Berman, a sympathetic interlocutor, seduced it out of me, I resisted revealing that to anyone, even to myself. Another human being's life was cheaper, I guess, than my own.

(I must note that when Paul Berman interviewed me and I decided at last to reveal the incident, so distraught was I that I kept calling the three young people "guys," not mentioning that one was a young woman. Yet, it's my image of her which is the sharpest and most poignant.)

21

"In the realm of totalitarian kitsch," Milan Kundera wrote, "all answers are given in advance and preclude any questions. It follows, then, that the true opponent of totalitarian kitsch is the person who asks questions. A question is like a knife that slices through the stage backdrop and gives a look at what lies hidden behind it."

I was now fully outside the compact mass, yet so indoctrinated was I in my Party, by my very birth, that I was able to give the answers without even being asked the questions. I was on automatic pilot. I was able to dissemble without truly being aware of it. My anger and my fear combined to protect me against my new enemy, my former self. I became impossible. Just say one word of criticism of the Comintern, the leadership, the line, and I was down your throat. I hated the very idea of giving up my nest, my mass, my friends. Doug would look pained, shrug, walk off. Joe might very well kill me. If Oscar Hunter, my political commissar—Mickey Mickenberg had by now called the commissariat at the front "comic stars"—knew what had happened to me, he said not a word. We carried on as before. Besides, suddenly we all had something to be exhilarated about; the great Republican offensive had begun in the center front for the relief of Madrid, victory after victory almost daily. There! It could be done. Followed by despair, for the Nationalist army had retreated in orderly fashion, then turned and regained all the territory it had lost.

The beds in the Murcian hospitals were again filled to overflowing. New smashed faces, more torn limbs, renewed screaming in the night. I began to help Oscar by making visits to wounded comrades, looking into their harrowed eyes with sympathy, with soft-spoken kind words. These were my comrades, the fallen, how could I ever leave them? It didn't help when the thought sneaked in that among the enemy men also visited wounded comrades, commiserated with the fallen, the broken.

And now there was Joe Gordon with yet another wound, a chunk of shrapnel in his thigh. Not quite the same Joe. Still ebullient, voluble, obscenity followed by obscenity, the world was fucked and he was fucking the world. He was meaner than ever before. Nastier. The shits were shittier, the incompetent even more incompetent. A new American battalion, he said, the George Washington, had shown up the first day outside the walled town of Villanueva de la Cañada. Fully armed, supposedly fully trained, they had entered the line and were immediately hit with heavy fire. What do they do? Bunch up just like we did at Jarama. The enemy behind the walls of the town must have roared with laughter. Decimated them, cut them in half. New rifles, brand-new machine guns thrown helter skelter, and those still standing ran like hell. The same old story. In the end, he said, we took the town, the old Lincolns, what was left of us, the Washingtons, too, what was left of them, the Franco-Belges, and the XIIIth Brigade. Yeah, and the English, but first they did something loco. On their flank, the Moors shielded themselves with villagers and the English stopped shooting, didn't want to kill the villagers. They took a lot of losses until they began shooting back. We took a lot of prisoners.

What followed were almost three weeks of war on the sunbaked manche, sleeping side by side with scorpions—you get hit by one of those and it's worse than a bullet—fighting the enemy in front of walled towns, in the hills, in the woods, those fucking Moors can fight, the enemy retreating real military-like. And the aerial bombings were hell. Who said that, war is hell? Still, we kept pushing on, he said. The only thing that kept us going was Steve Nelson, now there's a pol. And, Joe said, a crooked smile scribing his tough face, I got cited for bravery. Of course. He was indomitable. He was not alone.

The doctors told him they were leaving the shrapnel in his leg, it would stop hurting. They gave him a cane, told him to go about his business. We sang songs again, Stormy weather, Yes, we have no bananas, Life's just a bowl of cherries, Oscar joining us, laughingly telling us he was the only Negro in the world who could neither sing nor dance. Who cared? Oscar gave us a pass and we hitched a ride to Albacete with Phil Bard and his committee, come to see how the Americans were doing in Spain. Joe regaled them with war stories, skipping all the bad stuff. They wouldn't understand, Billy, they're just petit bourgeois fucks. Somebody oughtta tell Stalin about all these jerks leading us, he'd have their heads. No doubt.

In Albacete we met Doug; leaner, more reclusive, terser, drinking manzanilla—Spanish brandy—and drinking too much, his eyes red. After we embraced, he said, It was tough, very tough, bad. The enemy's good, don't run that easy. He had a wound in the fleshy part of his shoulder, it was all right, he would live. Saw Mickey Mickenberg, the meanest of the lot. The fucking comic stars don't leave a man alone. Know why we're called the Abraham Lincoln battalion? Because we, too, were assassinated. Those guys, pointing with his chin, Joe, Doug, and he shook his head in admiration. He was older than most of us by seven, eight years, and taller, too, his face lean and furrowed, his eyes little and mean, his thin lips pursed in anger. He seemed always to be angry, yet was fast with a quip, an anecdote. He could make us laugh, then have us sit up with awe as he recounted a battle scene, telling us about ourselves, heroes, giants, in a war movie. He reserved all his venom—and he was brimming with venom—for the comic stars, the incompetent commanders, the boy scouts, commonly called asslickers. We'd be playing cards, drinking manzanilla, and he'd lie down on one of the beds and sleep, ignoring the noise, the chatter. I'll be tired till the day I die, he said. Three weeks of sheer torture. I don't know why any of us are still alive. If not for Nelson, we would have quit, every one of us.

They were battle-weary veterans. I felt like a hanger-on, living the war through them. They babied me because of my wound, made an effort to make me feel one of them. I was no longer a believer. No matter what, they still believed. Hy Stone—a lieutenant, I think, in the infantry, a quiet man who'd lost two brothers to the war—Joe, Doug; they would be believers till the day they died. Not Mickey.

Daily we met in a room on an Albacete side street rented by Stone, a fellow named Rappaport, a dapper man who had been a business agent for the restaurant workers union before coming to Spain, and Yale Stuart, a tall good-looking guy who was later to lose an arm during the Ebro offensive. It was there we played cards, drank brandy, and when Joe could get us to cooperate, sang pop tunes. One morning, Doug, Joe, and I arrived at the room—I no longer remember where we slept during those days—and only Hy Stone was there. It could be others were there and soon left. Doug had his bottle of manzanilla brandy with him and was taking little sips. He was now rarely without the bottle, yet he never slurred his words, never showed symptoms of drunkenness, was always himself, spoke quietly, tersely. Suddenly that morning he began to talk about Oliver Law, he just seemed to have to get it out, and when he stopped for a sip, Joe picked it up. Thus, they alternated in telling me that awful tale of woe, how they'd killed Oliver Law at Mosquito (Mesquite, really) Crest. Life or death, Joe said.

As my friends told me this harrowing tale, I could feel their hurt, and I was right there with them, still feeling my own hurt. When they concluded and were at last silent, Doug handed me the bottle and told me to take a swig, it would help. As I laced my nerves with the sharp brandy, Hy Stone, who lost his second brother to the war in one of the ambushes

Law led them into, said, I thought we agreed not to tell anyone. Joe then asked me to promise to keep their secret.

Doug, it appeared to me, was suffering from guilt. Joe, it is true, was not; still, he had to get it off his chest, both of them had to. Its weight was heavy; they were believers, real ones, no wavering for them, and who better to tell than me, their closest comrade in the battalion. Raskolnikov talked to the organ grinder, Joe and Doug talked to me. Hy Stone, despite himself, confirmed the story.

The three of them were skeletal—there hadn't been much food to go along with the fighting and steady aerial bombardment—and deeply tanned from the murderous sun of the manche, even Doug was darker, but it is their eyes which to this day I can still see, lit up from inside their skulls, very bright, wild, savage, stripped of any civilized patina. Men at war. Joe and Doug made me run around with them, drink a lot, go to bordellos. I found it hard to keep up; then they would remember I was still suffering from my wound and would park me in a pleasant cafe near the bullring and order me to wait there for them until they returned and we could go eat a late Spanish supper at about eleven at night. Savage as they were, they were elated to be alive. As I say, Joe sported a cane to help him as he limped around, and Doug simply ignored the wound in his shoulder. Hy Stone came out clean, never wounded. I never got to know him well, he was a steel-spined bolshevik, tight-lipped, mouth clamped shut, as far as I've heard, to this very day.

I left my friends after a week or so to return to Murcia. We kissed and parted, Doug, Joe, and I. Hy Stone had retired from the fray early, and I saw little of him.

While I was in Albacete I received word from John Murra that Bill Lawrence wanted to see me in his office. Murra had been wounded at Cordoba, I think, and was then Lawrence's aide. Bill and I shook hands; I asked him if he'd heard from Malya, and he said, never mind. He went straight to the point. I was a little scared. Ruby Kaufman, he said, told me you received a letter from Lovestoneite friends. What's that about?

Yes, I said, Jackie Friedman brought it with him when he came to Spain. He ran into Ruby and asked him to pass it along to me. Jackie was given the letter by his father, Sam, one of the Painters Union leaders. Sam got it from old friends and comrades who became Lovestoneites. I knew them from the Communist Coops. Their son Natie used to play ball with me. They just sent regards and wished me well. Nothing else. I still have it, you want to read it? No, Willie, he said, smiling, and Bill Lawrence had a nice smile, reassuring. Just keep your mouth shut, don't talk too much. Malya still talks about you. She's all right.

That was the end of it. Except when I saw Ruby Kaufman next, I told him he was a prick. I told him that in front of Joe and other of his cronies and he was abashed, got red in his Uriah Heepish puss.

Bill Lawrence was a decent sort and treated me kindly; still, he was a Communist functionary possessed of bolshevik steel, and when some twelve men who'd been in Spain more than the promised six months went AWOL from the front and showed up at his Albacete office pleading for repatriation, he lost no time, placed them under guard and shipped them right back to the front via truck. They were allegedly tried and never seen again. Document 49 from the Comintern archives, addressed to Lawrence and shown to me by the historian Harvey Klehr, after mentioning the trial but not specifying the results, says anent those results, "Some questions may be raised in regard to the international complications which may arise. . . . It appears to me [not identified] inevitable that the international press will get hold of it." Of what?

No one seems to know exactly how many Americans were executed in Spain for desertion or whatever. My estimate would be at least twenty. But I note that in all the American wars since the Civil, involving some sixteen million men under arms, only one man was executed for desertion! What we Americans lack, of course, is bolshevik steel.

One morning while I was still in Albacete, Joe asked me to join him and an American comrade, who suffered from a head wound, on an errand to the I.B. headquarters to get our comrade a raincoat. For some reason I couldn't go. Later Joe told me that while there, trying to find exactly what it was our comrade needed, who should enter, red-faced, his mammoth beret bouncing on his big head like a giant flapjack, but our supreme commissar, André Marty. He began to scream at them and at the others there for similar purposes, calling them a bunch of Trotskyites, what were they bothering about, there was a war on, et cetera, et cetera. Joe kept calm, grabbed the arm of our comrade, and pulled him out of there in a hurry. As much in a hurry as he could, burdened as he was with our comrade, a cane, and a limp. Son-of-a-bitch, Joe muttered to me; that was all, just plain son-of-a-bitch.

Another afternoon, when Joe went to have his blind eye examined—it was causing him pain—Doug and I spent a quiet afternoon at a cafe drinking manzanilla, merely sipping it slowly. He told me he missed Ray Steele, who had been killed, I think, at Jarama. Ray had become the finest machine gunner in the battalion and asked to be sent to the new officers training school that had been set up. (First I learned of it.) His application had been rejected because he refused to join the Party. His contempt for Tony DeMaio, the battalion strongarm, was patent. Doug warned him to conceal his contempt, but Ray refused. Yearning badly to become an officer—he no doubt would have been a great one—he said he would join the Party. Immediately he was instructed to get ready to leave for the rear. As he readied his pack in his trench bunk, he was hit in the head by a bullet, and died instantly. It was Doug's belief that Tony DeMaio shot Ray Steele. That Wobbly bastard was not going to be an officer in our battalion. When I asked Doug how sure he was, he merely shrugged.

Tony DeMaio, according to rumors, scuttlebutt, sworn testimony, became sort of an evil Everyman. It seems he was everywhere at one and the same time. He was seen in Barcelona in front of the American consulate, on the lookout for American deserters, or in Valencia, nabbing deserters in a cafe, and at the same time at the front, waving his pistol at laggards during battle. Who knows? It is known for certain that he was made commandante of the International Brigades prison at Casteldefels. It is also known for certain that many I.B. men were executed there. For desertion? For drunkenness? For cowardice? For Trotskyism or Anarchism or POUMism or Francoism? Two Jews for consorting with "Gestapo agents." When, many years later, DeMaio returned to Spain, this time as tourist, Pete Smith said the first place he wanted to see was his old command post, the killing field at Casteldefels. There was an indoor cistern that ran from bottom to top of the castle tower. It is said that Tony DeMaio, when angry at a prisoner's refusal to confess guilt, would throw the man into the cistern and watch him drown. The graffitti etched by prisoners on the walls of the dungeon cells read Long Live Lenin, Long Live the Revolution, Long Live Stalin, Long Live the Republic, Long Live Liberty. My only experience with Tony was in Villanueva de la Jara when I saw him punch a man down because the man had asked simply enough after some unimportant vote, Why does everything need to be unanimous? Several of us stepped in to stop the beating. At that time we still didn't know what DeMaio's appointed task was. We merely knew him as a bruiser of a boy with the face of a Donatello angel. John the Baptist perhaps. He vociferously denies all the above. How can you possibly not believe a man who denies vociferously?

In the early 1940s, when I became reacquainted and then close friends with Mickey Mickenberg, he told me about the fragging of Oliver Law in the same details as related by Joe and Doug. He also added two details they had not mentioned: who it was that actually put a bullet into Law's gut (does it matter now?), and that Law lay dead for a couple of days, no one wanting to bury him. Strangely, and for the life of me, I can't now remember whether Mickey was a participant. Unconsciously, am I protecting him? If he wasn't, then either Joe or Doug told him, since they were close friends of his. Mickey also told me that when he was in Madrid shortly after the close of the Brunete offensive, he ran into Bob Gladnick and told him about it. Gladnick has confirmed that.

On April 22, 1983—I marked the date—when I visited Randall Pete Smith, who called himself a closet anti-Communist (we had become sort of sub rosa friends), then the official historian of the Veterans of the Abraham Lincoln Brigade (*sic*), he told me Nelson had done an in-house investigation of Law's death, and two vets had confirmed my version, and that Nelson finally said, Yes, Law was a mistake, but no one pissed on him as he lay dying, as I had reported. It would be nice to believe that.

An officer's runner who was alongside Law when he was hit has said it never happened, he was there. I wonder if he had a criminologist with him at the front to examine Law's body in order to determine where the bullet came from. Since he was so close to Law, I wonder if he can tell us who, as Law lay dying, expropriated his handsome John Brown belt and shiny, custom-made Spanish boots.

In July of 1986, at the time of the fiftieth anniversary of the beginning of the Spanish Civil War, Paul Berman interviewed me for the *Village Voice*. I told him, among other things, about the Law killing. After it appeared, both of us were called racists, and the newspaper and Berman were picketed by members of VALB and the Communist Party. Twenty-three members of VALB, headed by Steve Nelson, and including Hy Stone and the above-mentioned runner, attested in a sworn statement to the *Voice* that Joe Gordon had not fought in the Brunete offensive; ergo, my story was false. Berman produced proof from the Lincoln battalion's own records that not only had Gordon fought in the Brunete offensive, but he had been cited for bravery, as Joe himself had once told me.

Perjury is, of course, a universal vice, though most people try to keep it to a minimum; for the totalitarian mind, however, it is oxygen, impossible to live without.

22

Back in Murcia, now ensconced in an office on Calle
Nicolai, several blocks from the Street of Ragshops, I
worked on the hospital newsletter with the help of an
American boy who suffered from epilepsy. Why he had
come to Spain in his condition, I don't know. He had
been wounded, and frequently suffered from seizures.
When in high school I had had experience with someone suffering from petit mal, a boy who sat next to me,
and I had learned how to be helpful, putting a handkerchief in his mouth so he wouldn't bite his tongue, and so
on. In Murcia, the kid's name was Bercovici and he was
related to a writer who was to become one of the
Hollywood blacklisted.

Men were now being repatriated, but I didn't ask, nor
did Oscar Hunter, my pol, say anything to me about it.
The men now coming to Spain from the States were told
their hitch was only for six months. My group had not
been told there would be a time limitation; we just assumed it was for the duration. Later, the limitation was

arbitrarily rescinded. When men insisted they wanted to be repatriated after six months, they were vilified as Trotskyites or cowards or spies, and those who decided to leave without *salvo conductos* were called deserters. A number were shot. It got so bad that Tony DeMaio, as I've said, was dispatched to Barcelona to stand outside the American Embassy to nab those seeking refuge there.

In September, Joe showed up in Murcia and told me he was being repatriated, and so was I; unasked, it seemed. Oscar and Joe contrived it between them. I was doing nothing, simply marking time. At home I could make speeches for the cause.

The doctors gave me an X-ray picture, the bullet clearly marked, and an American surgeon advised me that back in the States I should make sure I saw a Dr. Davidoff at Beth Israel hospital in Manhattan; the top neurosurgeon in America, he said. Before leaving, Joe and I had a sad little party with Oscar. When we asked him if he would be going home soon, he said, They're keeping me here forever.

In Albacete I appeared before a panel of the Service Sanitaire des Brigades Internationales and was given my honorable discharge, with *"balle resté"* in spine, and lost capacity to work, "50%." The democratic government of the Republic of Spain owes me a work limitation pension of 50 percent. I'm still waiting. It would come in handy in my old age.

Then Joe Colbert, who was leaving with us, and I went to Bill Lawrence's office to retrieve our passports. John Murra told us to return the next day. When we did, hesitatingly, blushing—he was a decent man—he told us our passports had been with the trucks that had been lost on our way to the front. A stuttering falsehood. I said, You mean they thought our passports would be safer at the front than here in Albacete? He shrugged. It wasn't too many years later when the world learned that the passports belonging to those of us stupid enough to have turned them in had been used by the Cheka throughout the world. We would, Murra said, receive Spanish passports in Barcelona to use until we arrived in Paris. There we would have to go to the American Embassy to obtain duplicates. And what will we tell them there? I asked.

Certificat de repatriement pour état de Santé de la Direction
du Service Sanitaire des Brigades Internationales

Nom de famille ___*Harvay*___ Prénom *William*

Pays de naissance *U. S. A.* Lieu *N. York* Provce ___

Nationalité *Americain* Date de naissance *8 janv. 1915*

Profession *ouvrier*

Formation militaire: Brigade *15* Bataillon *17* Compagnie *C. M.*

Nature de la Blessure *Blessure par balle reg. cavic de col. esc. vertebr. Balle reste)*

Nature de la maladie (date de) _____

Perte de capacité de travail en *5?* %

Direction du Service Sanitaire Brigades Internationales,   La ComiMédicale d'A

Repatriation certificate for William Harvey

Still blushing, still unhappy with his task, Murra told us the *responsable* in Paris would instruct us.

Joe Gordon, Colbert, a fellow named Moran, and I left together via train. Murra gave me a large envelope with our personal dossiers to pass on to the Party *responsable* in Paris. I was still in Bill Lawrence's good graces, it seemed. I had dissembled well. A red hot, steel-spined bolshevik, that was me.

Doug Roach was nowhere around. Murra told us he was at one of the convalescent resorts on the Mediterranean shore, and that he would probably be repatriated soon.

In Valencia, where we lay over for several hours, as Joe Gordon and I were promenading we ran into Ernest Hemingway, who said he'd come in from Madrid for a day or two. He and Joe had met when he had come to the front to visit the Americans. Doug had permitted the writer to shoot off several rounds from his machine gun. We told him we were on our way home, and walked him to his hotel. There he gave us a bottle of Scotch and an address. We thanked him and left for the address he had given us. It turned out to be a lovely old casa, beautifully furnished, and attended by several pretty young women, obviously daughters of the upper classes, who spoke English. Hemingway had telephoned in advance and the treatment we received was munificent. We left the unfinished bottle with them. I never got to thank Mr. Hemingway; perhaps Joe did at another time.

In Barcelona, camions filled with singing militia on the way to the front rattled through the streets; still, it was not the same city we had entered on that awe-inspiring day back in January. Though the sun shone with its customary African fury, it appeared gray to me—gray with unfriendly faces. We were still wearing our International Brigades uniforms, and the eyes that examined us were filled with anger. After walking the length of the Ramblas to our hotel, I found the back of my blouse spotted with spit. We had destroyed their revolution; was this their way of letting me know how they felt about it? I was aware of it, but I doubt that my comrades were. After those at the front were informed by the commissars of the Barcelona events in May, calling the Party provocation an Anarchist and POUM putsch and insurrection, many had remarked that those treacherous Trotskyite bastards should all be shot. Of course, many were. Irving Goff, an American whose exploits behind the enemy lines were nothing less than spectacular, told Alan Rockman, who was doing research for a dissertation on the Jews in the Lincoln battalion, that he and several other Americans, including one Alex Kunslich, were hurriedly sent by truck with the XIVth (Guerrilla) Corps to the hills overlooking Barcelona and that he "was given a tommy gun and looked forward to mowing down the goddam Trotskyite bastards." He made a similar statement to Cameron Stewart, another researcher, this time adding the words "with relish!" Archie Brown, another Lincoln who was co-opted into the NKVD, boasted when he returned home that he had killed more Trotskyites than fascists in Spain. Still another, someone named Cohen (not Morris, who after Spain was sent to England by the NKVD to consort with the Kim Philby gang), amused his New York friends and acquaintances at a cocktail party with tales of how he was co-opted into the GayPayOo in Spain and was involved, ha ha, ho ho, in executions. And who were they? How right George Orwell was when he refused to join the International Brigades with the remark that he might have to shoot fellow socialists. His *Homage to Catalonia* is not the only written record of those days. The files of the Spanish Communist Party and the NKVD captured at the war's close now rest in Salamanca. How proud they were to record in detail their murderous accomplishments.

After my comrades and I obtained our Spanish passports and were told at what hour at night to catch the train for Port Bou and then Port Vendres, France, we decided to blow our remaining pesetas on a big meal in what looked like a very fancy restaurant. We were greeted at the door by a snooty maitre d' who examined us head to toe, and then said, *"No hay pan."* No bread. We said we didn't care if there was no bread, but he repeated, *"No hay pan."* The joint was filled with well-dressed people eating what looked like delicious food, and we were four hungry ragged veterans of the war. *"No hay pan,"* he said yet again, herding us out. Yes, Barcelona had changed. The Party had done its work well. Down with the ragged and the hungry! Up with the bourgeoisie! And at the front, this is what our comrades were supposedly fighting and dying for. Despite everything, how bravely they fought, going into battle time and time again against overwhelming odds. The ceaseless and ruthless use of the International Brigades by their commanders would lead one to believe that it was Stalin's orders that as many of these men as possible be sent to their deaths—they were just a bit too tough, too idealistic for his tastes.

Now angry and dismayed, we went to a working class bistro down near the harbor and finished all the tapas the bartender could muster, sluiced down with tepid cerveza. Moran, a merchant seaman built like a tank, drank six glasses with no more effect than if it had been water.

As we strolled towards the train station in the blackout, we were joined by an American in I.B. uniform who said he was returning to the front in a day or two. There were many women on the street offering their services. This guy kept stopping and asking something of one, then another. After three or so, one finally acquiesced to his demand and they went into a rather shabby building. He was down shortly and we asked him what it was he had wanted. To fuck a Spanish whore up her ass, he said. We shrugged and left him behind.

During the night, as the blacked-out train clanked hesitantly forward, foot by foot it seemed, we were bombed several times by Nationalist planes stationed in the Balearic Islands. I sat near Joe Gordon, and because he refused to reveal any fear, I also revealed none. We talked right through it. In the morning, we transferred at Port Bou for the Port Vendres train, and shortly we were in France. I don't know about my companions, but I cannot say I was unhappy.

23

I lived in Spain some nine months, and had not made friends with one Spaniard. I hardly knew what a Spanish man or woman thought, except by what I read in the papers. My only intimacy with any Spaniard had been with whores in bordellos. I did have Spanish nurses, mostly aides to women of the International Brigades. They were hardworking and friendly, but disappeared after work to homes we never visited. For nine months I lived under the aegis of Moscow-trained leaders, policed by men with guns on their hips. Wherever I went, Albacete, Villanueva de la Jara, the front, Murcia, side trips to Alicante and Cartagena, and later Valencia and Barcelona, I lived under the eyes of commissars and Party strongarms, apparatchiks, call them what you will. I might very well have been living in what later became an Eastern European Communist dictatorship.

For the Americans who fought at the front, many so bravely—despite the overwhelming fire power of the enemy, so valorously—the many who died, and the many who ran away, Spain was really an abstraction; we knew and learned little about it, except what our ignorant and biased commissars told us. As for those who ran away, most of them had been told their stint in Spain would be for six months but, once at the front, were peremptorily told they would have to stay as long as ordered; thus they believed they had earned the right to run away. Who is so righteous he can blame them?

Today, Spanish historians, both of the left and the right, give us barely a mention; our significance was just about nil. Would that the same could be said of the Soviet apparat in Spain. For Stalin, Spain was simply another card to be played in the international poker game. Long before the International Brigades and the Americans were withdrawn, and long before the war came to its bitter end, Adolph Hitler and Osip Djugashvili were already sitting together planning how they were going to divvy up their winnings.

Bravery on the battlefield is not uncommon, it is universal; tinker, tailor, Nazi, Communist, democrat. But the bravery to face up to and acknowledge uncomfortable truths is unique; to refuse to be a denier in the face of the compact mass can be called heroic.

> Our fight's not won till the workers of the world
> Stand by our guard on Huesca's plain
> Swear that our dead fought not in vain.
> Raise the red flag triumphantly.
> For Communism and liberty. . . .

So wrote John Cornford, English poet and Communist, who died defending Cordoba, a brave man. Were we all not brave men? He, and most of us, believed Communism and liberty were indivisible, and he wrote those words at the very time our leader, Stalin, was murdering millions of his own people, including Communists, who also wanted liberty. At the same time he was about to begin his crimes against the Spanish people who were fighting for liberty. For the arms Stalin sent and his cruel and brutish intervention, Spain paid him in gold bullion—its entire hoard—and we, alas, paid with our blood.

24

We were bedded in a small working class hotel in the upper reaches of Rue Lafayette, near the St. Martin canal. I still have a photograph of Joe Colbert standing at the rail of the overpass. He was a sweet guy, with a sly humor. By the way, Boishke—a fictional Boishke in her seventies, an imaginative leap forward from the Boishke of 1937—in my novel *Kill Memory* was to live in this hotel more than forty years later. Our *responsable,* a man named Friedman who'd been wounded on the Cordoba front, doled out four francs a day to each of us. It was soon apparent that Friedman and his comrade amie were living on a hell of a lot more, and I had to restrain Joe from bopping him one.

Friedman advised Colbert and me to apply separately at the American consulate for our duplicate passports. He also told us what lies to tell about how we lost them. The usual Party deal: first it steals your passport, then it advises you how to perjure yourself. The American consular officer, now leery of us, did not give them to us, but handed them to the purser of the *Normandie* when we boarded it for home a month later. I have frequently wondered what Cheka agent used my original passport—was it one of those bastards involved in the murder of Leon Trotsky in Mexico? Ah, I know, it was one of those guys who used to hang around Los Alamos because he loved the sunsets and had absolutely no interest in nuclear secrets. Perhaps one of those who used to send love notes to Stalin. Whenever I think of that great man, I get this image of Goya's dark painting of a giant eating a small human being. How tasty.

For a month we walked the streets of Paris and I got to know it so well that when Jeannette and I visited it in 1965, some twenty-seven years later, I knew my way around with no trouble. I found the little hotel and it looked, from the outside at least, exactly the same. I thought of the old days and was gloomy for a day.

We never were less than hungry, and could, on occasion, chipping in, take turns buying a beer and getting laid in one of those pleasant bistro-bordellos that seemed to be situated on nearly every street corner in those years when prostitution was legal in Paris. Friedman gave us free passes to hear the Red Army Chorus, too. How thrilling. Made up for the lack of a decent meal. Once I fasted for a day and went to the Salle Pleyel for an afternoon concert. Brahms, as I remember. It reminded me I was human after all. It was a beginning—I didn't really become interested in good music until I married Jeannette in 1948.

Joe Gordon didn't have a passport; remember, he had deserted the American army to go to Spain. He had to wait in Paris for a Party lawyer to buy him out of the army for five hundred bucks, the going rate at that time. I was not to see him in New York for quite a few months. We corresponded, however, and I still have one of his inimitable letters. He came home via freighter through the Panama Canal (probably without a passport), a very long trip but one which he enjoyed to the hilt, because the only other passenger was an acrobatic dancer who, he reported, taught him tricks he had never dreamed of.

When we first disembarked from the *Normandie* after a very pleasant voyage (I ate enough for three), Colbert, Moran, I, and a fellow whose name I don't remember and who joined us in Paris went straight to the office of the Friends of the Abraham Lincoln Brigade, an organization formed by the Party to collect money for the battalion in Spain and returning veterans. There I delivered to Phil Bard, who ran the organization, the manila envelope containing the dossiers of the men who had returned with me. He greeted me warmly. We also were hugged and kissed very enthusiastically by several young women who worked in the office and who had gathered around the returning heroes. I, for one, loved it. Then I went home.

My mother and sister were living on West 22nd Street, between Seventh and Eighth Avenues. Natalie was home alone, and of course we embraced and held each other long as she kept inquiring after my health. I assured her I was okay and that Phil Bard, who by then had married one of her girl friends from the Communist Coops, had already made an appointment for me to see a physician. I gave her a song and dance about how the defeat of fascism in Spain was imminent. (We continued to say that until Franco won.) She was duly impressed. As usual, she had a piano or dance class and soon left. Mama, she said, was working and would be home right after work. I had not, incidentally, given my family any advance notice of my return home. It was as in the old days. A young fool, I didn't think they really cared.

I changed from my suit, which had been bought for me in Paris, to my I.B. uniform, my only other clothes, and walked swiftly to West 26th Street, the union office. There I was greeted with what I thought was awe by Leon Strauss, the manager of the Fur Floor Boys local of which I was a member. He took me up to see Irving Potash, head of the Furriers Joint Council, and a central committee member of the Party. Potash treated me like a returning war hero, and told me whenever I was ready there was a job open for me, whether in the office or out in the field. I repeat, I enjoyed every second of this hero worship. Then several of my union brothers took me out to a local luncheonette for coffee and cake, and I regaled them with gory war stories. I was beginning to understand American Legion bullshitters better.

When my mother came home from work that evening, I was there waiting for her. We embraced and kissed passionately, and then she saw the bright scarlet scars on my neck and began to cry. I held her very tightly and whispered reassuring words until she caught hold of herself.

She turned to Natalie and ordered her out of the room, then commanded me to undress.

Mama, I said.

Get undressed, she said again.

Mom!

Every stitch.

I undressed to my underwear.

Naked, she said.

Thus I stood before her.

She examined me, every part of me, head to toe, fore and aft. When she saw there was nothing missing, she asked, What about the neck?

Phil Bard's already made appointments for me with the best doctors in New York, in Beth Israel, specialists.

Shaking her head, she said, So that was the school you went to?

Yes, Mama.

It was a good school?

Yeah, Mom, the best. I learned a lot.

As recommended by the American doctor in Murcia, I was admitted to Beth Israel hospital in Manhattan and placed under the care of Dr. Davidoff, considered one of the finest neurosurgeons in New York. After numerous examinations, he advised against an operation to remove the bullet and prescribed that I wear a shoulder, back, and head brace to stabilize it. I managed to get about rather easily with it, again enjoying the attention it brought me. I was becoming a half-assed prima donna. I wore it for about six months, as I recall, and it seemed to do the trick. I no longer suffered any pain, there was just the neck stiffness, numb toes and finger tips, and numb left thigh. My biggest problem over the years has been looking over my right shoulder to see if there's an oncoming car. Now that I'm in my eighties, there seems to be a thinning of the calcium which had formed around the bullet and there is an occasional lightning flash of pain. It reminds me to behave myself.

The hospital and doctor's expenses were free to me, sort of a donation to the cause of the Spanish Republic. Other expenses were defrayed by the FALB.

At Christmas, wearing my brace, I made what was for me a rare appearance at a veterans' affair, a dance held at, of all places, the Savoy Ballroom, my old haunt. I danced with my old friend, Leah, and was having a good time when I was suddenly confronted by a distraught young woman who stutteringly introduced herself to me as Marvin Stern's wife. Perhaps it was the neck brace I wore which led her to me. "What's happened to Marvin?" she asked. Embarrassed, with people all around me and not knowing how to handle it, coward that I was, I said, "I don't know," and turned away.

I was to meet her again, some two years later.

No sooner was Joe back in the States than he missed the war and his friends in the line and had to beg the Party to send him back to fight. Joe Colbert, too, seemed a bird in the wrong nest, and returned to Spain with Gordon. Before leaving, Joe Gordon dragged me to meetings of the newly formed Veterans of the Abraham Lincoln Brigade—Party agitprop thought brigade sounded more impressive than battalion—and at one meeting insisted on nominating me for treasurer, to oppose someone he disliked because the man had once revealed his fear in the trenches. Joe never, but never, forgave. Before I could even refuse the nomination the vote was taken and the man was elected with but one dissent: Joe's.

Both Joes left without even saying goodbye.

By that time I was working for my old union, the Furriers Joint Council. I sort of covered—guarded—Irving Potash's office. If some union member or whoever came along and insisted on seeing Potash without an appointment, it was my job to dissuade him or her nicely, but firmly. I did my job well. I was a Spanish war hero, so they listened. Potash and Ben Gold, president of the International Fur Workers and also a central committee

Sunday Worker

5 CENTS
28 Pages
IN TWO SECTIONS

Local—Increasing cloudiness with slowly rising temperature. Diminishing northerly winds

Vol. 111, No. 18   Published Weekly by Comprodaily Publishing Company, 50 E. 13th St. Subscription $5 a year.   May 1, 1938   Entered as second-class matter Jan. 3, 1928 at the Post Office at New York, N. Y., under the Act of March 3, 1879

200,000 MARCH IN GREATEST MAY DAY

Upper: Three wounded vets—left to right Bob Raven, Bill Harvey and Eugene Finick.

Lower left: Veterans of the Lincoln-Washington Brigades heading the vast May Day parade.

Center: Union painters—"Slums Must Go!"

Right: The colorful blue and white uniformed band of the painters led by pretty drum-major.

Photo by Sunday Worker Staff Photographer.

By ART SHIELDS

Two hundred thousand marchers, a mighty tide of unity, rolled down Fifth Ave. and Broadway into Union Square yesterday in New York's greatest May Day demonstration to the thundering slogan of "Jobs, Security, Peace and Democracy."

In the early afternoon the first contingents of marchers began pouring into the square to the stirring accompaniment of scores of bands and militant songs of workers.

They kept pouring in past the flag-bedecked reviewing stand when a drizzle began to fall in mid-afternoon, they were still pouring in when the sun came out again before sunset and they kept it up until the last marcher passed the stand

Representatives of more than 650 organizations, A. F. of L. and C.I.O. unions, peace groups, Spanish war veterans, Negro groups, religious groups, and countless spectators cheered Congressman John T. Bernard to the echo when the Minnesota Farmer-Laborite called for a united front "to crush the monster of fascism."

(Continued on Page 3)

Front page of the *Sunday Worker*

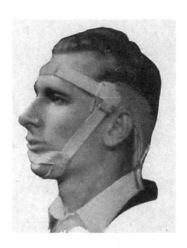

My photo in the FALB brochure

member, kept asking me when I would be ready to join the organizing staff. I kept putting them off, using my health as an excuse.

I was marking time, waiting things out. So far as anyone could notice, I was still a believer, true blue—more accurately, redder than a rose. I was sent out by the FALB to make speeches for the cause, and I must admit I followed the Party line, though I now believed little of it. I was lying and knew it; I had in my heart and mind become a POUMist and didn't know what route I was on, going east or west or north or south. In a sense, I was going nowhere. Besides, I wasn't about to give up the free medical attention I was getting, or a much-needed job. My mother was only working part time, my sister was now going to college, and every cent I made was needed. Evelyn had decided to rebel against her mother's wishes, and was seeing me regularly. We loved each other, and wanted to get married. I was earning about twenty dollars a week and it had to go a long way. The FALB had taken a mug shot of me wearing the brace, airbrushed my nose so I looked like a young John Barrymore, and placed it in a brochure asking for money for the heroes of the International Brigades. (When my good friend Joe Gordon saw it he wrote me a letter—you can read it on pages 230–32.) The brochure brought in lots of dough. I figured I earned what I was given.

Here I am, introducing two young Spaniards at a meeting in the
Furriers Union hall in New York City

A bonus, too. A civil service supervisor with clout was deeply moved
by my picture. She got in touch; she wanted badly to help me. I con-
sulted with friends. The beauteous Leah, my friend and dancing partner from Sunrise, advised me she had a friend who was a verbatim court
reporter, and that even during the depression he had made a good living. Why didn't I learn that trade? My admirer, whom I never met—it
was all done over the phone, and a good thing, too; my nose was not
John Barrymore's by a long shot—worked it out. The section for aid to
the handicapped of the New York State Department of Education
would pay for my training as a court reporter at the stenotypy school.
We all thought it was a good joke on capitalist America.

In the end, this little caper just about saved my life.

Dec. 14, 1937

Dear Bill Harvey,

Received your letter, and say chicken, thats a pretty cute mugging you got there, was just wondering how many broken down old women seen that puss of your's, and therefore sent in a few pennies to the F.A.L.B. Rehabilitation Fund. Everything here is about the same, promise after promise, nothing done yet, here's a confidential tip, if a control commission ever investigated Joe Klein's spending of money, goodnight. I know of the tremendous sums of money he spends, but can't prove it, Id love to see the axe fall, he's not worth 2 cents, and the guys whose ass's he sucked are about worth the same, in summing up, after Spain and Paris, here's my line, I'm a Communist, will be till the day I'm pushing up daisy's, right now, I don't think very much of the great majority of the Party leader's, they are mostly petit-bourgeois, intellectuals, opporttunists bootlicking bastards, "they better keep out of my way, cause I haven't heard the marxists interpretation on the rights and lefts to the button," and I don't give a damn how big or small they are. The Proletariat is the vanguard, what a laugh.

The same day I wrote the letter to you, I went out and got feeling pretty high walked into a cafe and seen a pretty french dame, sat down beside's her and told her what I thought of her and her whole goddam family, race, and all. After about 30 minutes of hard fast talking I stopped, she put her hand under my chin lifted it up, and kissed me square on the mouth, she didn't know a word of what I said, but she thought I was wonderful, anyhow to cut the story I've been living with her about 4 weeks now, what do you think of that huh? sunofabitch goddam me, if I ain't crazy about the bitch.

That jerk *Cooperman* who is home now, is got himself an O.G.P.U. mania, thinks everybody is after him, he'll probably never live it down.

Another jerk Tanz who is now in Paris says, tell the truth Comrades didn't I do the best job in Spain, "you stink, and not only that you were the lousyiest bastard we had, nobody else ever got a chance at your job, or they would have shown you a thing or two," was the unanimous opinion of the comrades here.

Very few people have come thru the last month, I understand there are hundreds waiting. Haven't heard from Oscar Hunter yet, except reports that he's doing good work.

Here's something, that dirty asslicking bastard, the rotten coward Sam Peck is now a captain, never a day at the front, I wish to Good Jesus Christ you expose that bastard to the fur worker's.

Eli Biegleman I understand is in charge of all the runner's in the 15th Brig. My Brother is now a commander in the Machine Gun Co, after the Belchite affair, I understand from reports he's real good.

Odette Friedmans girl *says* he's a no good rotten bastard, he has never written to her, she hasn't been working since she quit her job for him, I don't know if you know but he never was wounded he's a fucking liar.

Ive read, The Old Bunch, The American Testament, Red Star of China, and a dozen other short novels, its pretty tough for me to read.

You said a mouthful about not thanking me for the watch, cause some bastard swiped it already, but don't worry Billy. Now look cunyo, I don't give a rap how America changes. I ain't interested how the party squeaks or roars. I ain't worried about a job or how much money the F.A.B. puts out. (You know I worry night and day about you) All Im interested in, worrying about, is when and how Im going to get back, that goes for the rest also around here. Tell others to write, give my regard to all the boys, Murray Brown, tell Doug Roach to send me a line.

> Your Friend
> Joe Gordon
> c/o Bill Sherwood
> Hotel Minerva
> 20 *Bis* Rue Louis Blanc
> Paris

25

Doug Roach came home. He was not well at all. His back was killing him; some sort of spinal rheumatism, he said. Got it at Jarama. The cold nights. He was even terser than he had been in Spain. The FALB was supporting him. He ran around making speeches, earning his keep—for Oliver Law!

Huh? How can you? I asked.

A shrug; then, The dead's dead. That's what the Party wants. The Party. What else have I got? he said. Joe had said the same thing once. What else have I got?

The Party was the naysayer's refuge. The black man's. The poor Jew's. The sailor's on the beach. The Party had substance. It had a huge country behind it, ten or more front organizations, ran unions. What were you going to do? Join the Trotskyists, the Lovestoneites, the Socialists? Put them all together and they'd fit into one telephone booth. They stood alone, each the target of endless Party smears and lies. What else have I got? Doug said.

I arranged a lunch hour assembly in the union hall for Doug where I could introduce him, say what a great soldier he had been, what a marvelous comrade—not a papier-mâché hero, a real one—and how much I loved him. He giggled with embarrassment as he stood before hundreds of applauding unionists, but I could tell he sopped it up, that he wanted it and needed it. I spoke with great emotion, meaning every word, and stirred the audience so much it rose to a man and gave Doug Roach an ovation.

Hesitantly, he spoke a few words in his Hahvid Yaad accent, thanked the audience, and we went out for lunch nearby.

We saw each other infrequently, for lunch, for a walk, with no one else so we could be by ourselves, no Party bullshit. Once he said to me, You're lost, ain't yuh? He had eyes to see with. Yeah, I said, I'm lost. I was glad he didn't pursue it, because then I would have had to lie to him; I simply wasn't ready to make a radical change in my life. Joe was not back yet, the civil war kept going, Spain was dying, and so was Doug Roach. He was getting thinner and thinner, the pain in his back more agonizing. One day we said our goodbyes. I knew it would soon be over. Then one morning I received a phone call in the union office from Phil Bard: Doug Roach died last night. The funeral will be at such and such a place. Bob Minor will make the eulogy.

Who?

Bob Minor.

He hated Bob Minor.

Too bad, come anyway.

I didn't go. Besides, I'd said my goodbye to Doug.

If this were fiction, I would here give Doug a previous life, but I can't because this is a memoir. Strange as it may be, I know little about Doug other than that he came from Provincetown on Cape Cod, and he knew little about me. We were comrades, we were young, we lived in the present. Where or from whom we came did not matter. Obviously, we were both poor kids; we'd not been spoiled by money, that was certain. I saw him get really angry only once—other, of course, than when he'd spoken about Oliver Law in Spain.

It was in August 1937, when Joe Gordon and I were in Albacete after the Brunete offensive. Joe, Doug, Colbert, and I picked up a car at an I.B. truck and car depot. We were going to Tarazona, to the training camp of the Canadian-American MacKenzie-Papineau battalion commanded by our former commander, Merriman, still called Murderman by Joe. We were going there because Joe's brother Leo was a member of the unit.

When we arrived, the guards refused us entrance. We were veterans, all but Colbert wounded veterans. We insisted. They resisted. Joe Gordon said, You wanna start another war, comrades?

One left to fetch the battalion commissar, Joe Dallet. Tallish, ascot tie, high shiny boots, natty, handsome: the idyllic image of a movie revolutionary hero. You cannot enter this camp, he said. It seems we were the nasty, the mean, the ever-griping old Lincolns. He did not want us to upset his—his—troops, as yet so innocent, so pristine, so perfect, so untouched.

Joe kept insisting; we were wounded comrades, his brother would be going off to the front, he hadn't seen him in months. Doug laughed. How ridiculous.

We'll behave, Joe promised.

Dallet saw we were not going to leave. Who the fuck was this son-of-a-bitch to tell us we weren't good enough to talk to his troops? Maybe we'd give them some good advice! Finally Dallet relented after we all solemnly promised we would just say hello to those comrades we knew, and Joe would merely give his brother a hug and a kiss.

Joe did give Leo, a taller, less tough-looking Joe, a kiss and a hug. Then they went off to talk in private, and Doug, Colbert, and I went looking for comrades we knew from the States. We ran into Merriman, who still had his wounded shoulder in a wing-cast; he nodded to us and we nodded back—a very warm, friendly guy. We saw Bill Wheeler from the old Lincoln who'd been wounded at Jarama and who now showed up as an officer of the Mac-Paps. I met my YCL unit organizer, a fellow whose last name was Raphael or something like that. He was later reported killed. A name similar to his, Rayfield, showed up in a document from the Comintern archives as someone who'd been shot for being an Anarchist. If it was the same man, he could as easily have been accused of being a Martian. I must say we all kept our promise to Dallet. What Joe confided to his brother's ear, I know not. Sub silentio we learned that Joe Dallet, battalion comic star, was despised by his men. Rigid. A martinet. Unsympathetic. Revolutionary hero. What shit!

We behaved so well we were invited to the evening mess, where Bob Minor was to speak to the troops.

We sat together, of course, Doug between Joe and me, Colbert near Joe. I now sort of have a vision of a fifth man among us, perhaps Hy Stone; I'm not certain, though. We ate and then, all ears, we listened to Bob Minor, the top American Party man in Spain. The same old crap about how the enemy would run when confronted by our trained, courageous, and now well-armed troops. Then he said something about the Moorish troops in Franco's army. The POUM had urged the government to give Spanish Morocco its independence, not only because it was a socialist ideal, but because it would also stop the flow of Moorish troops to Franco. The Communist Party more than any other political force in Loyalist Spain castigated these troops as savages, barbarians, as makers of atrocities. Now, as we listened, Bob Minor, one of our leaders, said something about those blacks from Africa in a tone of utter disparagement. Joe and I heard a long throaty grunt from Doug Roach, another black man, and both of us turned to see him rising from his seat, his back hunched like a bull's, ready to tear into Robert Minor, major gasbag. We were certain we were about to see blood flow. Joe and I moved simultaneously and sat on Doug. He was a very powerful man and could easily have thrown us off; he tried for a moment, but I just said, No, Doug, you're going to hurt me, and he subsided. However, he stood and headed for the exits, and we followed him, the cynosure, as they say, of all eyes—and dropped mouths.

Back in the car, Joe driving, Doug let it all out: the massacres in the early days of Jarama, the horrendous yet victorious march through the arid manche during the Brunete offensive and in the end losing whatever had been gained, and now he had to listen to a Party leader disparage those black men from Africa. We sat silently as the car rumbled on. When he finally stopped talking, he began to drink from the brandy bottle which he had left in the car before we entered the training camp. He drank himself to sleep. No one said much on the ride back. Sad-faced heroes of the Abraham Lincoln battalion.

Now Bob Minor was about to eulogize him. Perhaps I was too much the purist, too angry, too self-righteous, but I did not go to Doug's funeral. I missed him for a long time.

Among the documents found in the Comintern archives in Moscow anent the Americans who fought in Spain is an unsigned letter, dated October 1937, to Bill Lawrence in Albacete, referring to a problem in the Mac-Pap battalion concerning Political Commissar Joe Dallet. It seems that the men did not like him, and that the distaste for him had reached a crisis and required solution. Removal, the letter states, from his post would not be considered. (As in the Law case, removal would have been considered an admission of error; the Party and, by proxy, its leaders never commit errors.) Shortly after the letter was sent, the Mac-Paps went into battle at Fuentes del Ebro. As the battle began, Joe Dallet withdrew his trusty .45 from its holster, ran far ahead of his battalion, and was killed. The rumors were not far behind. It was, one said, sort of a suicide, Dallet's form of self-criticism. Another said one of his own men shot him; still another, that the battalion control commission decided the best way to solve the problem was to have one of the Party pistoleros put an end to him. Any one of the rumors about his death could be absolutely correct. From my view of him, Joe Dallet was a vainglorious fool in a hurry to enter Stalin Heaven.

His widow, Kitty, to whom he wrote heroic letters, later married J. Robert Oppenheimer, the atomic physicist, and rumor has it she was

Steve Nelson's close friend during the period he was connected with the Soviet spy ring in the United States. Another rumor which could be absolutely correct.

It is said when the notorious Queipo de Llano, Franco general, ordered the murder of the great Federico García Lorca, he wrote, "Give him coffee, lots of coffee." The Lincoln battalion said it another way in a memo from the Battalion Commissar to the Cadres Service dated November 1, 1937: "We have had inquiries about Harry Perchik. He was removed from our battalion, the day before the battle at Belchite, with a high fever." High fever, indeed. Harry, a young Communist from the Bronx, was executed—no rumor, this—allegedly for desertion, but it was also known that he repeatedly complained, Bob Gladnick writes, that more Americans were killed thanks to the incompetence of CP-appointed officers than to enemy capabilities.

26

Before Jeannette, there was Evelyn.

When she told her parents she was going to marry me, her mother fainted, and her father physically threw her out of the house. She suffered black-and-blue marks on her arms, and a bloodied kneecap. Her father was a decent, hard-working man who belonged to the Pressers local of the ILGWU, and was an active union member. Her mother was the stereotypic tigress with her cubs. They were from Ukraine. Her gentile father and his brother protected her Jewish family during a pogrom. After marrying Evelyn's mother, he became Jewish without actually converting to Judaism, because they were without religion. I never thought of him as other than Jewish. I told Evelyn that within a month of our marrying her parents would be calling, asking us over for dinner, which is exactly what happened.

I fell in love with Evelyn, whom I met at a club dance near the Commie Coops, because she had a very pretty *simpatish* face and a glorious body. We had little in common other than being Jewish, working class, and loving to dance. She moved with a natural dancer's grace. She was even-tempered, as I was not. I have no idea why she loved me. She was very sentimental and always cried at the movies, yet she was a very sensible young woman except that she loved me and married me. It was her mistake. If her parents had not made it difficult for us, we would have dated, had some fun, realized our interests were incompatible, sadly kissed each other goodbye, and that would have been it.

My mother and sister were now living on Union Street, off Eastern Parkway in Brooklyn. Though it was longer for my mother to go to work in Manhattan, it was shorter for Natalie to go to school at Brooklyn College. Evelyn and I lived with them, sleeping on a couch which opened up in the living room. Evelyn was employed as a dues cashier for one of the ILGWU locals, and I worked for the Furriers Joint Council. Together we made about forty dollars a week. We believed that if we could make that amount of money for the rest of our lives, we would have escaped poverty.

I was happy to be married to Evelyn, yet by 1942, after three years, I was glad to receive my invitation from the army. At the induction center in Grand Central the lung X-ray revealed a beautifully defined Fiat machine gun bullet in my cervical spine. Where'd you get that? the officer of the day asked. Outside Madrid. 4F, he sneered.

So I didn't go off to war again. Having mastered the stenotype machine I was by now a freelance verbatim court reporter, with many thanks to my gorgeous airbrushed profile. I made a decent living, forty bucks a week already sneered at, and couldn't keep my hands off beautiful women. Discreetly. Evelyn never learned. Grow up, become a mature man, I told myself. Let's have a baby, I said to Evelyn, certain that a child would mature me, settle me down. A not unusual mistake. He was a red-headed boy, sickly yet charming. Seth David. I loved him very much, but no matter how hard I tried I no longer loved his mother. I felt great affection for her, I liked her, felt good being with her, but I did not love her anymore.

How do you solve that problem? I went to a psychiatrist, a Freudian. He never talked, and when he did he said I suffered from Don Juanism, a symptom of latent homosexuality. Why do you always wear turtleneck sweaters? I like them. Homosexuals wear turtleneck sweaters. I had one homosexual adventure in my life, when a boarder in our house kept after me to allow him to suck me off. Never after that; women, I love women. Now you tell me the more women I love, the more I am a latent homosexual. Yes, he said. You're full of shit, I said. Good, he said. As I've remarked earlier, I did get to hallucinate, see my father standing behind the doctor's back, and was able to tell him it was not my fault he had died, I hadn't killed him, and Pop let me off the hook. But I didn't stop cheating on Evelyn, didn't stop feeling guilty about it, and worried more and more about my son. I left Evelyn and I left him. I fell in love with another woman.

Seth died, he just hemorrhaged and died. His platelets did not reproduce. Thrombocedophenic puerpura. It can now be cured with a bone marrow graft. For three years I drove Evelyn and Jeannette crazy, and Seth, too. Then he died, and it was all over. I blamed my mother, I blamed Miss Veronica, I blamed Daniel the suck-off artist, only on occasion blamed myself. He was a lovely little boy, Seth was. Did not have one healthy day in his life. Rashes. Black-and-blue marks. Bleeding. He bled to death in a Los Angeles hospital, and we buried him in one of those cemeteries where they have no headstones, just a plaque. Evelyn said she didn't want a plain pine box, the kind Natalie and Bernie's little Paul had been buried in. For a while we believed we suffered from a family curse. Seth was buried in a fancy white box, the kind Evelyn wanted. I cried and cried. And then I got better. I married in New York, and Evelyn married in Cleveland. We never saw each other again. I did hear from my cousins, the Schreibmans, who had been so kind to me in 1934 when I stopped in that town for a night, that Evelyn had made a good marriage—real money—and was happy. I felt good about that. During our troubles she kept telling me I had ruined her life. I was glad to hear I hadn't.

Evelyn and I married in June 1939. The Spanish revolution having been destroyed by Stalin, and the Spanish Republic by Franco—talk about being caught between a rock and a hard place—the civil war was over, and all the Americans who survived the war had been home for many months. Joe, who lived through his second stint in Spain without further wounds, was sent to Party training school at Camp Nitgedaiget (Carefree). Several times I went up to see him. He was calmer, making an attempt to be less spontaneous, more mature, less brassy, a responsible comrade, as he put it. He even kept his hair neatly combed and brushed. He realized I was becoming more and more alienated from the Party, but our friendship prohibited him from pushing me about it. He, like everyone else, was a denier. We spoke frequently about Doug Roach, about how unhappy we were at his death. I tried to probe him about the Law fragging, and he shut me up fast. We will not talk about anything bad that happened in Spain. Forget it! Yet when he told me that his brother Leo had died a heroic death, he could not prevent himself from referring to General Murderman. Merriman had become XVth Brigade commander, and in April 1938, during the retreat at Gandesa, had led half his troops straight into the hands of the enemy. Leo had remained behind to cover the retreat and had been killed.

At Natie's house I ran into Comrade Fischbach, whom I knew from the Commie Coops. He was a Lovestoneite who had ignored the taunts and remained there, living with his family. His son, Ed, was a member of the Lincoln battalion. Ed was a poet, the sort who wrote for the *New Masses* in those days. When Ed returned from Spain his father called him, wanted to see him; after all, his son had been at war. Ed didn't want to see his Lovestoneite father, that comrade of the treacherous POUM. But Comrade Fischbach insisted. You're my son , dammit, I want to see you. All right, Ed at last responded, and set a time in the middle of the night in the center of Bronx Park so no one from the Coops would see them together. Comrade Fischbach told me about it and cried. What hath Lenin wrought, a boy doesn't want to be seen with his father? Edwin Rolfe, poet and Stalinist, died young. I hope before he died he'd become willing to be seen with his father.

I stopped going to meetings. I told whomever at the VALB that I was too busy at the union. At the union I told Potash and Leon Strauss I was too busy at the VALB to come to Party or YCL meetings. I have an honest face; they believed me, or denied not believing me. I was a badly wounded comrade, would somehow come around. The Party was in my blood, I could never leave it, could never betray it. True.

However, I was insatiably curious about seditious information, so I did go to public meetings held by Socialists, Trotskyists, and Lovestoneites. One I remember distinctly. I went with my friend Natie to hear Bertram Wolfe give a eulogy for Nicolai Bukharin, the most beloved of Bolshevik leaders. Wolfe was a passionate orator, and he made many of us cry. I cried loudest of all. I could not stop myself from seeing those Spanish kids in that eerie, greenish light in the stone church cellar. I had killed them, and now I had killed Bukharin. Guilt, shame, confusion was my name. I tried to jump the fence and didn't quite make it; now, wincing, I sat impaled.

I saw Natie frequently; he and Sarah—who was to become his wife—Evelyn, and I would go out together, to the ballet, the movies, a concert. Evelyn was bored by our continuous talk about politics or unionism. Sarah was a militant member of the Knitgoods local of the ILGWU, a local run by Louis Nelson, the most democratic labor leader in America. I felt close to the Independent Communist Labor League, which is what the Lovestone group now called itself. They believed in rank and file democracy, in a multi-party system after the revolution, in policies founded on American traditions and conditions. I found their politics very attractive.

In June of 1939, the same month Evelyn and I married, Bob Edwards, the English Independent Labor Party member of Parliament, was invited to the States by the ICLL. He had been commander of one of the POUM battalions in the Aragon, the very battalion with which George Orwell had fought. (At that time, Orwell was not yet a famous name even in England, let alone the United States. I, for one, still had not heard of him. Later I was amused to find that he and I had both been wounded in the neck, and proud of the fact that we had both read the war the same way. He was not only a great writer, he was also a great man.) There was to be a dinner at a hotel ballroom, after which Edwards and several others—Lewis Corey and Louis Adamic, as I recall—were to speak. It was one of those large, Times Square hotels, and I was there early, waiting for Evelyn to arrive before taking a table. To my chagrin, I saw someone I knew enter. It was Irving Fajans, who'd been wounded at Villanueva de la Cañada as a member of the Washington battalion. He was an active member of VALB, whose offices were nearby. Obviously, someone had seen me enter the hotel and knew my purpose. I had been acquainted with Fajans in Murcia and had liked him. I approached him, told him as nonchalantly as I could that I was waiting for my wife. He couldn't look me in the eye. He just turned around and left. Fajans was a decent sort, but in the world in which we both lived, being a decent person had nothing to do with it. As the Mafiosi say, It's nothing personal, it's strictly business.

On Monday morning—the Edwards dinner had taken place on Friday—Potash had not been in his office more than ten minutes when his private secretary told me he wanted to see me. What the hell was I doing at a lousy Lovestoneite meeting, the American backers of the POUM, among our worst enemies? I should know better, an old comrade like me.

I brazened it out. I told him I took the Party line seriously. We were twentieth-century Americans and I had just fought for democracy in Spain so I was only doing what democracy allowed me to do. Potash glared at me, then dismissed me with the caution that I behave myself.

I needed my job. Evelyn and I were looking for our own apartment, and I still required medical attention from the doctors the FALB had sent me to; also I was just a goddamned coward and couldn't make the final break. It was almost as if my body, every tendon, sinew, blood vessel, even a good piece of my heart, were still attached to the Party's corpus; only my head and the rest of my heart were off somewhere else. I behaved myself, as Potash had ordered—for several months. Then one of the ILGWU locals invited Norman Thomas to give a lecture, and I couldn't resist the temptation to hear what he had to say. He was a moderate Socialist, he was not a Marxist, I just wanted to know. Besides, it was my damned right, wasn't it? Within two days I was called in by a man named Ramsey, editor of the *Fur Worker,* the union newspaper. The VALB office had called Potash to say I was seen at a yellow Socialist meeting with several Lovestoneites—Natie and his father had accompanied me—and what the hell was going on with me? I gave him the same song and dance. He did not smile. You're taxing Potash's patience, he said.

I guess I wanted them to do it for me. A couple weeks later it resolved itself. That ingenious scam, the Popular Front, the League for Peace and Democracy, Against War and Fascism, blew up in our very faces. The Stalin-Hitler pact was announced to the world. Molotov and von Ribbentrop shook hands. Politics was only a matter of taste, they said. For forty-eight hours we were in a daze, confused, addled. Then the so-called anti-fascist Communist Party steeled its bolshevik resolve and became anti-anti-fascist. The war between the Nazis and the West was simply a war between competing imperialisms. My buddies in the Spanish Civil War who had boasted—and still boast—that they were premature anti-fascists resolved that The Yanks Are Not Coming. They, too, had become anti-anti-fascists. Now all those tens of thousands—suckers for the scam?—who had flocked to the Party precisely because of its Americanism and anti-fascism left in disgust. Some returned, of course, when Hitler's Germany invaded the Soviet Union, but it was never to be the same.

Natie Shlechter's father had predicted the pact several months before and I had yelled at him, told him he was crazy, he was going too far. Now my scream could be heard from one end of the union hall to the other. Stalin is a swine! The blood of our comrades is not yet dry. I knew precisely where I stood now, and let everyone know it.

It took a while. The Party leadership was stunned, dazed, and that included Irving Potash and Ben Gold, and I, after all, was of little consequence; but one Friday, when I received my pay envelope I found the inevitable pink slip and a note to see Potash.

You're fired, he said, you were only a temporary worker. Don't return on Monday.

I said something about how long was he going to take this shit from the Russians, and he coldly replied, jerking his head in the direction of the strongarm office, You know, sometimes it is necessary to use violence. I collected my stuff and left.

No, I didn't turn the other cheek, neither the one on my face, nor the one on my bottom. After all, I had not been brought up to be a pious Christian. For years I had walked picket lines for others. Now I decided to picket for myself.

Bob Gladnick, who had already broken with the Party and VALB, came to stand at my side. We decided to have a rollicking good time. Natie Shlechter called the Lovestoneite office for me, and they allowed us use of the revolutionary's tools: a typewriter and a mimeograph machine. Laughing, kibbitzing around, first we printed up a picket sign for me to hang around my neck: THE FIRST VICTIM OF THE STALIN-HITLER PACT! in large red letters. Then we combined to write a leaflet stating that yesterday I had been a wounded hero of the Spanish Civil War and today I had suddenly become an enemy of the people, or some such, I wish I had retained a copy for my then non-existent files. I hadn't yet thought of becoming a world-class writer. We ran off two reams; it turned out to be hardly enough. Incidentally, a friend of Natie's father wrote a piece in Yiddish for the *Daily Forward*. Unfortunately it took some time for it to appear; I do, however, have a photostat. Unconsciously, perhaps, I was already thinking of becoming world class.

We decided to hit the bricks at noon, just when every fur worker in the trade would be out on Seventh Avenue between 26th and 33rd Streets. Our luck held. It was a gorgeous fall day, and the streets were crowded with gesticulating, very talkative furriers eating their lunch from brown paper bags and discussing nothing else but the pact. Most of the furriers were Jewish, and Hitler was someone to talk about. The trade was buzzing, and then we came rolling down the street like two sailors off a just-docked freighter, shouting at the top of our lungs, The first victim of Stalin's pact with the Nazis! The furriers made a rush at us, couldn't get a leaflet fast enough. I ran out of one thousand sheets in no time. Bob and I had a bloody ball. As we headed down Seventh Avenue towards the union hall on 26th Street, whenever I espied a Communist big shot, a union official, I'd elbow Bob, and we'd block his path, click our heels, raise our arms in stiff Nazi salute and call out, "HEIL HITLER!" Then we'd step aside and allow the poor bastard to slink away. What could these valiant anti-fascists say? The line has changed again. The fur workers on the street laughed with us. They were just as angry as we were. One never laughs as much as when one laughs in anger.

In front of the union hall, we picketed before an ever-increasing union crowd, among whom were several union officers; Party people, most of them. They, too, were in a state of shock. One member of my old YCL branch made a move in our direction and I turned to him with hands fisted. I was dying to knock one of them on his ass. He slunk back against the wall. Across the street the sidewalk was lined with union strongarms, and not one made a move in our direction. I supposed Potash did not want to add to the tumult in the fur market which had resulted from the pact by an attack on a wounded veteran of the famed Lincoln battalion.

Suddenly the spit brigade showed up, composed of women union militants, a Party tactic. They spat at us, and if we hadn't known better, our first reaction would have been to slap a face or two. Then of course the strongarms would have moved in. How dare you hit a woman! We just laughed. Spit away, old crone. Now a new line of attack confronted us, the Fat Man, a mercenary of the union goon squad. I had had to pay him off many a time at Potash's instructions. The Fat Man never used his fists, fists leave marks. His big muscular belly was his weapon of choice. I had seen him knock men bigger than we on their cans just by heaving his belly at them.

As he headed our way, Bob and I figured we'd had our fun; enough was enough, it was time to jump the line, but since there is no comedy without tragedy, to our sorrow Marvin Stern's widow showed up as we

Original Yiddish article, in the *Jewish Daily Forward*

Translation from the Yiddish
Jewish Daily Forward, page 7
Wednesday, December 20, 1939

FURRIERS UNION DEPRIVES SPANISH VETERAN OF LIVELIHOOD FOR OPPOSITION TO STALIN-HITLER PACT

Bill Harvey, a former Communist and a veteran of the Spanish Civil War who was sent by the Communist Party to serve in the Abraham Lincoln Brigade in Spain, on Monday picketed the fur market and distributed circulars calling on the fur workers to help him get his job back in the Furriers Union.

The picket sign stated that he was a victim of the Hitler-Stalin Pact, and that as long as he agreed with the Communist Party line he was much appreciated and considered a great hero who had risked his life for Loyalist Spain. He was for that reason given a job in the Furriers Union which he held for almost two years. But as soon as he exhibited dissatisfaction with the Hitler-Stalin Pact he was thrown out of his job.

Bill Harvey was seriously wounded in Spain and is crippled for life. After Harvey walked around the fur market for a long time and attracted the attention of thousands of workers, he went to the Furriers Union and picketed the union office.

In the circular which Harvey distributed, he says as follows:

"I went to Spain to fight against fascism. Then, having been wounded there, I returned to America and the Furriers Joint Council gave me a job. As long as I believed in the Communist 'line' I was a hero. But once I could not toe the

line and acquiesce about all that the Communist leaders supported, and once I began to pose questions concerning the
Communist leadership in Spain and in America, Mr. Potash
ordered me not to attend any lectures delivered against the
official Communist Party line. It was not long before the
Stalin-Hitler Pact was concluded.

"When I began to ask questions about the Stalin-Hitler
Pact, Mr. Potash deprived me of my job. After I had worked in
the union a year and ten months, Mr. Potash suddenly discovered that I was a 'temporary' employee.

"It would appear that one can work for the Communists
only when one keeps one's mouth shut and does not tell them
what one thinks of them.

"I appeal for the return of my job."

Bill Harvey, Veteran of the
Abraham Lincoln Brigade.

crossed the street. The telephone wires must have been humming. "Do
you know what happened to Marvin?"

"Ask them," I said to her, because I still didn't have the courage to tell
her the truth. I should have asked her to meet me later over coffee and
then have told her, They killed him, one way or another, they killed him,
the fucking bastards. Yes, we had become they, us had become them.

Bob and I parted, satisfied with our day's frolic, and as I walked down
Eighth Avenue, Joe Gordon caught up with me. I guessed he'd heard
about the commotion we had caused at the union hall, he had old connections there, but he had come too late, and followed after me. As I
faced him, all the day's joy drained from me, and I can still remember

how hard the pulse in my temple beat. I could feel my lips go dry and tighten to the point of pain. I didn't for a moment think he was going to swing at me, and he didn't. I loved this man and there was a time I would have given my life for him, as he would, I was sure, for me. And that is what he said to me, his face ash gray, his blind eye staring wildly, his hair combed neatly now in his new responsibility as a Party functionary. Poking a stiff finger into my chest, he said, When you were in the Party, I'd have given my life for you; now you're out, we're not friends, we're enemies. Then, as he turned away, If the Party asks me to kill you, I will. That was just the tough guy talking. No fear of that, I wasn't important enough for the Party to waste a bullet on. As he walked stiffly away, I looked after him. He'd been a good friend. His vitality, his *joie de vivre*, even though he'd been half-blinded back in Murcia, had given me life, and had helped me in good measure to ignore the pain.

I felt terribly sad. First Marvin's widow, now Joe—ah, shit, there's just no fun in life. But I must say that by the time I got home, the sadness was tempered by a feeling wholly new to me, the lightness which comes with finding oneself a free man. At last. And unemployed, too.

Bob was soon gone. While our alleged anti-fascist comrades were resolving that the Yanks were not coming, it was an imperialist war, Gladnick took off for Canada, where he joined the Royal Canadian Tank Corps. He fought with distinction for almost six years, again coming out alive. After he returned, he worked as an organizer for the ILGWU in the American South and in Puerto Rico.

When I learned that Joe Gordon had gone down, torpedoed in the icy Murmansk Sea after Hitler's invasion of Russia, I could see him fighting to stay alive, adamant, tough, blasting the sea with obscenities. He was indomitable. He was a believer. I mourned him.

27

Fifteen years later, I got mine back. I gave as good as I got, but that queasy stomach of mine has never quite let me rest in peace. Vengeance is not sweet. I jumped the line, crossed it, did what I promised myself I would never do. I did it in part to protect the members of my union, The Federation of Shorthand Reporters. I had worked like a dog to help organize it; I had spent many unpaid hours to rear it and keep it alive, and I wasn't about to let its members be shortchanged because of me. But that's just one part of it.

It was that sad time in American life, those three, four years when Joe McCarthy just about destroyed the very honorable cause of anti-Stalinism, or anti-Communism if you will. He was the worst thing that could have happened to us. He shot with a blunderbuss instead of a single bore rifle. Our society can best be protected and enlarged by more democracy, not less, and McCarthy diminished it, bruised it, crippled it. He was disgusting. "Alger—no, Adlai," he said, trying to tarnish Stevenson with Hiss; you wanted to spit in that drunken face of his. Him and his aiders and abetters.

And who helped him along best of all? The so-called enemy, the fucking CP, the pusillanimous, the duplicitous CP. Can you imagine V. I. Lenin pleading the Fifth Amendment? Leon Trotsky? Karl Marx? Even Koba himself in the days of his heisting, bank-robbing youth when he was less a coward than he later became? Steve Nelson, as brave a man as ever fought a war, a revolutionary, a so-called Leninist, pleading the Fifth instead of saying outright, Yes, I'm a Communist and proud of it? If every goddamned fool who had followed the Party line had stood up and said, Yes, I am or was, so what, you bastard, what would have happened? That prize package of lard in the cowardly Congress of the United States would have refound his hole and slunk away, rat that he was. No sane human being could believe that the Congress and the courts would have allowed the jailing of one million, give or take a hundred thousand or so, Americans who were or might once have been Communists—not forgetting, of course, what the United States government did to I don't know how many Japanese during World War II.

But, still, let me admit it, it was satisfying to see the Commies squirm. It had been Louis Weinstock, national committee member of the CP, who had urged the Department of Justice during the war to indict and send to jail the Trotskyist leaders of the Milwaukee local of the Teamsters Union under the Smith Act. Eighteen men sent to the can for being Trotskyists, Leninists all. Now the Leninist CP was being harried by the self-same Smith Act, and how they screamed. Who but the CP had blacklisted—yes, you Hollywood geese, blacklisted wherever they had the power to do so, whether on movie set or shop floor—blacklisted, harassed, and driven men from their lifelong trades in Communist-led unions for opposing the Party? Who but the CP—and I plead guilty—had sent goons to break up Trotskyist, Lovestoneite, and Socialist meetings? Who but the CP during this time informed on Noah Greenberg, later an eminent choral conductor, when he worked as a seaman and as a Trotskyist opposed the tyranny of the Communists in the National Maritime Union? Not to mention the continual murder of oppositionists in the Soviet Union. Now those of us in the anti-Stalinist left could not but smirk at the spectacle of the cowardly CP pleading the Fifth like common criminals, those poor victims of McCarthyism, people who had never raised a voice at the slaughter of the innocent in the great, the pure, the unvarnished savior of the world, the USSR. Still, we detested McCarthy, despised him for besmirching our honorable cause with his bullying and half lies.

Yet, again yet, there were Chambers and Hiss and the Rosenbergs. Years later, when I worked as a court reporter in the U.S. District Court on Foley Square (I was forbidden to cover Communist trials), I asked the reporters who had covered those cases what they thought, and they told me—no one knows better what goes on in a courtroom than those who report a case verbatim—it was easy to see that Chambers was telling the truth and Hiss was lying, and just as easy to see that Julius was guilty of espionage and Ethel only of aiding and abetting, though Judge Kaufman, a brilliant but flawed man, obviously favored the prosecution. Reading the newspapers during the Rosenberg trial—those poor deluded fools—I could not but say to myself, there but for the grace of Natie Shlechter go I. But to kill them! That was sheer hysteria—as it always is when the state commits murder. Of course, when it comes to the likes of Hitler, Goering, Goebbels, et cetera, one wonders. Ah, to have seen Hitler hang by his neck. There are so many things to wonder about, aren't there?

In March 1953, year II in McCarthy's reign over the Senate—and I date it to the time when Osip Djugashvili, also known as Koba, alias Joe Stalin, mass slaughterer, died—my union, of which I was unpaid president (I worked days, helped run the union nights), went on strike against most of the employers in the freelance field. One of the employers, a man named Paul Hammer, an avid reader of the *Daily Worker* with whom I'd had numerous political arguments over lunch, mentioned at an employers' meeting that I had fought in Spain and had once been a Communist. During the master prick's reign, "had once" was equal to "being now." One of the bosses' lawyers, Joe Hack, Esquire, from a Wall Street law firm, who thought Joe McCarthy was king, contacted someone in Washington and shortly thereafter it was announced in the *Herald Tribune* and/or the *New York Times* that the Federation of Shorthand Reporters, among others, had been placed on one of those creatures of the day, a Senate committee's subversive list. Such was the nature of the time known as the McCarthy era.

The fact that the union had been tagged subversive stung its members, though not one suggested we cave in. It was the hope of almost every freelance reporter that some day he or she would be appointed as an official to either a city, state, or federal court. The way it looked in those sour days, having been a member of a subversive organization was not going to help. I felt responsible, but there was nothing I could do about it.

Shortly thereafter, while I was subbing in the Pleas and Sentences Part of the federal court on Foley Square (the reporters in that court had signed a union contract), who should show up during a recess while I was out in the corridor having a smoke but a broken-nosed pug who shows me an ID with the name of McTighe or O'Toole or some such, an investigator for Wisconsin Joe. I supposed that some employer had heard I was putting in a day's work in the federal court, no less, and had contacted Joe Hack, Esq., and he in turn had made a phone call.

I had come in contact with quite a few investigators, FBI agents and the like, as a freelance verbatim reporter, and had learned a very simple and easy lesson: if you spew out a stream of obscenities when speaking with them they soon accept you as one of the boys. A true blue American, that's me. So I say to this guy, What the fuck can I do for you, bud? Can I help him with this name or that name? Look, buddy, what the fuck you asking me about these fucking guys for, I've been out of their fucking circuit for over fifteen years. Well, he says, what if we subpoena you? If you subpoena me, fella, I'll say I was a Commie years ago, and after that, you guys are so democratic, I'll stand mute and you'll have to send me to the fucking can. He laughed. All I'm doin' is my job. Yeah, I know and you can tell that buddy lawyer of yours to cut the shit.

He shrugged and said, Okay, guy, and started to leave. I called after him, knowing I had his number, Do me a favor, tell that boss of yours to take a flying fuck for himself. He just shook his head, a big smile on his face.

In the same court, the same day or the next, I can't remember—the bosses thought they would enjoy embarrassing me, here I was working in the U.S. District Court, for God's sake—another recess, another guy. This one was button-down, clean cut; for goodness sake, he could have been a sibling of Alger Hiss, spy. His name I no longer remember, but he was from the House Un-American Activities Committee. I used up all the fucks I knew and then added some more. It impressed him even more than it did O'Toole or McTighe, whatever. Same routine. Same result. This time I told him to tell his lawyer friend or whoever it was who'd called him to take the flying fuck for himself. Just doing my job, he said. Yeah. Your job.

I never heard from either of them again.

One day I'm in the union office surrounded by dejected strikers—striking is a bitch when what you want is to be out there earning a dollar—when the phone rings. I answer. Yes? An FBI agent calling for Mr. Herrick. That's me. I'd like to come over and have a chat. That's just what I wanted, an FBI agent coming to the union office, with my members sitting there hoping against hope that the bosses were calling to say they wanted to settle this blasted thing.

The FBI office was just about around the corner on Chambers Street and Broadway, and the union office was on Park Row in the old Herald Tribune building. No, I said, I'll talk to you in your office.

In short, the Department of Justice was mounting a case against VALB for being a Party front. The case would be heard by the Subversive Activities Control Board, another creature of the time, but at least they followed the rules of evidentiary procedure, with rights of cross-examination, calling of witnesses, and appeal.

Did you, I asked, receive a call from Joe Hack, Esq., of such and such?

No, nothing like that. We know you've been on the outs with VALB for a long time. Other vets are going to testify, we thought you'd love to get even, too. He seemed to know all about me.

No, I said, I don't want to testify. Just leave me alone.

I tell you this, I did want to get even. They had informed on me, I figured I owed them; after all, loyalty is not a given, it has to be earned, but the thought of crossing the line made me shrink inside myself.

Think about it, he said.

You know, I was surprised. He was a nice guy, didn't try to push me around, didn't even hint at a bribe, didn't say a word about getting my union off that subversive list.

Okay, I said, I'll think about it.

No, I kept saying to myself, don't think about it, you just can't do it.

Mickey and I were old and good friends by now. He was working alternately for the ILGWU and the Textile Workers Union in the South, still at that time a very nasty place to be doing union organizing. He was in town, and we met for dinner at the old Lafayette Hotel restaurant in Greenwich Village. He told me he wanted to testify, wanted to get his back. Besides, he said, it's time I said under oath what I've been saying all these years to anyone who'll listen, that the International Brigades were a Communist deal from top to bottom and had absolutely nothing to do with anti-fascism or democracy. It's time the lie was shoved down their cowardly throats.

I told him I had turned the FBI down. I just couldn't cross the line. I reminded him that I'd been born into the movement, had been taught even before the ABC's that to cross the line, to testify against the Party, was the greatest sin a man could commit against the movement.

Bob's going to testify, too, he said.

You guys are different. I can't do it. (Bob never spoke to me about it. He never even mentioned my name to them.)

Look, Mickey said, they suffer from totalitarian (a new word in our lexicon) gall. Like the Mafia they can do anything they please, even inform on you. Pay them back and you're a goddamn rat. I didn't, after all, take the Mafia oath of *omertà*.

What he said was true, of course. I'd thought about it for years—why can they inform, lie, kill, and still feel self-righteous if you peach on them? I myself judged harshly those who had had lunch with a comrade one day and then had informed on him the next. Everyone had his own reason, his own rationalization. I wanted to get my union off the hook, and I wanted, like Mickey, to shove the lie down their throats. And the lure of vengeance was very tempting. Still, when Sabena Cerone, the FBI agent, called and in his nice way asked if I had changed my mind, I said, No, I haven't.

It occurred to me one morning—it was constantly on my mind along with the strike, which was going badly—that I was being a coward. What was holding me back was the same old business, What would people say? A bad reason, a very bad reason.

I called Cerone and told him I would accept the subpoena without a fight.

We lost the strike, and much of it was due to mistakes I had made. If we had compromised we could have settled and come out ahead, but I had to show my members that I was more militant than everyone else. A bad way to lead a strike, to lead a union. And we were still on that subversive list.

However, no sooner did I report to government counsel on the appointed date than they tell me the attorney for whatever Senate committee had us on its list wanted to see me. I could not but smile.

What, the attorney asked me, about so and so, naming one of my union members whose family is well known in Communist circles? Look, I said, not using one obscenity, as I had not to Cerone, if there are any Communists in my union they're not about to let me know. To them I'm a dirty Lovestoneite-Trotskyite bourgeois enemy. I just don't know. He asked me about several others and received the same response from me.

I was very convincing, and, aware that I was going to testify for the government as a friendly witness, he told me they would remove the Federation from the subversive list.

Yeah, victory. The next thing I know I'm sitting in the witness room. I suddenly have a fever, a very high fever, I'm burning up. I feel sick to my stomach. I'm going to cross the line, join up with the capitalist society against my former comrades. I'm scared shitless. If I could get out of it now, I would; be cited for contempt, go to jail. I realize that if Joe Gordon and/or Doug Roach were still alive I would never have agreed to accept the subpoena without a fight. I would remain mute. I could never cross the line no matter how much my erstwhile compadres had earned it. I breathe deeply, in, out, in, out, slowly, catch hold of myself. It is too late. I am committed. *Tochiss afn tisch.* I'll go in there and answer the questions truthfully to the best of my recollection, as every witness should. How many deposition witnesses had I sworn in as a verbatim reporter, a notary public? Do you swear in the testimony you are about to give to tell the truth, the whole truth and nothing but the truth, so help you God?

I do.

One of the government lawyers is asking me questions: my name, what position I hold with my union, had I ever been a Communist. Then a wholly irrelevant question, with no objection following, about the little job I did in the South for the Party and a guy named Marchand, and then I perjure myself—I give false names of the two people who lived on Collins and Fifth in Miami Beach who had acted as liaison between Marchand and me. Then we come to Spain.

Government counsel is sticking to my condition for agreeing to testify; I would only give them names of people who are known publicly as Communists: Browder, Joe Stalin, Charlie Krumbein, Steve Nelson, people who make their living working for the Party, so that my testimony cannot lead to them being fired from their jobs. In essence, my testimony concerns what is known universally: that the Abraham Lincoln battalion and the International Brigades were organized, dominated, controlled, and massacred by the Communist International, a tool of Stalin. I also relate how I was informed on by Boishke in Murcia and Fajans in the States, how I was fired from my job with the Furriers Union, and how Gladnick and I picketed the fur market. Though I mention how I had been harassed by Comrade Neumann, I do not say anything about the executions in the church basement. I had never told anyone about it and had no intention of revealing it to anyone.

Cross-examination begins. I, who had taken the testimony of hundreds, perhaps thousands, of witnesses; I, who could write a handbook on how witnesses should behave on the stand—just listen to the question and answer it, adding nothing, do not stray, keep your cool—I lose my temper. Mr. Clay, VALB lawyer, is being fed questions by Moe Fishman, the secretary of VALB. Is Herrick your original name? No. Is Harvey your original name? No. What was it? Horvitz. What was the purpose of that line? I am asked to name members of my YCL unit in the Fur Union. I stare at Fishman, what is he up to? I say nothing, just stare. The question is repeated. I give the name of Leon Strauss, by then a well-known public Communist leader. I give another name, Cohen, and can't help smiling; if the FBI is going to look for a no-first-name Cohen in the City of New York, it will undertake a task as difficult as that of Sisyphus. I give another no-first-name—I don't remember which, I have no copy of the transcript—then hedge, wait, and finally a different question is asked. I'm still wondering what Fishman is up to. And I'm sore and let them know it by giving snippy answers. A bad witness.

Suddenly I'm asked by Fishman, via Clay, to name the men who were on the *Normandie* on the way to Spain. There is colloquy, I do not now remember what, and I am told to give their politics. I wait for Fishman-Clay to withdraw the question. Nada. Rien. Nothing. I stare at Fishface again. If I could get my hands on him, I'd throttle him. I now understand what Fishface is up to. As in Spain, so here: throw the rank and file to the wolves so he can label Horvitz/Harvey/Herrick an informer. They were fucking me again, those bastards. I hem and haw, searching for names of men who were on the *Normandie* with me and who had died in Spain. Rodolfo Armas, the Cuban leader, a Communist. Akalaitis, our squad leader on the way to Spain, a Greek Communist. Kavorkian, an Armenian Communist. Chelebian, another Armenian Communist. I should have mentioned then and there that they were dead; perhaps then Fishface would have caught on to what I was up to and stopped urging me on. How many names did the bastard want? The

260

courtroom clock was approaching 4 P.M., so I knew adjournment would soon follow. I gave several more names of dead men, taking my bloody time; finally, adjournment was announced. On my way out of the courtroom I made certain to pass Comrade Fishface so I could give him a sharp elbow. Glad to get out of there.

On the following morning, cross-examination continued by Fishman/Clay. I was asked to continue giving names and their politics. I eke out several more names. I am ready to leap from the stand to commit murder. More names, please, and my memory, addled as it is with distemper—here the unconscious is at work—I give the name of the much alive Ruby Kaufman, the very same Uriah Heep who had informed Bill Lawrence in Albacete about the letter Natie's parents had sent me via Jackie Friedman. Silence, then Joe Colbert, also very much alive, but I catch myself and add that I do not know if he was ever a member of the Party or the YCL. I remain silent, waiting for Fishman/Clay to ask me to continue. But they now turn to another line of inquiry.

Soon it is over, and I feel as if I have just been through a battle and come out alive, though they—they—have managed yet again to wound me.

I never advised government counsel that the names I had given were those of dead men. I doubt if they much cared.

An apostate Catholic I knew once told me that even then after many years outside the Church, when he committed a so-called mortal sin, inwardly he cringed; the fear is still there, is he going to hell? I feel much the same. Ambivalent is the word I am looking for. I still cringe, but have no doubt those bastards deserved it.

Over the years, confronted with my sin I have felt regret, but for a reason few would understand. It was the old bolshevik in me. Not only had I jumped the line, but it had been bad agitprop. Those pious few who do not think beyond what they are expected to think turned their backs on me. Humbly, I say, Fuck you!

Within two weeks after my return to New York from Washington, I ran into a man named Wallach whose ass I had protected when I spoke to the lawyer for the Senate committee. Said I didn't know what I in fact did know. Yes, I lied for him. Unknowingly, he reveals to me how right I was about Comrade Fishface's reason for asking me to name names. I understand, he says, you gave a lot of names. Yeah, I say, dead ones. Unfortunately, you were not among them.

(This Wallach is not to be confused with the Albert Wallach who was last seen being ushered from his cell in Casteldefels, the regal domain of Anthony DeMaio. Albert was accused of everything from desertion to American spy. He was executed. We wonder, in our naiveté, who were the judge and jury?)

As I said earlier about my interlude with Orson Welles, if you get too close to an employer, he begins to think he owns you. So it is with investigatory agents. Sabena Cerone, a nice guy, was no different. He asked Mickey and me if we knew a man named Bennett in Spain and we both answered yes, but, lying, we said we didn't know his politics. But that was not the end of it. We were both subpoenaed to appear at a nickel-and-dime case against Bennett, who worked in a government library around Washington, I think. Though we both testified that the International Brigades had been organized and dominated by the Third International, we added that not all volunteers were Communists; when we were asked the critical question, we both lied under oath that we did not know Bennett's politics. He was acquitted. Later, Mickey ran into him on West Eighth Street in Greenwich Village and he sent regards and thanks.

Another time, Sabena Cerone tricked me. Nice guy. When I ran into him on the corner of Chambers and Broadway in Manhattan, he offhandedly asked me if I would testify in a case against someone named Hartman and another man whose name I do not now recall. No, for God's sake! I said. Sabena smiled. Now he knew I knew Hartman, the Party name of a fellow reporter who had worked with me when we organized the reporters' union. He and the other fellow were official reporters in the state Supreme Court. No, I won't! I repeated, and, sore at him as well as myself, I left him. I never heard from him again. Neither Hartman nor the other man, I was glad to hear, was fired from his job.

If there were any I inadvertently may have harmed, one of those innocents who never even heard of the Communist underground in the United States, whether Comintern, NKVD (KGB) or GRU, I ask that I be forgiven. But where were you, my dear comrades, when harm was done me? I still await your apologies.

Several years later, shortly after the death of Joseph McCarthy, on the way home from work I stopped to have dinner with two of my elderly friends, Esther Goldfrank, the anthropologist, a specialist on the American Indian, and her husband, Karl August Wittfogel, author of the classic *Oriental Despotism*. It was Karl who told me that in 1933, when Hitler assumed power, Karl, as one of the leading Communist theoreticians in Germany, attended a meeting of high Communist Party leaders and comrades to discuss a plan to call the German working class into the streets, and that a courier arrived from Stalin ordering them to cease and desist. Now was not the time for going into the streets; Hitler would be the icebreaker for the revolution. Karl and several others dissented. After the meeting, at which it was decided to obey Stalin, Karl asked the world famous literateur and Hungarian Communist, Georg Lukács, how, knowing better, he could have agreed. Lukács, the great seeker for truth, replied, "I would rather eat shit than ever leave the [Communist] movement."

Lukács, like so many other intellectuals, was to eat so much shit it began to ooze out of his very pores.

After an affable and delicious dinner with Esther and Karl, as I was preparing to leave they told me they were going to Carnegie Hall to attend a memorial meeting for Joseph McCarthy. I knew that Karl and Esther had become rightwingers, but I hadn't thought they had gone over the edge and I said so. They responded they were merely curious, and wasn't I? I had never attended a meeting of rightwingers in my life and, yes, my curiosity was piqued. Okay, I said, I'll go along; I'm always game for a little fun.

They had tickets for a loge from which when seated I could see not only the speaker on the stage but also the entire audience, a well-dressed, well-behaved crowd. The only speaker I remember is William F. Buckley, Jr., the conservative nonpareil, a man who in some strange way always reminds me of Max Shachtman, the very unorthodox Trotskyist. Both Buckley and Shachtman, as opposite as ham and hot pastrami, are and were saved from their respective orthodoxies by their marvelous sense of humor. You can't be a Francisco Franco or a Robespierre tongue in cheek.

At any rate, Buckley, after a speech that I no longer remember, asked the audience to stand in silence for the late senator. The entire audience, and it was a full house, rose to its feet, no dissenters there, except for one. Me. Stand for that prick? I heard Esther and Karl move as to rise, but seeing that I, their guest, did not, to their honor they refound their seats out of respect for me. Soon the entire audience became aware of us and before I knew it some three thousand people were staring up at our loge. What an eerie feeling it was to be the target of those thousands of hostile eyes. What could I do? I squared my jaw and stared right back.

I was pleased to read recently that William F. Buckley, Jr., seems to have changed his mind, and from his conservative point of view has joined those of us from the old anti-Stalinist left, R.I.P., in believing that McCarthy had been a sheer disaster to the cause of democracy.

28

Mickey's testimony took two full days. In hours, mine equalled less than a day. He told me he had a great time, no weak stomach for him. He covered just about the entire length of the Americans' stay in civil war Spain. It is probably the best history of the Lincoln battalion extant. Insightful and witty. He was not the battalion comedian as someone has said of him, he was the battalion wit; irony was his sharp-edged weapon against the comic stars.

On one of the Lincoln battalion documents found in the Comintern archives—hundreds of names of men vilified as spies, Trotskyites, deserters, thieves, including two Jews as having had relations with the Gestapo— Mickey is tabbed as defeatist, suspected of Trotskyism. Never a defeatist, always hoping for a Republican victory, nor a Trotskyist, he was not even sympathetic to the POUM. Still, they never touched him. He served a good purpose in the battalion; he vented the men's grief and anger for them. The rank and file had great affection for him, and when he was finally expelled from VALB for his dissension, Earl Browder himself had to be called in to attend the meeting; they even used Mickey's best friend in Spain, a man whose life he had saved at the Ebro, Yale Stuart, to testify against him. Later, the *Daily Worker* called him a deserter. He sued and they were forced to retract their slander by notice in the press because he produced his honorable discharge papers to prove they lied. Lies, lies, they smothered you in lies.

In 1960, at age fifty-two, having just returned from yet another stint trying to organize textile workers in what was still a violently anti-union South, tired, bitter, cynical, his wit sharper than ever, he died of a heart attack.

Mickey fought the fascists with a lousy gun and few bullets, and the comic stars at his back with wit and anger. I daresay he faced the dangers of the anti-union South the same way. For two years he was his comrades' voice, their shield against their own leaders. Yet those same comrades, after they had no further need for his courage, his voice, and his anger, turned their backs on him like the jackals they were—and some still are—because he refused to kneel to commissars as he refused to kneel to fascists and goons. That was his bitterest defeat, and he wore it longer than any other.

He was a voice, a raging sardonic voice, who fought against the conquest of man by man's enemies—a voice that I never heard waver or whimper.

I still miss his friendship, his voice, his wit, and his unconquerable will.

29

Jeannette was born in Worcester, Massachusetts, to Anna Schnaerson and Eli Valodovsky, a name which on entry in Ellis Island became Wellin because it was easier for the immigration officer there to spell and say. Anna and Eli came from Kiev, Ukraine.

Jeannette was a twenty-two-year-old widow when I first met her in a freelance verbatim reporting office. Margos Margosian, her husband of nine months, was killed by a Japanese bullet in New Guinea during World War II. He had been a comrade and officer of the Shoe Workers Union local for which she had become an organizer at age seventeen, when she worked in a shoe factory sewing gussets to vamps. She was brought up in a Communist household, and her father was the type of secular Jew who made it a point during Passover to carry a loaf of un-wrapped bread under his arm through the Jewish neigh-borhood in which they lived. Anna, a sweet-tempered, timid woman, would be embarrassed about it, but could say nothing to her husband because he had a violent temper. He was a blacksmith and was strong enough to tear telephone books in half. He died when Jeannette was fourteen years old, leaving a wife and seven children.

Jeannette had two brothers, four sisters, and a Downs syndrome brother who died in infancy. They were a very poor family, and Jeannette had to work after school from an early age. She was an A student.

When I first met her and told her that Stalin was a murderer, she stared at me aghast. How can you say that, it's like telling me my father was a murderer. But she did not stop going out with me, so I knew her ties to the Party were tenuous even though she herself did not know it. Some members of her family tried to get her to break with me, and she was just about ordered to do so by her Party unit organizer, but she never faltered, and married me. It took four years of arguing, fighting, yelling—I yelled, she didn't, she was and is quiet-spoken and never even yelled at the kids though there were times when she should have. One day, without my being aware of it, she read my copy of *The God That Failed,* was particularly moved by what Richard Wright and Ignazio Silone wrote, and told me she was quitting the Party. We didn't celebrate, merely went on as if nothing had changed. There just was less yelling on my part.

We, of course, had much in common. When I told her about Lyovka, that love of a man, she told me about Paul Skurz, a comrade who went to the Soviet Union for a long visit and upon his return told his comrades that it was far from Utopia. Within twenty-four hours he was ostracized and spat upon when encountered in the streets of Worcester. We both remembered the night Sacco and Vanzetti were electrocuted, and that the blinds in our homes had been pulled down in solidarity with them. When I mentioned that the Italian Anarchist leader, Carlo Tresca, had told several of his comrades and me that Sacco had been guilty and had compromised Vanzetti, she bit her lip and looked terribly pained. (Tresca, a vigorous anti-Communist, had only recently been murdered on a Manhattan street by a Mafia hitman on a contract put out, it is said, by the Triestan Stalinist leader, Enea Sormenti, alias Vittorio Vitali, alias Carlos Contreras, himself a brutal Comintern hitman.) Jeannette went to many meetings, picketed, marched, attended demonstrations; during the war, when she worked in Boston after her husband's death, the Party ordered her to attend USO dances in order to proselytize soldiers, sailors, and marines to join the Party. One of her assignments was to bring Party documents for reproduction to the office of Herbert Philbrick, who had a ditto machine. Philbrick led three lives, one of which was being an FBI agent. When Jeannette was eight years old, Ann Burlak, a young comrade from the mines of Appalachia, came to hide in her house from the Red Squad. Late one night, as the police knocked on the Wellin's front door, Ann went out the rear window. I knew Ann Burlak. Three years before she fled from the Red Squad, she appeared in the Young Pioneer camp in Lumberville, Pennsylvania, where I was world champion of track and field. The Party had sent her there for a rest. She was a tough cookie, but a sweet and generous comrade loved by all of us. When I first learned Jeannette was from Worcester, I told her about a kid from that city in the Lincoln battalion who, when ordered over-the-top on February 23, 1937, ran as fast as he could towards the fascist lines. Perhaps he hoped to conquer the enemy army all by himself. Or perhaps he thought that was the best way to forget his fear. The burial unit found his body as close to the enemy lines as one could be without being invited in to share a vino rojo. His name was Al Goldenberg. Jeannette not only had known him, but his family as well. When Al was in Spain, she and her girl comrades would visit his house, where his stepmother feted them with hot chocolate before they sat down to cut and baste hems to make red kerchiefs, which they wore with their white middy blouses during May Day parades, or at Party picnics. When she was nine, she and several other kids were sent to teach the ABC's of Communism to Italian children whose parents were being wooed to join the Party. The bosses are bad, the workers are good. America is bad, the Soviet Union is good. A. B. C.

But she was a rebel against the Party without even knowing it. She loved books, and no one could tell her what to read. We had that in common, too. She read Dostoevsky and Proust, those terrible decadent bourgeois novelists, and Joyce, too. She still reads them and says the more times she does, the better they get.

The first time I looked into her eyes, at that time so terribly sad, still in mourning after three years for her young husband who had died in the war, my heart fell open, a reminder of my mother's sadness in the years after my father's death. I fell in love with her. Now, after fifty years, no less, but only more so. By the way, she sings in a lovely alto voice. She looks nothing like Miss Veronica.

We have three children, Jonathan, Michael, and Lisa, and four grand-children, three girls and a boy. One grandchild, Jake Matthew, died when he was but fifteen months old. We still mourn him after six years.

My Seth, Natalie's Paul, and Jonny and Pearlyn's Jake did not die from related illnesses, so we cannot say it was genetic; it is just, we were told, that boy children are generally weaker than girls. And men are weaker than women. Ask anyone.

When my brother Harry lay dying, my mother pleaded with the God she did not believe in to take her life instead. Her plea was rejected and Harry died at age forty-eight. Nathan, my father, died at age thirty-six in 1919, and Eli, Jeannette's father, at age forty-four in 1937. Her mother, Anna, didn't go until deep in her eighties; my mother in her eightieth year.

Jeannette and I no longer follow a line. We vote our conscience, make up our own minds. We have many differences. Like many Americans, we are skeptical of power, of government. (Sometimes I think that Americans are the most anarchistic on earth.) Still, we believe a worker should be given an even break, and the lives of the poor and the unfortunate ameliorated. We bemoan the fate of the world, its wars and its atrocities, its injustices and its chicaneries. We no longer believe our way is the only way.

Voltaire said that history is not only battles. It is the measure of man that he even had to say that. He also said, and I paraphrase him, in the age of reason it is necessary to laugh, to live tongue in cheek. I have tried to write with tongue in cheek, have failed more frequently than not.

It is just one big joke, so why do we cry so much?

Jeannette

30

How much of the above is true? I have related it from what I incorporated into my life as I lived it, so it is true because I believe it to be true. We write our own histories, we believe our own histories. In any event, we believe what we wish to believe. I have tried to be honest. (Who would say otherwise about himself? Would Iago admit he was a villain?) Time recalled is tricky, and when you have devoted a great part of the last forty years to writing fiction, it is trickier still. I have found writing a memoir more difficult than writing a novel.

When I sat down in 1956, at age forty-one, to join my colleague, verbatim reporter Charles Dickens, at the desk, it never occurred to me to write other than fiction. I had read novels all my life, and when I thought of writing I thought not only of that estimable shorthand writer, but of Tolstoy, Trollope, Dostoevsky. Of Hemingway, Fitzgerald, and Dos Passos, whose *U.S.A.* is one of the great American novels of the twentieth century. Read it, and you will know our time better than any historian, and you will understand better what this country is all about. Of Isaac Babel, that most brilliant of prose writers, murdered by Stalin for absolutely no reason. Just senseless murder. Also of Orwell and Ignazio Silone, both of whom I love, and Camus, whose *The Fall* and *The Rebel* (non-fiction) have influenced me as much as any. While I was writing the first of many drafts of what was to become *¡Hermanos!,* my Spanish Civil War novel, I read what I believe is the best war (ergo, anti-war) novel written in our time, *Parade's End,* by Ford Madox Ford, that most generous of writers. The war he wrote about, World War I, was just about the most useless, idiotic war fought by the warlike human race in its long history, and no one has shown its obscenity better than Ford. My war was a just war destroyed by the duplicity and brutality of a revolutionary cause gone awry, a cause totally corrupted and finally demolished by its very own innate moral principle, that to reach its goal any means were acceptable. Arthur Koestler devoted a good part of his work to that, and I learned much from him. And I have returned to that war time and time again in at least five of my novels. People have asked me why, and I have answered, if you got the point, you would not think of asking. Like Camus's old Sisyphus, perhaps I have wasted my time. Still, I've enjoyed every minute of it, hard labor though it was.

I don't know how many times I've heard Calderón's great line, "Be my brother or I will kill you." Still, it never sounds trite to me. Isn't that what Joe Gordon said to me, and just about the same to Mickey Mickenberg? Franco to the Republic? Stalin, Hitler, Mao to the entire world? They were sincere, they meant it. "Be my brother or I will kill you."

I wrote about revolutionary politics for the same reason Jane Austen wrote about Mansfield Park. She knew and understood it and its people. What else does one write about? She wrote comedies, novels of manners. I wrote tragedies of manners.

Jake Starr, the Communist hero, putting a bullet into the skull of the poumista Daniel Nuñez in *¡Hermanos!,* Boishke informing on the young American in *Kill Memory,* General Alfara, falangista, murdering the poet Federico García Lorca in *Shadows and Wolves,* weren't they just doing what was expected of them in the society in which they chose to live? Manners are very important. Except for those askew, of course; my, how they upset the compact mass.

I was using politics subversively—to undermine the use of power, for I am skeptical of all power. My books are anti-political, that is the joke I unconsciously played on myself. And I was using politics to get at something deeper; the people, my characters, where did their need for revolution and violence and amorality come from, and where did it lead them? Who, I was asking, were Nechaev's mama and papa? It wasn't poverty he came from. Neither did Lenin or Trotsky. And what better way to get at this need for revolution than through fiction, where you are permitted to construct a life and to dig deep into the heart and mind of the character you have invented? There are few assumptions; the character, after all, is your own invention. You imagine events to reveal your characters, just as you imagine characters to reveal what goes on in the world you have chosen to write about.

I feel embarrassed going on this way about how and what I write. It is for the reader to say what he or she gets from a book, what the book is all about. For a writer—or a painter and sculptor for that matter—to explain his/her work strikes me as condescending and, perhaps, as advertisements for him/herself. Others may feel the need to do that; it is not for me. If you want to know what my books are about, read them.

It was my friend Natie who so many years ago encouraged me to become a novelist, and when I finally found the time and the courage to sit down to it, I discovered it to be the most difficult task I could possibly have imagined. It took me ten bloody years of hard, obsessive labor—and I mean hard and I mean obsessive—to finally get a book published, and that was the one that only took a year to write, *The Itinerant,* a semi-autobiographical novel. Then it took another year to write my pariah of a book, *Strayhorn, a Corrupt Among Mortals,* my second published novel. Pariah because it is out of print, and is a book some have called evil, to which I have responded, You don't know how to read. Every night I would trudge up to the attic against my will (from down below, Michael's Procol-Harum, Lisa's Joan Baez, and Jon's Rolling Stones produced an exuberant youthful cacophony), sit down at my desk, and by magic a page would be ripped out of me; then, depleted, dead tired, I would go down to bed. Fat, mute, beautiful Madeline Dearing, once a great operatic diva, seemed to have emerged from my marrow, and I still both weep and laugh for her. My third published novel was the first one I wrote. It took me nine years to write it. Eight or nine drafts. It was the book which taught me how to write a novel. It was the book which built up my stamina; how to run a marathon without dropping dead. *¡Hermanos!* I stood stark naked, stuck out my jaw and said "Go ahead, throw your best right hook." It still lives and I still stand. It was the book which taught me that simple words in short declarative sentences worked best for me. No literary stuff. After all, English is my second language, Da Gutteh being the first.

Seven more books followed in the next twenty or so years. I disown none of them and none of my characters, but one character I love best of all, no offense meant to the others. Clara, the old revolutionary, the old one, in *Love and Terror* (I'm sorry about the title, it should have been *Terror and Love*), I created her out of two sentences Bob Gladnick wrote me about a woman he met in Israel. A beautiful woman in her fifties, harbormaster in Haifa, who'd been permitted to leave Poland with one suitcase during the anti-semitic purge in the Polish Party, and who had been a nurse in the International Brigades. I gave her a full life. Her veins run with blood, not ink. Her life had been bitter, heroic, tragic, and still she survived as a fully sane, strong woman, without the smell of skunk, no phony romanticism or nostalgia for her.

I have written how I pleased and what I pleased. Only one human being on earth has been permitted to look over my shoulder as I worked: George Orwell, whose photograph hangs near my desk. Should he disapprove, I would plead, Not Guilty, George; I've done the best I could to live up to your standards. What the hell more do you want?

I have had ten works of fiction published and, like most writers I know, wish I had a chance to rewrite every one of them. There was only

Cecil Eby's photo of me revisiting the battlefield at Jarama in 1967

one Flaubert. It took him twenty years to write *Madame Bovary,* but I bet he, too, would have loved to have the chance to rewrite it. I'm certain even that master could find several words to change, more than one sentence to recast.

It has been the longest road I ever bummed, and the most difficult. Bone-freezing days, days too hot to breathe, but good days, too, the best being those when at work. Ah, those days at work.

I regret none of it.

31

On Friday, January 10, 1997, I was eighty-two years old.

I was born during the second year of World War I. It seems to me it has never stopped. Perhaps the Marquis de Sade was right: we are one with nature, and nature is violent, cruel, unjust, criminal. You are a crotchety old man of seventy-five and you are standing at the open grave of your fifteen-month-old grandson who one minute is a perfectly healthy child, and the next is murdered by an aberrant disease whose name you can't even pronounce. Peaceful interludes are but rare: listening to Glenn Gould playing a Bach suite; standing open-mouthed before a Rembrandt self-portrait.

We have learned nothing in five thousand years. We must fight nature—and that includes our own—endlessly, or it will overcome us and destroy us. Still, still, there is always a fatal contradiction, and I am not referring here to economic contradictions as enunciated by that nineteenth-century romantic, Karl Marx, but the contradiction that is ourselves, that insane desire to transform ourselves into angels. The more we try, the more we change ourselves into beasts; the more fervid our desire to raise ourselves, the more we lower ourselves. I am paraphrasing Michel de Montaigne who said that some four hundred years ago. How did he know? Who has listened? The crematoria and the mass graves in the frozen earth of Kolyma and Karaganda are but the most emphatic affirmation that no one has paid attention. We have learned nothing—only the weapons are more deadly, and the means of communication infinitely faster, the easier to repeat ourselves.

Today, as I worked, I stopped to listen to Vaclav Havel on the radio. It seemed I was listening to the only sane voice in an insane world. Thoughtful, witty, tongue in cheek. He is wise, human, I thought. What does that word mean? Human? Himmler and Beria, Idi Amin and Pol Pot, and their aiders and abetters were human, sprung from the loins of men and women. Beware; aiding and abetting are crimes. When I say Havel is human, I suppose I mean our aspiration should be to be like him. Measured, sane. Leave your fucking gun at the door! How I would love to sit and talk with him. I am certain it would make me more human. There, you see, can't help myself. I want to be an angel, too. St. Just, Marat. Soon the tumbrils will roll. Good or evil, moral or amoral, one is no more or less human. That is the pure hell of it. That is the human contradiction.

Don't get me wrong. I am not a pacifist. I believe in freedom and democracy—and let's not be wiseass about it, we all know what that means—and I'm willing to fight to the death for them.

I'm getting on. Soon I'll be eighty-three, a goddamn relic. I need my seven-year-old grandson to work the video for me. I prefer sitting on my butt to almost anything else on earth. Listening to good music, reading a fine book. I'm getting accustomed to the fact the rod has lost its steel.

Though Jeannette is also electronically illiterate, luckily for me her energy has not yet begun to flag. Sitting on her butt is the last thing she wants to do.

We have had a good life together, though we have had our troubles and tragedies, as who hasn't, and we do not think too much about the end.

My mother's silk thread, like Ariadne's, unwinds without breaking. Her life continues. Once as a kid when I came home bawling, having been knocked on my ass in a fight, she said, "It's better to fight and lose than to live like a vegetable."

I have not lived the life of a vegetable, and, by a long shot, I have not lost.

Tolstoy to Gorky:

> *Heroes—that's a lie and invention;*
> *there are people, people and nothing else.*

Wisconsin Studies in American Autobiography

William L. Andrews
General Editor

Robert F. Sayre
The Examined Self: Benjamin Franklin, Henry Adams, Henry James

Daniel B. Shea
Spiritual Autobiography in Early America

Lois Mark Stalvey
The Education of a WASP

Margaret Sams
Forbidden Family: A Wartime Memoir of the Philippines, 1941–1945
Edited, with an introduction, by Lynn Z. Bloom

Journeys in New Worlds: Early American Women's Narratives
Edited by William L. Andrews

Mark Twain
Mark Twain's Own Autobiography:
The Chapters from the "North American Review"
Edited, with an introduction, by Michael J. Kiskis

American Autobiography: Retrospect and Prospect
Edited by Paul John Eakin

Charlotte Perkins Gilman
The Living of Charlotte Perkins Gilman: An Autobiography
Introduction by Ann J. Lane

Caroline Seabury
The Diary of Caroline Seabury: 1854–1863
Edited, with an introduction, by Suzanne L. Bunkers

Cornelia Peake McDonald
A Woman's Civil War: A Diary with Reminiscences of the War, from March 1862
Edited, with an introduction, by Minrose G. Gwin

Marian Anderson
My Lord, What a Morning
Introduction by Nellie Y. McKay

American Women's Autobiography: Fea(s)ts of Memory
Edited, with an introduction, by Margo Culley

Frank Marshall Davis
Livin' the Blues: Memoirs of a Black Journalist and Poet
Edited, with an introduction, by John Edgar Tidwell

Joanne Jacobson
Authority and Alliance in the Letters of Henry Adams

Kamau Brathwaite
The Zea Mexican Diary
Foreword by Sandra Pouchet Paquet

Genaro M. Padilla
My History, Not Yours:
The Formation of Mexican American Autobiography

Frances Smith Foster
Witnessing Slavery: The Development of Ante-bellum Slave Narratives

Native American Autobiography: An Anthology
Edited, with an introduction, by Arnold Krupat

American Lives: An Anthology of Autobiographical Writing
Edited, with an introduction, by Robert F. Sayre

Carol Holly
Intensely Family: The Inheritance of Family Shame and the
Autobiographies of Henry James

People of the Book: Thirty Scholars Reflect on Their Jewish Identity
Edited by Jeffrey Rubin-Dorsky and Shelley Fisher Fishkin

My Generation: Collective Autobiography and Identity Politics
John Downton Hazlett

William Herrick
Jumping the Line: The Adventures and Misadventures of an American Radical

Women, Autobiography, Theory: A Reader
Edited by Sidonie Smith and Julia Watson